Politics & Rhetoric

Politics & Rhetoric
Coming to Terms with Terms

George E. Yoos

palgrave
macmillan

POLITICS & RHETORIC
Copyright © George E. Yoos, 2009.

All rights reserved.

First published in 2009 by PALGRAVE MACMILLAN® in the United States—a division of St. Martin's Press LLC, 175 Fifth Avenue, New York, NY 10010.

Where this book is distributed in the UK, Europe and the rest of the world, this is by Palgrave Macmillan, a division of Macmillan Publishers Limited, registered in England, company number 785998, of Houndmills, Basingstoke, Hampshire RG21 6XS.

Palgrave Macmillan is the global academic imprint of the above companies and has companies and representatives throughout the world.

Palgrave® and Macmillan® are registered trademarks in the United States, the United Kingdom, Europe and other countries.

ISBN: 978-0-230-61746-9

Library of Congress Cataloging-in-Publication Data

Yoos, George E.
  Politics & rhetoric : coming to terms with terms / by George E. Yoos.
    p. cm.
  Includes index.
  ISBN: 978-0-230-61746-9 (alk. paper)
  1. Rhetoric—Political aspects. I. Title. II. Title: Politics and rhetoric.
P301.5.P67Y66 2009
808'.001—dc22   2008051389

A catalogue record of the book is available from the British Library.

Design by Scribe Inc.

First edition: August 2009

10 9 8 7 6 5 4 3 2 1

Printed in the United States of America.

To the memory of Arthur E. Berndtson,

1913–1997

Previous philosophers have almost always directed their attention to the answers given in reply to philosophical questions. Their disputes were all concerned with these answers, their truth or falsity, their truth or refutation. The new point of view [linguistic philosophy] differs from all the others in that, from the start, it ignores the answers and directs all its attention towards questions. . . . The great mistake of philosophers up to now, which has led to so many misunderstandings, is that they have produced answers before seeing clearly the nature of the questions they have been asking.

    F. Waismann, Late Reader in the Philosophy of Science, University of Oxford

There is no limit to language games, because there is no limit to language. Language, it has often been said, makes infinite use of finite means. There are only so many sounds, letters, words, and grammatical constructions in English. But they can be combined in an extraordinary number of ways—ways that are to all intents and purposes unlimited, for the simple reason that each day the language changes, offering new possibilities of ludic expression. Each turn of the road, indeed, can provide a fresh source of language play.

David Crystal, *By Hook or by Crook*

Der Ursprung und die primitive Form des Sprachspiels ist eine Reaktion; erst auf dieser können die komplizierteten Formen wachsen. Die Sprache—will ich sagen—ist eine Verfeinerung, im Anfang war die Tat.—Goethe, *Faust* I.
The origin and primitive form of a language-game is a reaction; only from this can more complicated forms develop. Language—I want to say—is a refinement: "In the beginning was the deed." Goethe, *Faust* I.

Ludwig Wittgenstein, *Culture and Value*

Contents

List of Figures		ix
A Preface on Rhetorical Studies		xi

I Paradoxes in Talking about Meaning
1. One-Sided Rhetorical Critiques about Meaning ... 3
2. What Is the Meaning of Life? ... 9
3. Making and Discovering Meaning ... 21
4. The Meaning of What You Would Like to Mean ... 35

II Theories of Language and Communication
5. Language Use and Language Usage ... 47
6. Rhetorical Use and Usage ... 55
7. Limits of a Code Theory of Language ... 67
8. Definitional Proposals and Definitional Reports ... 81
9. An Inferential Theory of Language ... 95
10. Figurative and Literal Language ... 103

III Interpretation and Definition as Historically Developed Concepts
11. *Interpretation* and *Definition* as Umbrella Terms ... 117
12. *Interpretation* and *Definition* as Correlative Terms ... 129
13. Contrasts between Definitions and Interpretations ... 139
14. Nominal, Conceptual, and Real Definitions ... 143
15. Rhetorical Definition as a Generic Term: Talking and Walking the Talk ... 153

IV Logical Definition, the Language of Control, and Rhetorical Criticism
16. Logical Definitions by Class and Differentia ... 169
17. Logical Definitions by Necessary and Sufficient Conditions ... 187
18. Pigeonholes and Rational Numbers ... 193
19. Coming to Terms with Terms about Application and Control ... 199

20 Interpretations as Hypotheses and the Contexts of
Interpretation in Rhetorical Criticism 207

References 215

Index 223

List of Figures

12.1	Model of Contrasts (Between Synonyms and Antonyms)	136
12.2	An Application of Model of Contrasts	136
16.1	Venn Diagram of Two Classes	173
16.2	Venn Diagram of Complementary Classes	174
16.3	Venn Diagram and the Definition in Terms of Two Generic Terms	174
16.4	Venn Diagram and Conjunctive Possibilities of Combinations of Two Terms and Their Complements	175
16.5	Venn Diagram and Conjunctive Possibilities of Three Terms and Their Complements	177
16.6	Limitations of Venn Diagrams with Four or more Terms	180

A Preface on Rhetorical Studies

What I propose to do is to reframe the whole focus of the discussion of interpretation and definition by putting these modes of discourse into new rhetorical frames. They are frames that will give us a restructured and a radical reinterpretation of what we most often are doing in the name of interpretation and definition. Instead of looking at human communication from theoretical and conceptual frames derived from linguistics, formal semantics, formal theories of syntax, cognitive science, cognitive psychology, brain science, or neurophysiology, I prefer to look at these scientific perspectives on language use from outside the technical frames and the technical vocabulary of these disciplines.

I propose to look at interpretation and definition in terms of terms found in our ordinary discourse whereby we interpret the implications of their use for any discussion of communication and rhetoric. I want to discuss the issues about interpretation and definition from rhetorical frames by using terms found in our ordinary ways of speaking about clarification and meaning. I especially want to reframe rhetorical frames to probe issues about the arts of creating, making, and discovering meaning whereby we identify and communicate with each other. Although I am in one way looking at interpretation and definition from the view that it is our social politics that shapes meaning, much in the spirit of some current authors such as Edward Schiappa and Barry Brummett, I do not see meaning essentially as simply socially constructed in the manner that they describe. Rather I want to look at the shaping of meaning as a personal affair, as language play, as a refinement of usage. It is from such creative language sources—where authors, even scientists and humanists, try to say something original—that language can be found that can be assimilated politically and functionally into practice much in the way that social constructivist theorists of meaning describe.

To be able to do this reframing of the discussion of the issues surrounding interpretation and definition, I start from personal political perspectives on meaning that look at the processes and functions of the use of language spoken in the pragmatic applications and dynamics of human interaction. I especially see it in play in the terms that now shape our politics. Such language adapts to complexities by making refinements of the things we do when we communicate in particular and especially in unique and unconventional situations.

And the refinement and increased capacity of language to adapt to the complexities of life through communication is dramatically and exponentially increased by the increased power of written language to enhance the power of practical thought through new language creation. I. A. Richards aptly described a book as a tool to think with (I. A. Richards 1965). But it is also a tool to think differently. And this creativity is equally true of visual and mathematical schemata. Creation of meaning in such visual schemes has equally exponentially increased the power of our coming to terms with terms especially in the sciences and in the continuing explorations in the humanities.

For clarity and better understanding of the communication modes of written language we need to reframe the discussion about the clarification of meaning in the uses of terms to come to terms. And in using ordinary terms to talk about the clarification of meaning we find that when interpretation and definition are considered as rhetorical modes, it best helps us to come to terms with the terms of our language, and in our special case the English language. Interpretation and definition as I propose to come to terms with them are the two important rhetorical modes that shape best terms that we use to talk about both our social and cognitive actions. They are the modes we use to best analyze and create the language that we count on and whereby we can best guide, advance, and improve upon the values that we define as key to our civilization. And that judgment about the value of words is a matter for our social politics, as many writers presently would agree.

The rhetorical frames that I propose to discuss and use in talking about interpretation and definition are frames that I have developed out of my own readings and writing about what has been going on in rhetorical studies in the last forty to fifty years. By reframing my conception of rhetoric in newly defined rhetorical modes, as I have recently done in a recent work on politics, I hope to show that our conception of what it is to interpret and to define takes on new meaning within these newly, revised rhetorical frames (Yoos 2007).

Many specialists in rhetoric conceive of rhetoric as a separate branch of study independent of communications and composition. And if this proposal were accepted, would there not be, then, three distinct and separate arts, the art of speech, the art of writing, and the art of rhetoric? And if so, how should we draw the lines between these seemingly three important separate arts? There are some very practical difficulties raised when we try to teach speech and writing independent of the other. Speech communications and written composition from a rhetorical perspective are both about language use and usage. Should they then not be pedagogically inseparable, as we find with those who combine all the language arts into language arts programs, as they do in elementary education?

Speech communications and written composition tend to be arts overlapping with each other. Each needs to connect speech to written scripts and to connect writing styles to the tonalities, phrasings, and rhythms of plain speech. It is difficult to master speaking and writing skills independent of one another, especially as today more and more oral rhetoric, as we see it prepared today, is first scripted for the speaker so as to create a written text for an oral interpretation in the speaker's presentation. It was for this same reason that some people think speech and writing ought to be taught together on the college level in the same academic departments. Could it be that "rhetoric" should be the compromise name for this new focus, this conjunction of skills, as some rhetoricians have thought? But the Berkeley experiment with this sort of integration within its Rhetoric Department has not been repeated in higher education with the same success on the same scale elsewhere outside the University of California, Berkeley.

There is a great deal of academic departmental politics being fought over names. And there is a great deal of academic quest for status among those having different sorts of specialties in communication studies. In English departments there are turf battles being fought between those who teach English literature and those who are composition specialists. The literary people seem usually to win out in this battle. Comparably, there are similar turf issues that traditional speech departments face, especially given that communications departments are now large alliances between all sorts of communications and performance studies, specializing as they do with their different media studies, studies of group formats, and studies of different communications platforms with their different social interactions and performance functions. The National Communication Association (formerly the Speech Communication Association) bridges across many humanistic scholarly specialties, such as performance studies, public address, argumentation and forensics, public sphere studies and public policy studies, rhetorical theory, history of rhetoric, ethics in communication, critical and cultural studies, discourse studies, and now, lastly and importantly, mass media studies.

And historically, self-proclaimed rhetoricians and academically trained rhetoricians have struggled in their alienation within their departments with the diverse communication specialists for academic recognition, power, and professional status. A great deal of this struggle is over the allocation of grant money and fiscal resources for developing and expanding rhetoric as a specialty on the graduate level. This is especially true among those who are engaged in the teaching of reading, writing, and speech pedagogy, together with all those who promote advanced forms of literacy that is so much needed for academic success and for achievement in the workaday world that requires communication competencies.

But rhetoricians trained in the classical traditions of rhetoric in the late nineteenth century lost this fiscal game over status and fiscal resources in English departments to literary scholars. And in that loss of academic turf, theoretical and applied rhetoric were both exorcised from departments dedicated to the study of English literature. Rhetoric, then, in these literature departments was reduced to the minimal adjunct status of simply a name for written composition. Nominally, then writing skills as taught after the demise of rhetoric in literature departments was mislabeled "Rhetoric and Composition."

And ironically English composition until recently was taught with little attention, if any, to traditional rhetoric. And now with the new resurgence of interest in the teaching of rhetoric since the late 1960s in English departments, rhetoricians again are starting to reintroduce the teaching of rhetorical competencies into composition courses with much more emphasis on such rhetorical elements as invention, argument, and arrangement.

The only significant place that classical theoretical and applied rhetoric retained any past status as a subject matter in academia after the nineteenth-century demise of rhetoric was in conjunction with the teaching of public address and argumentation in speech and communications departments. And then, in the late 1960s, when there was a resurgence of interest in rhetoric among English composition specialists, it was to the speech traditions of scholarship and their work in historical studies about rhetoric that English scholars turned.

It was in this reaching out and as a result of the initiatives by compositional specialists in English in the guise of a new rhetoric that the Rhetoric Society of America was born in 1968. As a philosopher and as an early editor of the newsletters of the society, and later as editor of the *Rhetoric Society Quarterly*, I acted pretty much as a go-between in those early days between speech and English, bringing the two sides together about matters of common rhetorical interest.

But there is another ancillary and back-door way rhetoric has been finding its way back into other fields and disciplines in academia. It was my job as editor of the *Quarterly* to canvas these interests in rhetoric outside speech and English. Not only has the history of rhetoric played a part in the intellectual and cultural history of Western society, but many of the writing, reading, speaking, and listening skills taught historically in rhetoric are comparable to the teaching of analytic and interpretive skills found in other disciplines both in the humanities and in the social sciences.

Noteworthy too after the 1960s there was a renewed interest in rhetorical criticism, not only in speech communications and in literature departments but in many other academic fields, especially among those disciplines interested in politics and in the study of the diverse patterns of culture. And this type of criticism spilled over into newly developing programs in cultural and ethnic studies. Especially noteworthy is that rhetorical issues and topics found their way into women's studies, religious studies, and other ethnic and minority programs.

And about the same time there developed within analytic philosophy a parallel focus on critical analysis and argument critique. This linguistic turn in philosophy found its way into the course work in informal logic, which developed out of the introductory philosophy courses that were once the legacy courses in traditional Aristotelian logic (Yoos 1995). Much of this effort in informal logic later fell under the rubric of critical thinking, with its special concerns for such topics as public relations, propaganda analysis, and unmasking logical fallacies, the deceptions of advertising, and the ploys and ruses in politics. Many of these efforts came to fruition in the informal logic movement that came together and has been centered in the University of Windsor in Canada with the founding of the journal *Informal Logic: Reasoning, Argumentation Theory and Practice* (Johnson 1996).

The works of Chaim Perelman (1968) and Stephen Toulmin (1958, 1984) are exemplary examples of work in the new rhetoric by philosophers in the new types of rhetorical critique of argumentation and the critique of everyday reasoning that has always interested classical rhetoricians. And again in English studies there was the work of I. A. Richards (1965) and Kenneth Burke (1966) that helped lay the foundations for new ways of thinking about shaping meaning and fashioning rhetoric. Together these authors propelled rhetoricians in new directions and into revised conceptions about rhetoric that have given impetus to the renewed interests in rhetorical studies.

And beginning in the 1970s critical thinking began to achieve interdisciplinary status across academia and among educational proponents. And along with it there was another somewhat parallel, national interdisciplinary movement, "writing across the curriculum." Its specific purpose as a movement was the introduction of writing along with critical thinking into the classrooms across the curriculum. Critical thinking especially became a part of many new developing academic programs, not only in the humanities but in the social sciences, and even in the sciences, and even in such disparate fields as psychology, education, engineering, and philosophy.

And too it needs to be remembered that like the new rhetoric, classical rhetoric too had been all about problem solving, invention, discovery, arrangement, and especially the limitations of memory in communicating. Rhetoric as a discipline has traditionally dealt with what now are considered many of the contemporary topics of interest in the new rhetoric. Classical rhetoric had been about methods of inquiry into the processes of communication—about such modern concerns as modeling, framing, organizing subject matters, types of genre, and using appropriate tones and types of appeal in writing and speaking styles.

All these new ways of looking at rhetoric and communications were the same as the traditional classical rhetorical concerns about invention, strategic planning, and the value of heuristics for finding things to say about various subject matters. All these issues had been historically entertained by traditional modes of rhetoric so as to make writing and speaking relatively persuasive and interesting, in addition to making writing readable and clear to different types of audiences.

Traditional rhetoric in that it had focused on the skills for designing effective strategies for communicating, for the composing of speeches, and for the compilation and organization of written texts, once was considered an architectonic rhetoric. Much the same has been true of the developments in the new rhetoric. It too like traditional rhetoric has focused on the wide-sweeping compass of rhetoric in the curriculum. The new rhetoric as a movement proposes a reconsideration of the overall aims and goals of rhetoric in the college curriculum.

But there is a certain abstract emptiness in such wide surveying and theoretical talk about what rhetoric is and about what its uses are. Understandably, there are those who are dissatisfied with global talkers and prefer to work with the concrete and the specific details of rhetoric in action. Thus there has emerged a controversy within rhetoric itself over the range and scope of rhetoric that is now labeled or characterized as *big rhetoric* versus *little rhetoric*. (See Gaonkar 1993; Mailloux 2000; McCloskey 1997; Petraglia 2003; and Schiappa 2003.)

I have found comparable parallels of division in other disciplines. For example, I was astounded to find that phenomenologists seemed to want to talk about phenomenology rather than do phenomenology. There is the same parallel in the natural sciences. There are those who want to talk about it, its history and its methods, and there are those who simply want to do science and not talk about it. But this is true of many disciplines. And I find this also to be true in philosophy. There are the doers and the talkers about it.

Traditionally, classical rhetoric, then, was "big time rhetoric." It was conceived as an overarching discipline of many disciplines. Very much like architecture it was thought to be an architectonic art. Philosophy and history too have traditionally have had this proclaimed status. Just as we can have a history and a philosophy about just any discipline, so the same claim can be made for rhetoric. Just as there can be a history of philosophy and a history of rhetoric, there can be a philosophy of history and a philosophy of rhetoric. Equally, there can be a rhetoric of philosophy, a rhetoric of history, and equally there can be a rhetoric of all the lesser arts and disciplines. Now there is a rhetoric of architecture, of painting, of music, of religion, of science, of politics as well as of economics.

At the present time we find that rhetoric is in an object of public ridicule, opprobrium, derision, and derogation for all of its past asininities and its alleged pretentious misdeeds in promoting high-toned propriety, elegance, and pomposity. Rhetoric is thought to be dedicated to bombast and charming talk, dirty tricks, and now politics and propaganda. Right now rhetoric is popularly thought to be about verbal emptiness that flimflams the unsophisticated much in the spirit of advertising and public relations specialists who with their marketing skills are producing all the contemporary deceptive spin about pharmaceuticals and politics. People now talk mainly about studying rhetoric to expose such duplicity. And as a result rhetoric is being justified by the desperate advocates of change as a proper course of study for self-defense against some of its own alleged tricks and verbal misdeeds. Some now want to teach it as an antidote to counter its own sins much in the spirit of Aristotle's *On Sophistical Refutations* (1941) written to counter sophisms.

But this limited application of rhetoric to rhetorical criticism reduces its role and function in academia. In that role of making dirty tricks transparent it will always be adjunct to those concerned with social critique. But importantly, such critique is the business of "small rhetoric." Small rhetoric is by its own definition becomes an adjunct interest. It is an interest with limited aims. It is an art with specific critical skills that address circumscribed issues in communications studies such as style, eloquence, and persuasion. And small rhetoric is the major type of research and scholarship that we see going on at the present time in diverse communications specialties where uses of argument and the study of modes of persuasion are auxiliary. But nevertheless small rhetoric is pervasive in studies of practical concerns in all the different sorts of communication specialties. It is at the heart of all language and cultural critique. One cannot deny the importance of such activities for social and cultural critiques especially in politics.

It is not much of a confession for me to say that my heart has been with big rhetoric because I came to rhetoric from philosophy, from Informal Logic, and critical thinking (CT) where the big issues about language and pragmatics are at the forefront of interest in practical logic. And as such you will find that this book is about big rhetoric. I see it as an interdisciplinary discipline that seems to be a confusing oxymoron in categorizing any specialty. But interdisciplinary or not, it is within the frame of big rhetoric that I want to begin my lengthy analysis of what I consider to be two fundamental and significant rhetorical modes, interpretation and definition.

George E. Yoos
Clear Lake Minnesota
November 2008

PART I

Paradoxes in Talking about Meaning

CHAPTER 1

One-Sided Rhetorical Critiques about Meaning

There is something self-referential about any talk about meaning. To talk about the meaning of the term "meaning" presumptively assumes that we know what we are talking about. We are asking about the meaning of the very term that we are using in asking about the meaning of "meaning." There is often a sort of dramatic irony that is hopelessly being played out in the paradoxes we get into when we ask about the meaning of a term that we have already assumed to have a meaning in the very act of using it in our asking about it.

I want to explore this drama of unending questions that we spawn in asking about the meaning of what people say, especially when some things that they say may have no meaning at all. Such questions parallel the frustration that we have with children who persist in endlessly questioning, "Why? Why? Why? How do we reasonably stop these never ending questions asking for explanations about what it is to have meaning that seem so central to such puzzling questions as, "What is the meaning of meaning?" (Ogden and Richards 1947).

What I am proposing is a new way of facing up to some of these paradoxes in talking about meaning. I am *not* proposing a theory of communications, nor a rhetorical theory. What I am proposing to do is to provide my reader with a method of critiquing communications derived from rhetorical frames that center on what is said in ordinary terms to be "an interpretation" or "a definition." Interpretation and definition are I contend the rhetorical modes that we use to attack problems about creating and comprehending meaning. I want to frame together some new distinctions from rhetoric that will help us better to understand these rhetorical processes so central to the study of the creation and the clarification of meaning.

I want to deal with *interpretation* and *definition* as historically developed terms. They are general terms that have come to be the names for a variety of processes of clarification whereby we come to think about how and what things mean, or even more to say what things actually are. And importantly for my analysis of interpretation and definition I want to treat these two terms semantically as "umbrella terms." My definitional proposals about numerous terms used in clarifying these two rhetorical modes, as you shall see, require a great deal of justification and amplification to make it clear about the many different uses of different terms that have been developed in talking about interpretation and definition.

I want to show how interpretation and definition as rhetorical processes are interactive in shaping how we talk about both language use and language usage. What these two terms interpretation and definition have in common is that they are used in a way whereby they work together to furnish us with the meaningful foundations for refining our cognitive and adjustment endeavors. They do so by inventing and creating words and expressions with new meanings and with new applications. Interpretation and definition are the essential rhetorical modes we use to explain the role taking that makes possible our comprehension of what goes on in each other's heads.

Analytically I want further to look at interpretation and definition in part as correlative terms. This point follows from the fact that correlative terms are involved in the definition of each other. I will further explore and expand on this point about correlatives as I move through the course of the book. Furthermore not only do I want to deal with the topics of interpretation and definition from the perspective of logical definitions, where we are able to find words that we can reliably stand on, but I also want to treat interpretation and definition as rhetorical modes used to generate new words and new types of meaning. Through interpretation and definition we are able to generate new meaning and new terms for all the different genres of communications. We do it not only in the sciences and in the technologies but in the creative arts and in literature, and especially in ethics, where we are dealing with the ins and outs of the sorts of negotiations that take place in politics, especially noteworthy as seen in the formation of legal language (Schiappa 2003).

It is a linguistic fact that language as a synchronic system of signs evolves from interpretations of our uses of signs in personal contexts and from the singular events of rhetorical situations. Developments in language use and usage start in everyday speech engagements. All communication starts as *parole*, "speech" in unique contexts and in singular events. These unique communication events of speaking our language are the places where we develop new meanings. But even more importantly, writing sets the precedents for what becomes established, recorded, developed, and accepted as language usage. Writing lays the foundation for definitions of usage, but it also lays the foundation for further innovations that go on into further refinements and changes in language both in speaking and writing.

The problem of meaning is finding interpretations and definitions that will define what it is that we are doing in talking about meaning, which on the surface appears to be a highly circular, blurred, and muddled topic. In talking about meaning, we circle through our own word uses when we try to communicate to others what is meant. Language in a context of action is foremost used in our communicating with each other. And foremost, language is to be understood in the way it creates its own clarifications about itself so as to make what it says better understood.

It is in the acts of opening up to others about our own experiences that we communicate. It is in the development of new words and new expressions with new meanings that our public advances and accumulations of what we consider knowledge are made possible. New words and new forms of expression make us aware of the possibilities and the potentialities that we have for gaining new knowledge for facing up politically to our futures and for looking forward to the future of our civilization.

Throughout the book, I shall try to illustrate that figures of speech are modes of indirection that allow us to focus on issues from new innovative or novel perspectives. The least we can say about figures is that they engage us from refreshed perspectives. Note that a figure takes more time to process its meaning than does a literal expression, and thus redundancy as a rhetorical strategy in interpreting figures gives us even more and more processing time to fully grasp its figurative meaning. This is one of the instrumental values of extended metaphors. In rhetoric by using figures we achieve perspective reversals by using different rhetorical devices: by using syntactical anomalies, by semantic anomalies, by devices that trigger surprise references, by unexpected allusions, and especially by introducing newly reframed perspectives. Figures provide us with new contrasts and new comparisons by playing with ambivalent and shifting references. Redundancy as I hope to illustrate in the extended text keeps something in focus for an extended time so as to keep triggering the implications it has for the topic at hand. It is for this reason that I will deliberately use redundancy interpretively as a rhetorical device to explore meaning contrasts.

Traditionally in the many studies of semiotics (science of signs) there have developed many modes and methodologies whereby we can clarify meaning. Some want to speak of their critique of meaning as logical analysis. Others want to speak of it as semiotic analysis. Others want to talk about the meaning of signs, about iconology, and about iconography. Others want to talk as Ludwig Wittgenstein does about language games. Others want to see literary criticism as the basic mode of language critique.

Others want to frame such critiques in the strategies and modes developed in rhetorical criticism. Some want to talk about such critiques as interpretive criticism. For some the key to understanding meaning is to be found in the art of the paraphrase. Others want to reduce the study of meaning to pragmatic analysis where syntax and semantics are anchored in the conventions of communicative action. Others want to reduce meaning to what is given to consciousness in the phenomenological reductions of the intentionality to be found in acts of communication. This is a general description of Edmund Husserl's method of phenomenological reduction.

Others want to categorize meaning clarification as hermeneutics, which is an aggregate name for all the methodologies involved in the interpretations of texts. Hermeneutics as a growing movement had its historical origins in the disciplines that sought to determine the meanings of the scripts of sacred texts. As a field of interpretive studies it has extended its scope, as I am trying to do in what I have to say, to all modes of interpreting meaning. So in a way what I am doing within my own critical frames might be simply called one more mode of hermeneutics. But insofar as I want to integrate what I am doing with logical analysis, what I am doing is additive to traditional critical work labeled hermeneutics.

All these modes of clarification, when considered singularly within each of these diverse theoretical semantic frames, I want to show are for the most part one sided and fraught with paradoxes about how best to approach and unravel these puzzlements that we get into when we talk about meaning. Each is fraught with the paradoxes that we get into in talking about interpretation, such as the one now frequently labeled "the hermeneutic circle," in which interpretation continuously grounds itself in and upon its own interpretations. Such a cat-endlessly-chasing-its-tail methodology based upon circles of interpretation leaves truth seekers with none of the foundations necessary to arrive at the certainties that they think they need to know to understand what someone is saying.

What I am proposing to do in my own critique of the problems of meaning—that is, the problem of what it is to mean—is to integrate many of these seemingly disjunctive and opposed semiotic traditions that each in different ways appears to be explaining on different levels problems about meaning. For the most part these different semiotic traditions in logic and linguistics can in part be traced back to two historical figures.

There are the semiotic traditions following the work of Charles Sanders Peirce (1960), and there are the European traditions of linguistics with its beginnings in the semiology of Ferdinand de Saussure (1972). I do not propose to engage in any sort of historical critique of these two major historical figures, nor do I examine any of their early work and trace the effects they had on the developments of semiotics.

Rather what I want to do is to introduce some of my own revisions of the frames that I have found in the study of rhetoric that attempt to encompass the directions that the work of these two figures historically has taken. I have found these rhetorical frames useful to talk about meaning both in reading and writing, which is ultimately the only way we have of coming to terms with terms in any fixed way in the languages of this world. I have found some of my revised notions of rhetorical modes useful for exploring issues of meaning that are explored on the advanced levels of rhetorical critique, in those critiquing strategies found not only in rhetorical criticism but in the critiquing strategies found in the arts of rhetorical invention, in the arts of composing speeches, in the composition of written texts, and especially in fashioning moral, ethical, and political appeals.

In my own critique of the problems in discussing meaning I want to show how the theory of reference that emerged out of a representational theory of knowledge (so prominently discussed in analytic philosophy), when it itself is subjected to logical analysis, becomes a mere one-sided and misleading approach to the study of meaning. And I also want to show how the theory of difference and the systems of contrast said to be found in language that emerged from the linguistics of Saussure too are equally one sided in discussing meaning. Discussions of meaning following Saussure fail to discuss the creative aspects of how new meaning is generated by acts of linguistic refinement. They fail to recognize the role that prescription and acceptance plays in the sciences and technology. They fail to discuss adequately diachronically (through a cross section in time) how our words are born, live, and die (Crystal 1997).

Both structuralism and the later poststructuralist thought, I maintain, are one-sided explanations about what it is that we do in the name of interpretation and definition in talking about meaning. Both movements for the most part have failed to show how we actually innovatively create meaning in all the practical aspects of living as we carry out the work of our daily lives. They fail to explain how we create the language that we can stand on in our applications of words to actions in the working out the problems of our daily lives.

Written discourse, as the deconstructivists or postmodernists maintain, ultimately is the standpoint we use mutually in the last analysis to comprehend and understand each other. It is in written discourse that we state necessarily and sufficiently where we stand exactly in talking about the meanings we deal with in dealing with each other. And we use language foundationally, not in the logical sense of truth functionally based definitions of the logical positivists, but we use it by clarifying our meaning by two rhetorical processes that I propose to describe as *rhetorical interpretation* and *rhetorical definition*. Rhetorical definition as a mode of clarification is especially important in written texts. As I hope to show, rhetorical definition is ultimately the rhetorical standpoint we need to take in all our practical dealings with the world. Rhetorical definitions create the standpoints we need to take toward anything and everything that we do in this world, and even more importantly, it includes even how we are able to deal and to come to terms with ourselves.

But first, in order to probe our search for our standpoints that we want to take in our use of words, we need to deal with the treachery and the deviousness of so much word play committed by so many in talking about meaning. We need to clear away the infelicities of those who ask us questions about meaning to which they have no clear answers. It is such hocus-pocus in the word play about meaning that drives many of us to despair about the meaning of so many different things that people say, and especially about the meaning of that notorious puzzling question already mentioned about "the meaning of meaning."

It is these tricks and diversions into the shifting senses of the meaning of words that get us into these verbal traps that so frequently and constantly lead us astray. It is these tricks and verbal blunders in talking about meaning that prompt many of the stupid questions people ask about what is the meaning of this or that, whether they be about the meaning of visual forms, musical forms, words, concepts, or just things. All are things said by some to have meaning. The word *meaning* slides undetected and unnoticed from one aspect of experience to another without the least awareness that there are these meaning shifts about what is meaning occurring across so many different activities whereby we communicate with each other.

To confront these paradoxes, deceptions, and puzzlements about meaning, I propose, then, to discuss some of the frames developed in the critical thinking movement, especially by using some of the logical frames used in linguistic or analytic philosophy. Many of these critical methods I have found previously developed in logical studies. But I also want to combine this work derived from logical analysis and embed it within rhetorical frames that I have found in the new developments of rhetoric, especially those found in some of the existing methods exercised and now currently in fashion in rhetorical criticism.

CHAPTER 2

What Is the Meaning of Life?

As an introductory step to both my analytic method and my rhetorical critique, I want to take on in some depth an exemplary example of a quest for meaning that constantly is being asked and that tends to baffle a great number of people. For me "What is the meaning of life?" is a razzle-dazzle question. It is the prime example of what I like to consider a "dumb" question about meaning that can have no straightforward, precisely direct, defined answer to it.

The question is a question most frequently asked of philosophers, as if philosophers are the ones who search for answers to such a question. And it seems when asked to be a condemnation of philosophy, implying that philosophy cannot come up with any satisfactory answers. Some may think of the question as a fair and common-sense question, but when you think about it, there is just no common sense to it. And that raises many questions about the question itself.

The question with this question, as with most questions, is just what sort of question is being asked in the asking of it. The question from one point of view suggests that the questioner is in ignorance of the truth and wants to know a true answer about the meaning of life. But such a presumption that there is possibly a *clear* answer begs the question whether there is an answer *at all*, and at the same time it implies and seems to deny the real possibility that there is no answer to it. And if the latter is true, then the question should be, "Why is there no answer to it?"

Either way of asking, whether life has meaning or not, presumes that the question is clear and avoids altogether the issue whether the question is meaningless or hopelessly confused. It also avoids the question whether the question is ambiguous, since the term *meaning* in the question may have multiple senses that leave one up in the air about just what is meant. And in another way the way the question is asked diverts attention away from the questioner's purposes in asking the question in the first place. And that raises the question why anyone would ask a meaningless or ambiguous question. Why would anyone ask a question with terms of indeterminate meaning? What was their agenda?

To begin seriously my critique, it should be noted that there are various possible senses of the word *meaning* that need to be interpreted, analyzed, or defined before a response to this all-too-popular question can be attempted. Do we mean by *meaning* "a sense of purpose"? "having significance"? or "being of importance"? If life has meaning, can we just know intuitively what it means for life to have meaning?

But importantly for many there is the question or suggestion about whether there is such a thing as an ultimate meaning to life. Is it possible that ultimate meaning is about what is everlasting or eternal and that what is ultimate in meaning is a part of a divine design or destiny for all human beings? In talking about *destiny*, is there just one single meaning or a single end in the living out of our lives for all of us when life seems to be many sided with so many different meanings and destinies for so many different people at different times? Or to put it another way, if life has meaning, why can that meaning not be multiple and varied depending on the meaning we personally want to give our life at any one given period or point in time? Why can it not be a meaning that varies with our own choosing?

But most of us fail, unfortunately, despite all our internet servers, to make any connections to God's answering machine. And those of us who fail to find the link to it find it difficult to imagine what an inner religious revelation would be like, even if we were to chance upon it. If we perchance were to see the Divine Light, how do we know we would be seeing the divine in it? And to pique us, the answer usually is that God's light needs no outside test or confirmation. The answer we would say, is actually to be in the light of it.

But I suspect in my cynical fashion that the question about the meaning of life has a devious, religious motive behind it. It is, I suspect, asking for a *deus ex machina* sort of answer about the meaning of life, and that sort of answer suggests that God is a joker in a game of celestial poker and that we can use that joker to answer every question about the meaning of life. And the problem with that sort of answer is this: how do we come about understanding what the meaning of life is if it is dedicated to such an all-powerful God? How do we go about getting fixed answers from God or his surrogates as to how we should give meaning to our lives?

Noteworthy is that we find in the multifarious contexts of religious preachings only proxy answers proposed by numerous divine mediators. Or maybe luckily we can try to take the initiative ourselves to find the answer and seek to find our own direct connection to deity without the help of someone's divinely mediated advice about how to make that divine connection. How many mega preachers with microphones and rock star amplifiers are today soliciting money, infamously recommending what they think is their proprietary ownership over those Internet connections that they have to God's Web site? It seems they want you just to contribute to their radio and TV networks to help them further their material prosperity as messengers to spread the blessing of their message. Any notion of self-evidence requires a great deal of self-confidence to tell others about it. And so the circle of trust and faith goes around and around as infinite religious paradoxes surround any notion of finding the meaning of life in an inner light and in having faith for faith's sake about what you are seeing in that supposedly revealed and revelatory light.

But to get a better slant on this dumbfounding question put to unbelievers about the meaning of life, I suggest that we first turn from questions about divine revelations to some naturalistic questions about what it is to have meaning. "Do stones have meaning?" "Do the stars have meaning?" Surely in one sense stones and stars merely exist in the same way as our own existence exists. We just are. As some naturalists want to maintain, we got to be just here where we are by all those causal forces that have been coming together by selective biological choices. But in the end could it be that we and stones just happen from causal events in nature? What we are is just a matter of natural occurrences. Just as dogs chase rabbits, we are here simply chasing what we love to chase. We just exist like stones and stars. We have been just deposited wherever we are and doing what comes naturally.

But why all this questioning about the meaning of life if life is just a natural event? The question is odd. Or is the question when asked a genuine attempt to ask how we should want to live out our lives? Is it not a question about whether life is worth living? Certainly this last question is deeply personal, and the answer is personal and individual and not subject to commands, especially if we were to have a God who has given us liberties about the kind of life that we want to live. Has God given us free will to suffer the consequences?

For the most part the answer about our various choices that we make from day to day depends upon how we feel about events at any given moment. Some of us have different answers about what we think to be important. It should be noted that for some people meaning in their life for the most part is just having kids and living for their kids. Each one and everyone in the long run is simply after what gives them their kicks. Yet there are some who despair at having to answer a question about how their lives can only have the meaning they give to it themselves. And if anyone feels that they are in total despair about themselves, that appears to be to some just a sure sign of severe psychological depression, and for that they need psychological help. Most of us, though we may at times probably feel that though life may be not so rosy, at least we find life to be worthwhile most of the time. And if at times nothing seems worth much in our lives, we at least have to admit that it is better than nothing.

Questions about the goodness of life are very complex and have no simple answers. Answering such questions about our personal love of life requires an infinite capacity for judgment and careful assessment of our individual lives and our potentialities; most of us, in our all-too-short period in life, wish it lasted longer. Sometimes the question about the meaning of life seems to be asking for an overarching explanation of why everything or anything happens. And in addition, such a question seems at times to be asking about how we should be living out our lives, located as it is in the grand totality of our limited perspective that we have on "everything." And it is this need for a unifying perspective on "everything" that extends beyond our ken that motivates those who pursue metaphysics. It motivates all those who speculate on astronomical cosmologies about all that flying, fiery debris that seemingly and endlessly fulminates and fluxes out there, either expanding or filling up space.

But is there any meaning or significance in all those boiling energies that we speculate about that fill up space? Is there any more meaning in everything that we find out there than that which we find simply existing in stones? What place do we have in just existing for ourselves in that grand order of everything that exists? But surely naturalistic explanations do not give us the "meaning of" why there are stones, or why in the evolutionary processes there are living things. It is these very thoughts that prompt those who think about intelligent design. But note the ambiguities in all this asking for the "why" of things. Are we, in asking for physical explanations, asking for reasons, or again are we asking for purposes?

When we look at all those asking questions about purposes or explanations about ultimate ends of life, they all appear to be no more than desperate attempts in one fell verbal swoop to give us a final and a conclusive answer to all the many questions about life's uncertainties. They are questions for many about the consequences that follow after our ensuing final departure from our lovely green, earthly pastures. And we find that some religious advocates suggest that the afterlife is of much greater importance than this one, and that its importance dims any importance we might have for "this sorry life." The glory of this life is thought to be a mere shadow of the glory in the next. This was the subject of Pascal's wager. The odds on a bet made on a measure of the good of the finite against a measure of infinite good ends up being zero. What an infinitely small price to pay for paradise? It is a question that persuades suicide bombers.

But there is another perspective on meaning and purposes in life that I wish to point out, one that is completely ignored in all this game of religious cat and mouse about who has the secret and who has the mission to reveal it. If we carefully think about the question "What is the meaning of life?" we find that in one way it does not make sense to say that our lives have no meaning. Our lives are full of meaning and full of purposes. Is it factually true, as many speak of life, that it has no meaning for people? And of course those who believe in religion do, as they say, find that their lives are full of meaning in believing whatever they believe religiously. But we can say the same for megalomaniacal fools who believe in their own divine destiny. Certainly, Hitler had meaning in his life. But what gives religious advocates the belief that others, who do not believe in their religion, have no meaning to their lives? This question about the meaning of our lives is comparable to questions asked by religious advocates about the impossibility of an ethics or a morality that is not based on religion.

And again too is this disbelief in the validity of any naturally based rational morality at all based on fact? Does belief in fairness and justice require a belief in God? The analogous question for morality is, "Can there ever be any ground for a secular ethics or a secular morality?" Beliefs that without religion life can no meaning and that without religion there can be no sense of right and wrong simply are false presumptions about how many actually think. Such presumptions are contrary to what we observe about human beings and the lives that they live. It is these obviously false presumptions about life without meaning and a life without any moral sense that create the beliefs generating many of the dumb questions about sources of meaning and morality. Dumb questions, I repeat, are ones that simply rest on obvious false presumptions that in turn generate questions that beg answers to issues about life in question. Note the question "Why do you beat your wife?" It is a dumb question, for I do not beat my wife. Beating my wife is a false presumption held by the person asking the question.

All these contentions about life having no meaning, nor that there can be no justice without religion, are refuted by the very fact that many people do have both meaning in their lives and have a sense of justice. Many understand how justice can be obtained in practical ways in the way they live out their lives. And the questions about meaning and justice are also controverted logically again in theology. It is controverted by the fact that actions based upon divine demands without a divine sense of justice must ultimately be demeaning to an omnibenevolent and compassionate deity who believes in benevolence and justice. Such a deity would have a rationality and a moral sense identical with those who believe in justice without divine commands based upon their own moral sense. They would have a belief in the need for the practical value of reason and justice, such as the belief that a society is based upon mutually accepted agreements on how to get along with other people. It is a belief derived from a sense of justice that a good society requires good will and justice to progress and survive.

What we are giving allegiance to in this case in our theology is not to divine ordinances but to rational justifications for good will and justice. Such rational grounds are based simply on the recognition of a need for benevolence and justice if we are going to have functional societies, especially societies politically structured to enable us to live together in prosperity, security, and peace. We must grant, then, that many situations are arguably unfair without any appeal to religious issues. But we also must grant that many events have no meaning for us in the way we live. But equally on the other hand, we must agree that many events do have meaning for us in the ways that we do live.

It is only our ignorance that perpetuates our despair at not succeeding at much of what we strive for in life. We must admit that we are all ignorant of much that surrounds us, and we are especially ignorant of much of what has happened in the past. And we are equally ignorant of much of the world that is immediately about us. Much of the world is a blank and a mystery to us. And that ignorance means in one sense that what we do not know has no meaning for us in the long run, as we have no positive knowledge about those things that we do not know anything about that would make a significant difference to us.

And that is life! The meaning of our futures is always cloaked in probabilities, and in living we have to face up to those probabilities; we especially have to take advantage of options when there are favorable opportunities open to us. Or again we have to face up to those other probabilities that threaten us with disaster. Preventive medicine is certainly an option we should rationally pursue.

But how can we say that there is no meaning at all to everything that we do? Why should we not just think of life as an experience where we know the meaning of what many events have in store for us? But for many things we need to admit there is no meaning in them at all for us, and we need to admit that there is little we can do in facing up to some of life's spectacular, unfortunate uncertainties. It is the ordinary condition of our lives that we do not know everything, but what we do know is that there are many situations and encounters that are meaningful and important to us. And in those cases there are things that make life meaningful, significant, and important in each one of those passing moments. But in the end we have to reconcile ourselves, as the saying goes, to death and taxes.

But in all this digression about "meaning," "significance," and "importance" we should note that these three terms at times appear to be correlatives. We find each involved in the definition of the other, which is again to chase after the meaning of these terms in terms of the other terms. Having significance we have meaning, but not always does meaning have significance. How, then, do these terms overlap and interact as correlatives? These sorts of questions take us again and again full circle and back again to the problems we have in defining one term in terms of the other. How do we cut through this circle in asking and talking about the differences in the meaning of terms, such as the meaning of the term *meaning*, or again the meaning of the term *significance*, or even the meaning of term *importance*? We are circling again through synonyms that seem at times to be no more than empty synonymous abstractions. How does one get out of such a meaningless circle with any definitional precision?

To get out of an airplane spin, you give a hard kick to the rudder opposite the spin. You put the plane into a dive to regain the lift on your inner liftless spiraling wing. You need to regain that lift back on that unstable wing. So too likewise we need to abandon the generality of terms such as meaning, definition, and interpretation on the abstract level that have put us paradoxically into our verbal spin. On certain levels verbal abstractions tend to be nothing more than empty abstractions that give us no cognitive lift. And that is to say these verbal abstractions on one level have no practical direct applications to the world around us. These words, like airplanes when they have no lift to support their flight, cannot fly; they are empty, having no cognitive lift. Like an airplane that is stalling, they lack any ground in the applications of the controls that we have in using those words.

Instead of trying to define terms on an abstract level, I suggest that we should try instead to give these terms uses for talking about practical meanings in specific everyday applications. We should ask about the specific situations in which abstract, correlative, or umbrella terms, such as meaning, definition, and interpretation do in fact apply in bringing us into direct contact with the world.

On concrete levels of applications such terms as *meaning*, *significance*, *importance*, and *purpose* at times do have clear senses in which they do in fact apply. The same holds with many of our inexact synonyms. They do apply on certain levels. And new, often subtle, uses of these terms can be discovered, refined or even invented for the use of them as we extend their use in new contexts and unfamiliar situations. I suggest that we tend to underestimate the generative potential of the imagination to find new applicable uses of words in new and different contexts on various levels in quite new and different situations.

Note, then, the temporal aspect in concrete applicable circumstances of the meaning of meaning, of the meaning of significance, of the meaning of importance, and the meaning of purpose. Such terms are applied relative to times and places. In certain circumstances such terms certainly have very direct applications. What are we to make of this momentary, transitory sense of the importance of meaning and significance, a sense that we have in the past attributed to long-ago, chance meetings with people we talked with but which are now long forgotten? How difficult it is to remember each and every one of those whom we met for a moment on one particular day that had significance and importance for us on those long past forgotten days! And we must then admit that we are ignorant of experiences we have had with so many people we have met in our life. And those meetings were important to us for the moment or two that we had with them, but now they are completely forgotten.

Note that teachers have many students, and their importance to teachers is equally temporary. Teachers and students forget each other. And that forgetting of moments of past importance in classes especially holds for most students now after they have left and are out of school. How important grades were in high school! And in no time at all they were no longer important. How many remember the names of their teachers?

One interpretation we might make of the question about the importance of importance is that it is a devious, empty, tautological question. We are being tricked by the question into pursuing the meaning of a tautology: "To eat beans you have to eat beans." In such sentences the predicate adds nothing new to the subject. It is a redundancy that rhetorically adds nothing enlightening about what is being talked about in the name of importance. But another interpretation of the meaning of the question about the importance of importance may be that it is simply a confusing question about different senses of the meaning of the term importance. We might interpret the meaning of importance, for instance, in different ways: it could refer to a significant purpose, what is best, or even what is thought to be an ultimate value. The questions, then, in all three of these cases are about the meaning and the interactions of the meaning of different expressions about importance, as we use these different interpretations differently in different contexts. And usually context helps us know and interpret that difference.

In other words the word "meaning" in any question about "the meaning of life" may have many different senses in its use, and we consequently are at odds about how each of the different senses of meaning is being used. And since we do not know the meaning of the question about the meaning of life, why in the first place does anyone ask a question that we know to be ambiguous? Since the question's meaning is logically indeterminate, is it not just another one of those trick questions that are used to confuse us?

Note in the interpretive jargon of critical analysis, a word is said to be *multivocal* when it has more than one usage or sense. A word is said to be *univocal* when it has only one use or one sense in its usage. That terminology is to be contrasted with term *equivocal* which means that the word can convey more than one sense in the context where the speaker seems to be talking about only one thing. To say that an argument equivocates is to say that it violates the rule of argument that the terms in one's conclusions should have the same meanings they have in one's premises. Note that by introducing the terms univocal, multivocal, and equivocal we have reported on the meaning of technical language that logicians have defined to talk about varying senses in the uses of words within logical arguments.

But note that these technical logical definitions are reducible to terms taken from ordinary usage. Such logical jargon might be helpful in talking about words with multiple senses, but logical jargon such as multivocal are not terms that we necessarily need to use in ordinary ways of speaking. We need as a substitute just simply think of our words as "having multiple senses" in a context. Why, then, use technical jargon when ordinary words will do just as well to talk about the different senses of a technical term? The need for using the technical jargon of semiotics is a question I need to consider seriously throughout this book, for sometimes jargon can be useful as an aid to introducing new meanings and new distinctions to talk about meaning. But in the end we should be able to understand our technical senses of terms in the language of everyday usage.

But either way we interpret our question about the meaning of life, whether with or without jargon, it ends up being a question that has multiple senses (i.e., it is multivocal) for which we cannot give a fully determinate, meaningful answer, given the question's ambiguities (multivocality). But importantly there is a much more important critical task involved in asking about the meaning of life. We can also ask what is *implicitly being asked*. In this case one interpretation of the question about the meaning of life is that the question suggests (i.e., *contextually implies*) that presumptively we have no psychological or naturalistic answers for it and that we can only give religious answers to it. As such the question thus becomes a lead-on question made by those who want to purvey their religious beliefs.

And this suggests that the person proposing the question has religious answers, especially if that person has a declared dedicated mission to provide those answers. And the question, then, contextually implies that those people themselves have meaning to their own lives in being missionaries proclaiming that their lives have meaning. Certainly, that mission assuredly gives them meaning to their lives. How comforting it must be to know that the way you are living your life has the answer to how the rest of us ought to live out our personal lives.

Implicit suggestions are *implicit implications* (contextual implications). "Implicit implications" is not a redundancy. Implicit implications cannot be formulated except by means of interpretations that we can rephrase or turn into explicit statements. And the job of critical interpretation is to make manifest in explicit language what is implicit or suggested. Such interpretations are about the implicit implications of a text. What they are is a much more complicated affair than simply asking for a definition or for an explanation of the literal meaning of what is being said. As I hope to show, contextual implications are central to the pragmatics of meaning and basic to the conceptions we have for any talk about interpretation and definition.

Religious answers to our question about the meaning of life often wrap mysteries into enigmas generated by the ambiguities of the question. Note that religious language talks a great deal about "what it is to have faith and trust in God." And often many of these advocates of certain religious faiths use this sort of language by treating the terms *faith*, *belief*, and *trust* as if they were synonymous terms when in many cases they are not.

Note the claim that "to have faith you have to have trust." *Faith* may mean "trust," but it could also mean "conviction" or "belief." The statement is either the tautology "to have trust you have to have trust," which is nonsense, as the logical positivists liked to say. Or if we mean by faith belief, then the question is raised, "How can trust produce belief in us?" And that question raises the additional complication about what we mean by belief. Is belief a type of feeling, a disposition, or something we think we know that is based on good reasons? Such language that uses the terms faith, trust, and belief is ripe with abstract ambiguities that generate more and more confusion.

In discussing mysteries, we need to accept our ignorance as a limiting condition of how we live out our lives. Our language and memory can only encompass a very narrow compass of the details that we experience in the living of it. We have little reliability of knowing very much of what will occur outside the small perimeters of our awareness and the memories we have that define the limits of our existence. And we have little knowledge of what will happen to us in the future. The best we can do from day to day is to make the most of what we know and what we think we know best in the small circles in which we live out our lives. The best we can do is to think out the problems and issues that we face in a clearly defined way as best we can each and every day, and then we must make the most of these definitions of problems and issues to guide what causal applications we have available to us and to use them as best as we can in controlling the circumstances of our lives.

The limitations of our language usage, I suggest, make it difficult to make sense of questions that use multiple senses of words (multivocal terms), especially when we use abstract terms such as meaning and importance, as well as other general terms, such as *freedom*, *responsibility*, *love*, and *justice*. To repeat, if we examine the usage of such abstract terms in everyday discourse, these abstract words in their general application and in our abstract discussion of them have very limited practical use in making decisions, especially about many of the important issues that today we find discussed in ethics and politics.

Abstract concepts function better not on the level of generality but on the level of specificity, where they are applied to the concrete details and difficulties in situations requiring specific judgments. "We *meant* to have you over for dinner." "It is not *fair* for you not to keep your promise to meet her tomorrow." "Feel *free* to take what you want." "I *love* ice cream." What is meant by these expressions requires minimal interpretation. Note that the senses of these terms in these applied cases are easily interpreted or paraphrased in these contexts. There is very little ambiguity to be had. We simply know what is meant if we are competent speakers of the English language. Why would any one agonize over the meaning of these useful abstract words in these specific everyday contexts?

Thin concepts used in hortatory rhetoric, such as concepts of justice, meaning, liberty, and happiness, have definite applications when we try to apply them to particular incidents in our lives. In those specific contexts those seemingly abstract words light up and become full of meaning. "You know that cheating on your wife is unfair to her." "You get my meaning. I don't have to explain." "You are free to go." "What you say doesn't make me happy." Such is the game of life that we live from day to day in ways that are down to earth in talking about justice, meaning, liberty, and happiness. In those specific contexts such terms are not empty.

CHAPTER 3

Making and Discovering Meaning

In what I propose, then, to say about interpretation and definition, I see rhetoric as the overarching art embedded in all studies of language use and usage. I see it as fundamentally tied to all the arts of making, creating, and using meaning. I see it as an art used for all sorts of different practical purposes in studying communications, especially for dealing with those issues being analyzed and studied by what I have referred to in my preface as little rhetoric.

But in making this big claim about big rhetoric and the importance of the rhetorical modes of interpretation and definition, in no way do I want to deny the importance of little rhetoric. My statement merely stresses the importance that big rhetoric has in defining the overarching issues about what is going on in little rhetoric. Little rhetoric is a garden of its own, full of designs and strategies that reveal all the fascinating facets of personal, social, and political communications that are going on in human society.

There is presently a large amount of self-critique and a great deal of reflection among humanists on the current loss of interest in the humanities. But now in the humanities I find, despite its recent decline in academia, a renewed reassessment of its importance for the future of civilization; I especially find it going on in the present-day enthusiasms of rhetoricians. And in that reassessment of the humanities I find that there is an important role for rhetoric to play, especially that initiated by the new rhetoric that emerged in America in the late 1960s.

I find that the importance of the humanities is best exemplified in the studies of hermeneutics and rhetorical criticism, which for the most part is about little rhetoric. I want to show how the work that I am developing here on interpretation and definition emerged, as I have said, from my own studies in critical thinking, anchored as they have been in rhetoric. And finally I want to show how our conceptions of interpretation and definition are at the heart of issues about the value of hermeneutics for any cultural or any critical critique, especially those made of written texts by those working within the humanities.

Interpretation and definition are fundamental topics for all branches of education. Rhetorical knowledge, as with interpretation and definition, are fundamental to literacy in speaking, in writing, in reading, and above all in listening. Rhetorical knowledge is fundamental to how we think about what we say and how we best can say it. And that is why I have structured my book around the expansion and clarification of two basic, but in a way ancillary, modes of rhetoric, interpretation and definition.

And to do that I am expanding and enlarging on our senses of what it is to be an interpretation or on what it is to be a definition. To accomplish this end, I propose as a first step in my critique to introduce a newly proposed basic semiotic axiom of meaning. Instead of talking about meaning in terms of a theory of verification, as has notoriously been done by logicians such as Alfred Tarski, I want to start from a point of view taken by Ludwig Wittgenstein, where meaning and language games emerge from the refinement of primitive human reactions to the conditions in the world. Language is not simply a preexisting condition developed out of names for things in this world. It is something that grows and evolves out of social conditions. It grows out of the emerging new roles that language plays in the changing forms of social cooperation. In that view languages grow, live, and die within the history of different geographically isolated and segregated groups of people. It lives and dies in the face-to-face relations in dealing with families and friends (Crystal 2005, 2007).

I call my statement my basic semantic axiom, as it is for me a starting point for my analytic expansion of the key terms used in formulating a number of hermeneutic maxims that I propose to develop for use as strategies to talk about clarification and meaning. For me my statement is only a beginning point, not an end point for talking about interpretation and definition. And the following statement is no more than an oversimplified interpretation and an expression of it derived from my awareness of what I conceive as my own usage of terms in my native English.

As formulated, my basic semantic axiom is not easily practical or immediately applicable by any direct use. Without amplification of my statement of it as an axiom, it is too abstract to apply directly in any practical way. But I want to use the axiom in the beginning as a starting point to talk further about interpretation and definition in terms of other different, seemingly synonymous and related, terms that help me clarify the meaning of what I want to convey by my axiom. The following, then, is a statement of my basic semantic axiom with a few preliminary interpretive comments added that I think can be made about it: "In talking about meaning, it makes more sense to say, 'We interpret sense, we both define meaning and interpret meaning, and we interpret language use and define language usage.'"

From my perspective it logically follows from this proposed axiom about *sense, meaning, use,* and *usage* that it is simply *my interpretation* (*judgment*) of how these four terms are frequently used in conjunction with the terms interpret and define. And from what I know of English usage and my own use of these terms, my interpretation of the frequent use of them in this manner is for me *by definition* a valid interpretation of what my axiom means.

Note again how self-referential all this language is in talking about meaning. This is why such talk appears to be so paradoxical. Such a condensed and abbreviated interpretation of how we talk about sense and meaning appears at first glance somewhat cryptic and aphoristic and seemingly merely an empty epigram. At best it amounts to no more than an intuitive sound byte. But nevertheless, we can amplify and expand on it, which I shall proceed to do throughout the course of this book.

And in the process of such definitional expansions through some interpreted senses of closely related synonymous terms and antonyms of these four named terms in the English language, I want to show that we can practically carry out a careful analysis of related terms that reflexively apply to them. Rhetorically, we can through interpretations of these terms related to interpretation and definition generate reports of English usage that are both ordinary and at times technical, and that in the end these reports end up being practically applicable in talking about problems about what it is to have meaning.

These interpretive reports of the use of these logically critiqued terms will provide us with new distinctions whereby we can expand on our common-sense conceptions of sense and meaning. We need thus to give a full account of the use and usage of these related terms, whereby we talk about different levels of meaning, and especially we need to face up to some of the awful paradoxes we get into in talking about meaning, as for example, in such puzzling self-referential questions as that about the meaning of meaning. Is questioning the meaning of the phrase the meaning of meaning a quest for a definition? Is it simply a request for an interpretation of the various senses of the uses of the term meaning? Or, is the phrase simply a garbled a bit of meaningless nonsense?

Note too how puzzling it is to ask for a definition of the sense of the expression *common sense*. It is asked presumptively as if such a concept as common sense nominally could have a defining referent. But note the ironic tone in speaking of common sense in saying, "There is nothing so uncommon as common sense." Is "uncommon common sense" just an oxymoron with a subtly implied ironic meaning about "good sense"? Note again the play on the root sense of the term *sense* in saying that what one is doing or saying is "not sensible." There is something strange about saying that what you are doing or saying doesn't make sense when our actions and words do seem to have a modicum of sense in our making use of them in the very saying of it, even if vague and ambiguous.

Even better yet, it is strange to say that what you say is "nonsense," especially when, again as suggested, the offending terms do have senses that make some sense when they are used. Such verbal twists on the terms *sense* and *nonsense* appear to be mere play on words that positivist philosophers such as Rudolf Carnap (1969) and the early Ludwig Wittgenstein (1922) made at the time and by which they were able to deceive others including themselves about what they were declaring to be nonsense.

How strange to talk about meaningful nonsense! When someone says what you say is nonsense, do they mean that what you say is false, or do they mean to say that what you say has no meaning at all? Yet note that logical positivists talked about emotive meaning. Is emotive meaning nonsense? And is not a confused sense of meaning nevertheless still a meaning, a blurred meaning? How can we avoid these endless verbal circles that we get into when we ask puzzling questions about the senses of the meanings of words as if words by themselves have meanings apart from the contexts of their use?

And thus one suggested perspective to take in asking such puzzling questions about sense and meaning is to interpret and expand on the various senses of the meanings of the ordinary uses of the terms *define* and *interpret*. And in that examination we might, as I suggest, find enough related words, some even technical, that we can use, that we can stand on and practically apply, when we talk about defining and interpreting. It is my thesis that not only are interpretation and definition logical modes, but in a fundamental sense they are foremost as I propose rhetorical modes of clarification. But they as modes do more than just clarify. They are important ways that we have in creating and finding language that we can act on. And they are the ways of finding or creating language that we can rely on in communicating with other people about things that they little understand or even know very little about. We need definitions to convey knowledge.

And we need definitions to actually *create knowledge*, which in one way seems to be a contradiction, for do we not often just speak only of discovering knowledge and not creating it? Such a question about discovering and creating knowledge divides many in the sciences from students in the humanities who strive for new and innovative meanings to express what they find to be the case. But the answer to any question about creating knowledge depends on how we conceive of knowledge. And in a sense much of our scientific knowledge is made possible by the creation of language in the sciences.

If knowledge is about the "about," which means about what is out there in the world independent of our conception of it, then we do not create it. In that sense words do not create reality. If, however, we need words with new meanings to discover what is true, then it follows that without the words there could be no truth. Without just those words that we have created there would be no knowledge. In that case knowledge is found embedded in the very words we formulate. Knowledge is absolutely dependent on the words that we create to know what we claim to know about.

To approach "definition" and "interpretation," we need, then, to understand the various senses of the uses of these two terms. To do that, I need to context my analysis by uncovering the communicative presumptions that we have and others have when they try to reach some sort of mutual understanding about what we say to each other. Such is the perspective of this book, which as a whole is a definitional expansion about what goes on in the name of clarification. Both of these rhetorical modes, interpretation and definition, as modes of clarification lay the foundation for mutual understanding whereby people communicate with each other.

The traditional rhetorical modes have been narrowly restricted to narrative, argument, description, and explanation. Each of them requires clarity and understanding in our uses of them. We need in using them to use words and expressions that define and interpret for the listener or reader what the speaker or writer wants to make clear in using these different traditional notions of modes. Speakers and writers seek clarity about what they are doing and saying on many different levels of discourse. Some do it by direct reference, some do it by indirection, some do it symbolically, and some do it even figuratively. Each requires a different level of interpretation and definition. And just focusing on any one level gives us a one-sided view of the complexities of communication. And it is for this reason I seek to bridge the gap that presently exists between Anglo-American and European semiotics, which have divergent views of how we communicate.

But I have found that there are two other ancillary distinguishable modes along with interpretation and definition that are little talked about in rhetoric that are also useful for clarification. They are *noting* and *reminding*. They are the modes that I primarily use in this book to make my case for the importance of a better conceptual understanding of what it is to define and to interpret. These two ancillary modes have never been treated in the literature of rhetoric as conventional or traditional rhetorical modes. Fundamentally, they have been treated in linguistics as speech acts. But I suggest that both of these ancillary modes can be conceived of as rhetorical modes that are very closely related to other types of pointing and referring, such as traditionally we do in logic in talking about defining. In a way noting and reminding as terms are used in ways comparable to logical designating expressions such as *denoting*, *designating*, or *making ostensive references* which as terms dominate most discussions of epistemic realism, the view that there is a reality independent of mind.

Denotation or ostension have been the traditional logical modes for directing our attention to what we are talking about. But there are other rhetorical modes of reference that sometimes explicitly and sometimes tacitly refer to what we mean. We find in rhetoric other stylistic genre and tropes of reference such as *allegory* and *allusion*. Both allegory and allusion as genre call attention to background knowledge in the minds of a listener or a reader. And we might add that it is these background assumptions that are equally important in the understanding of figures of speech, which function too by reminding us of our assumptions that we hold in the way that we look at the world.

Not only is my aim to note and remind in this book, but it is also to *appeal* to my readers to accept the validity of my interpretations of many noted distinctions that I find rhetorically useful, many of which others may not have noted before. These interpretive analyses will make up the body of this text. My aim is to get my readers to recognize that my analysis of these distinctions makes more sense than do the standard theories of interpretation and definition that we find in logic and literary studies. Even more so, my aim in this book is *to respond* and not to argue for any particular theory of meaning. I try to eschew theory. You will find for the most part that my rhetoric is what I call a *response rhetoric*. By response rhetoric I mean a rhetoric of *explanation* that gives readers what I think are the best ways of understanding what goes on in the name of interpretation and definition across the whole range of discursive practices (Yoos 1987).

Overall there are numerous dyadic relations or contrasting concepts about meaning and clarification that I wish to point out. We need to examine them to discover the important semantic interdependence that exists between these concepts that are relevant to any talk about interpretation and definition. There is a shifting back and forth of meaning going on between what I am calling interpretation and definition. It is that instability that is going on in these meaning shifts about these modes that needs to be carefully analyzed and questioned.

I want in addition to show how the oppositions between these designated dyads that I shall list are importantly contrastive rather than simply comparative. They are as contrastive terms often defined as *correlative terms*. Speaking of them as correlative shows how each term of a correlative pair involves the meaning of the other term in our interpretation of it. In doing this, I have found that there has been little discussion about the contrastive role in Aristotle's logic that *differentia* play in defining terms by genera distinctions.

Traditionally in an Aristotelian frame definition focuses on the overlapping contrasting *genera* of the defining terms. We tend to focus in defining on the role that the *genus* plays in identifying the term defined. The focus has been on properties or attributes held in common by a species rather than on the *differentia* that contrast with the *genus*. Aristotle's definitions are for the most part based on a logic of comparisons. But importantly, contrasts, I want to show, play the bigger role in defining than do logical definitions in terms of positive attributes or traits. Consequently, I find that there are limitations in defining the uses of terms by a logic of classes or by a set theory, which logically are analogous to Aristotle's predicate logic that uses predicate nominatives whereby definitions are formulated by only considerations of positive attributions.

I have found, for example, that in discussing correlative terms it is the contrasts that make correlative terms so fascinating. It is not their distinctions in terms of common defining attributes that dominates their meaning. For example, when we speak of an interpretation generically, a paraphrase appears to be a statement belonging to the genus interpretation. A paraphrase is an interpretation. But what is most interesting in thinking of paraphrases is how they contrast with interpretations. A paraphrase is more than an interpretation. But how much do the two differ? What makes them contrasting? Likewise a definition in one sense seems too to be a paraphrase of meaning. But in another way definitions importantly contrast with paraphrases. But how do they differ? These questions, I suggest, are fruitful in helping us to explore and to understand the differences between interpretation and definition.

Note the traditional philosophic discussions of "cause and effect," "means and ends," and "rights and responsibilities." They illustrate well the importance of contrasts in understanding the uses of these sets of correlative terms. It is around such concepts that many of the traditional aporia of philosophy have been generated. It is these differences and contrasts, as discussed in the philosophy of Jacques Derrida (1978), with his notion of *difference* ("*différance*"), that have made his way of looking at language seem to make such good sense. We need to explore, then, why deconstruction as a mode of semiotic critique seems to be descriptive of our use of language and how semantic confusions about meaning result in our uses of it.

In discussing aporia, for example, Derrida finds it is the differences between gift giving and economic exchanges treated as correlatives that are what generate the inconsistencies in our discussions about gift giving. In defining gifts and exchanges, Derrida finds the perplexities that we have in expecting anything in return from the recipient of a gift. For example, in giving should we expect any respect or gratitude for our generosity? The antinomy between giving and exchanging comes into being by the very inconsistency generated by the definition of a gift as not being an exchange.

Note that the term *exchange* is amenable to a positive definition. We give and we receive in exchanges. But do we not on many occasions in an exchange expect something back from the giving? A gift apparently ceases to be a gift when we receive or expect something in exchange. By definition a gift is paradoxical when we contrast acts of giving with our conventional acts of giving, for thoughts about generosity create expectations of wanting recognition for it and wanting something in return for our generosity. Any such expectation about gratitude amounts to making our act of giving an exchange. In my ironic moments I like to say that we have an obligation to allow people to be generous toward us.

Much in this fashion I find that the following listed topics, when considered as conceptual dyads, can be considered as correlative terms. When they are considered as such, you will find that they are subject to some of the comparable paradoxical issues that you will find relevant to any talk about defining and interpretation. All these dyads in what follows are to be treated as contrasting topics based on distinctions of difference. Their discussion throughout the book will be based on their contrasts and their differences.

List of the Dyads to Be Discussed throughout the Book

interpretation and definition
use and usage
illocutionary and perlocutionary acts
code and inferential theories of language
words and sentences
signs and symbols
literal and figurative
noting and reminding
logical and rhetorical definitions
analytic and synthetic
cardinal and rational numbers
numerator and denominator
application and control
saying and doing
conceptual and real definitions
talking the walk and walking the talk
interpretation and paraphrase
topic sentences and summary abstracts
interpretive summaries and interpretive commentaries

Some of these conceptual dyads are derivative of uses of technical language and some are not. I shall base my analysis of the technical language in explications of their proposed use or usage that is reducible to ordinary language. Each term in these dyads will help us get straight the meaning of the others, which in turn will help us hopefully understand in the long run what I am trying to do in the name of interpretation and definition.

Correlatives appear to be isolated conceptual dyads. But is that the case? Do they always stand alone separately in our thinking from other dyads? There is nothing in the way of saying that the term of one correlative dyad may be correlated with another term to form other sets of dyads that equally can be seen again as another pair of correlative terms. Such interconnections suggest that there are important limiting factors about how words relate that interanimates meaning across the whole spectrum of a language use. We see it in the linkages between synonyms and antonyms. We see it in the limits of our vocabularies (Urdang 1975; See *Webster's Dictionary of Synonyms*).

Note in the above pairs, interpretation and definition are one dyad. And interpretation and paraphrase are another. Paraphrase and translation might be said to be another. Note all four terms interpretation, definition, paraphrase, and translation, may be discussed by linking correlatives together in comprehensive statements about the meaning of what is being said in a language. The meaning of each of these terms in different contexts can be seen contrastively to animate the meaning of the other.

And as I explore each of the above dyads, you will find that all have some correspondence or correlation with the notion of "something having meaning." Each in a way, as I will speak of these dyads, can be shown to be defined in a context with the other. In other words, as the expression goes, we use other words to make comparable contrasts and distinctions. And we are always seeking in *other words* to understand what is the meaning of terms that we use. This always makes linguistic meaning a "merry-go-round that goes around and around," and where our quests for meaning end up we may never know. And sometimes, surprisingly, we may end up creating meaning that we want to stand on and live by.

This endless circling in search of meaning has been called the hermeneutic circle. We never end in our chasing after words through words to reach absolute certitude about the meaning of other words. And such a seemingly hopeless prospect of endless verbal chasing makes linguistic absolutists cry, "Relativism!" But as I shall show, the trip on the verbal merry-go-round does go a long way to help us clarify many of our paradoxes about the meanings of words and the meanings of our use of the word *meaning* in reaching an understanding about what is being said. Each of these contrasting dyads that I am proposing to discuss reveal the problems we have in keeping rhetorically straight what we are doing in rhetorical criticism in the name of interpretation and definition. Each of the above dyads forms and connects with others dyads in clarifying the different levels of meaning we use to talk about whatever goes on in life.

And thus in going through our circle of words we are led back full circle to what we are doing rhetorically, that is, clarifying meaning by defining and interpreting. Note that our circling through our vocabulary reveals the power of language to allow us to derive meaning through verbal and nominal interanimations between words. It enables us to find new ways of clarifying the meaning of what we see, what we hear, what we speak of, and ultimately what we write about. It ultimately gives us a place to stand in communicating with other people. It ultimately gives us greater understanding of the meaning of the words that we use in dealing with other people.

I want to make one final important note about the derivation of the semiotic frame at the center of my analysis in this book. You will find that frame presented in part in H. P. (Paul) Grice's *Studies in the Way of Words* (1989). His analysis of verbal meaning is first found in his classic essay "Logic and Conversation," in which he proposes his Cooperative Principles of Conversation (the Cooperative Principle): "Make your conversational contribution such as required, at the stage at which it occurs by the accepted purpose or direction of the talk exchange in which you are engaged."

And he goes on to say, "One may perhaps distinguish four categories under one or another, under which will fall certain more specific maxims or submaxims, the following of which in general will yield results in accordance with the Cooperative Principle."

And as he further notes, "I have stated my maxims as if this purpose were a maximally effective exchange of information; this specification is, of course, too narrow, and the scheme needs to be generalized to allow such general purposes as influencing or giving direction to the actions of others."

For me this amendment by Grice is much about rhetoric. I find this extension of Grice's maxims as he moves in the extended direction from *talk* to *nontalk*, to *nonverbal exchanges*, that he is going in the direction that I am taking in using revised rhetorical frames that equally apply not only to textual but to visual and spectacle types of rhetoric.

As Grice adds, "All [exchanges] are based upon the awareness of mutually held assumptions by the constituent members of social interactions who come to understand together each other's social behavior."

And instead of focusing simply as Grice does upon the logic of such conservational exchanges based upon both conventional and conversational implications ("implicatures") of such conversation exchanges, I prefer instead to talk about conversation as taking place in the much larger rhetorical frame of what Lloyd Bitzer has called in his famous article "a rhetorical situation."

To keep my beginning analysis simple, I prefer to frame my talk about a rhetorical situation not in terms of an information exchange, as Grice does, because in rhetorical situations I find *meaning* and *purpose* and not *truth* (logic) to be the major issue. And thus instead of framing my analysis in terms of "Logic and Conversation," as in Grice, where truth conditions are the major issue in informing and in arguing, I prefer to think that my analysis is about the larger rhetorical frame that I would prefer to entitle "Presumptions and the Rhetorical Situation."

But let me speak first to Grice's account of his maxims to show how his maxims are relevant to rhetorical issues about informational exchanges. Grice proposes four presumptive maxims that operate in a cooperative context. They follow from his roughly stated Cooperative Principle: "Make your conversational contribution such as is required in the talk exchange in which you are engaged." He then presents four specific maxims derived from the Cooperative Principle labeled "Quantity, Quality, Relation, and Manner."

In my own approach to Grice's terms and problems of communication, I prefer in what I want to say about what he says to concentrate on his maxims of *Quantity* and *Manner*, as they are most relevant to my semantic and pragmatic issues about meaning and issues about clarity of meaning. Quality and manner, then, are not just focused on logical issues where truth claims are basic. For me, meaning as an issue is always prior to questions about truth. Where we have truth we first must have some sense of the matter that we are being true about.

But let me state the four types of the Conversational Maxims that Grice defines:

(Note in the brackets below that I have named rhetorical topics related to the maxims that are of special interest both to informal logicians and practical rhetoricians.)

Maxims of Quantity

Make your contribution as informative as is required (for the current purposes of the exchange). [semantic inadequacy] [unwarranted assertability]
Do not make your contribution more informative than is required. [fallacies of diversion and distraction]

Maxims of Quality

Do not say what you believe to be false. [lying]
Do not say that for which you lack adequate evidence. [alleged certainty]

Maxim of Relation

Be relevant. [diversionary fallacies] [inferential theory of communication] [presumptions]

Maxims of Manner

Avoid obscurity of expression. [vagueness]
Avoid ambiguity. [ambiguity]
Be brief (avoid unnecessary prolixity.) [perspicacity] [focus]
Be orderly. [incoherence]

The maxim of quantity raises questions about what are the necessary and sufficient conditions for communicating. The maxim of quantity is about the adequacy of words to communicate a sufficient amount of information, but also it is about the important semantic problem of words not adequately referring to referents. In other words, words in logic fail in their practical applications in contexts of action in which they purportedly are said to apply but at times actually fail to do so.

Interestingly too, there is in a second part of Grice's maxim of quantity, the problem of saying more than what is being asked for. We commonly make the mistake in communicating of using words having more precise meaning than called for or giving more information than is actually called for in a situation. Precision and abundance of meaning are sometimes irrelevant to the purposes for which the words are being used. This second point is necessary to make in order to show better why the words of ordinary language in their definitions do not always require the precision of scientific terms that are used to replace them in scientific studies such as in physics and chemistry.

We do not need to think of gravitational forces ordinarily in talking about weight. And we do not have to think about water vapor pressure to talk about humidity. It is such issues about precision that make for confusion about the vagueness of terms in ordinary English usage of such words as *warm, cold*, or *hot*. Terms need to be as precise or as adequate as necessary for the purposes of their use in everyday contexts. As we shall see, there are these same sorts of issues arising about everyday uses of words, such as with our terms definition and interpretation. It is important to understand the different ways these two terms differ in meaning in the different contexts of their use. For certain purposes more precision in their use is needed than in other contexts. Thus, sometimes there is a need for logical definitions.

And a final point, as described by Grice: the notion of relevance is important to any determination of implicatures. He uses the term *implicature* to refer to the various types of implications that we speak of in ordinary English. The concept of implicature is key to the inferential theory of communication presented in Dan Sperber and Deirdre Wilson's *Relevance: Communication and Cognition* (1986). What these last two authors give in support of their inferential theory of communication plays a key role in what I shall later have to say throughout my book on the topic of interpretation and definition. The sort of distinctions that they present in their work helps define the basic problems one has in fashioning a rhetoric for different rhetorical situations. They help us develop types of rhetoric that are focused on the different discourse conventions and on the different contextual presumptions that we make when we interpret and define.

And that brings me back to what first led me in my first struggling beginnings in philosophy. It all began in my reading George Herbert Mead's *Mind, Self and Society* (1932). His theories of social interaction led me first to speculate on the foundations of grammar and later into thinking about the dynamics and differences between rhetorical situations. I found this topic very much enriched by what I found later, with the advent of the new rhetoric in the late 1960s in the studies of argumentation by Stephen Toulmin (1958, 1984) and Chaim Perelman (1968).

And it is thus from these perspectives that I have derived in a piecemeal fashion from Mead, Grice, and Sperber and Wilson my own rhetorical frames that I am using for my discussion of interpretation and definition. My work with these authors for me comes under the rubric of big rhetoric. I. A. Richards, in *The Philosophy of Rhetoric* (1965), urges that rhetoric be "a study of misunderstanding and remedies." Such a perspective on reading and understanding I find in harmony with what goes on in critical thinking.

Rhetoric and critical thinking are in many ways overlapping interdisciplinary programs that have been proposing remedies for the malaise of deception and misunderstanding to be found in public communication. Studying interpretation and definition should be seen, then, as addressing questions about these misunderstandings, about deceptions, and about bad-faith issues that are so pervasive now in contemporary public discourse, and especially within what we see now going on in the merchandizing of products and in the politics of destruction that is going on in the mass media.

CHAPTER 4

The Meaning of What You Would Like to Mean

Many philosophical questions about the meaning of certain concepts throw us into the verbal dithers, as I have already illustrated by pointing out the circular definitions that exist when we try to define terms by oppositions or contrasts. Such ambiguities throw us into endless questioning and word-chasing loops. Such questions are often thought of as paradoxes, which by some definitions are said to be apparent or seemingly true statements that are contradictory.

The emphasis usually in talking about paradoxes is on the "apparent" or the "seeming" and not upon the "contradiction." The question is how we get snookered into the trap of trying to escape such "merry-go-round defining verbal circles" that seem to generate only contradictions in talking about their meaning as if the statements being made were true. How do we go about escaping these verbal traps without denying that they are nothing more than simply contradictions? When that occurs, paradoxes end up merely being based upon false statements that logically yield no logically determinate conclusions.

Much of what I have to say on the topics of definition and interpretation, if useful, should help quell some of our puzzlement over some of the paradoxes we get into in talking about meaning, especially those paradoxes we find in speaking about "the meaning of meaning." But to do it I want to be helpful by illustrating some steps we need to take in trying to explain the basis of the semantic disconnect we get into when we talk about the meaning of certain terms. In particular, I want to examine the disconnect that exists between *what we mean to say* and *what we end up actually saying*. That paradox is introduced by our talking about two sorts of meanings both labeled confusedly by a single common term *meaning*.

There exists in the meaning of these two expressions an important contrast in talking about their meaning that needs to be noted. There is a sense of *meaning to say* and the sense of *the meaning in saying it*. How in talking about interpretation and definition do we keep the distinctions straight about the meaning of what we want to say and the meaning of what we actually say? How do we do it without descending into paradox?

A quest for the meaning of what we intend to mean appears often to be seeking something indefinite that at times seems to be something conceptually impossible to grasp. And what we have actually said in words is often something in contrast open to all sorts of different descriptions or explanations of what was said, some of which may be accurate and even correct. Such descriptions or explanations are equally said to be interpretations. And it is by an analysis of the expression "the meaning of a meaning" that we discover how we get entangled into paradoxical ways of speaking about meaning as well as talking about interpretation.

Paradoxes thus are problems about the meanings of the words that we use in the very formulations of our statements about those words and what in those statements those words actually stand for. Often, I suggest, paradoxes are nothing more than the difficulties we have in dealing with empty generalities and abstractions. They create puzzles in situations where the words used are resistant to any consistent rhetorical interpretation or resistant to any confident analysis of them by using definitions. If we want to be straight in our minds about facing such semantic paradoxes, we need to see how our brains get wracked up trying to untangle such verbal conundrums that usually are about what we are doing in our way of defining our terms.

Such verbal puzzles have been intriguing to philosophers, logicians, and mathematicians since antiquity. Philosophers love to argue *sacré bleu* about their verbal aporia, their professional "sokudus." Attempts to solve them in philosophy become all too verbally clever. There is St. Anselm, with his "none greater can be conceived," and St. Thomas Aquinas, with his analogies of infinite causation, and there is Immanuel Kant, with his dead-end antinomies. Many of the word plays on "perfection" and "infinite" have acted as a stimulus to philosophers in doing metaphysics to escape the paradoxes in talking about deity. Paradoxes have been much of the impetus behind the generation of all the systematic theorizing and speculation to be found historically in metaphysics.

And even now we see such attempts to escape such theoretical inconsistencies when astronomers and physicists frame cosmologies by the use of theories whereby they try to explain everything. But in a backdoor way, such dealing with many paradoxes in astronomies and physics, we must admit, has turned out fruitful, as with Albert Einstein's thinking about the limits and the untimeliness of our simple concepts of location in space and time by modifying notions such as simultaneity. Mathematicians, in trying to escape paradoxes in the developments of mathematics, have too generated many interesting and fruitful explorations into the logical foundations of newly created systems of mathematics, such as theories of sets of infinite numbers and theories about modal logics and alternative universes.

The kernel of the problem, then, with paradoxes is that they are statements thought true that lead us apparently into logically contradictory conclusions. And the problem with that is that they seem to make us commit the basic logical error, first clearly stated famously by Aristotle in his use of *reductio ad absurdum*. For Aristotle the *reductio* was the basic and foundational principle of logic. It was the essence of proof. If what we assume to be true leads us to a contradiction, something must be wrong with our premises. But those who treat paradoxes seriously often reverse the issue and question the logic and not the truth of the premises.

For example, the famous paradoxes of Zeno attempt to prove the impossibility of motion, since objects move through an infinite number of points in moving from point to point. And since motion must advance through an infinite set of points between two points in a finite time, motion must be logically impossible, even though we see that there is motion in the world with our very own eyes. Perception of motion, given the logic of the definition of motion, therefore must prove to be illusory. But again note that Zeno's paradoxes have been thought by many to have been largely dissolved by the calculus, which permits other different descriptions of motion. Obviously, something must be wrong with a definition of motion that is a description if we accept that motion exists in our experiences and our conception of it leads us into a contradiction. Here what seems at issue in Zeno's paradox is whether there are other descriptions of motion where motion is not illusory.

And one can avoid many of the seeming philosophical paradoxes found in the philosophical problematic by redescribing what in the first instance seemed to be the meaning of the words that seem so paradoxical. Such was the method of Wittgenstein in addressing the philosophical problematic. And today such a method is prominently displayed by recent work of the philosopher John McDowell (1994). Each gives interpretations of language and events that allows us to see that there is no paradox if we make different descriptions in different frames (and in different language) that do not lead us into seeming contradictions.

Many skeptics, however, have been less sympathetic with any notion of saying that paradoxes are only "apparent." Instead, they treat paradoxes as nothing more than logical contradictions. But first, to show that paradoxes are actually contradictions, we must show that the meanings of the terms in stating them are at first definable. Logic requires using defined terms. And if the terms of paradoxes have no acceptable precise definitions, arguments about them end up being impossible. How can we argue about things that have no precise definition of whatever it is that we are talking about? If we are arguing about the definition of a term that we cannot define by definition, we have tried to do what is impossible! Supposedly even God cannot create round squares. Supposedly, even God cannot do what is logically impossible.

We have in paradoxes what Rudolf Carnap has called pseudo problems. They are problems fundamentally caused by our uses of terms (Carnap 1969). And that has been the positivists' accusation against traditional philosophy. We often hear it asked, what is the good of philosophy as a mode of inquiry if it gives us no satisfactory answers in addressing its problems, which are mainly nothing more than self-inflicted paradoxes generated by logically unanswerable questions generated by the meanings found in the use of terms?

There is the Platonic adage that philosophy begins in paradox. But maybe Ludwig Wittgenstein's fly in the bottle is the better metaphor for thinking about philosophy. And I suggest at this point in our analysis that we continue to follow Wittgenstein's suggestion. Philosophy should aim at showing how the fly got into the bottle. And of course, the answer to that is that the fly must have been put there by some professional philosopher asking questions with indefinable concepts.

And we might say the same sorts of things about a great deal of religious language that is used to talk about God. We cannot talk about a concept of God, as most philosophers admit, without being paradoxical. Can God create a rock that He cannot lift? How can God be a person and be infinite at the same time, since persons by definition are finite? Or how can God know everything and still know the result of our free will choices? Or how can God create a world full of evil and still be a God of love and still be infinitely good?

And consequently it is said that religious language is ripe with many seemingly rational inconsistencies. And any acceptance of religious paradoxes must end up with our acceptance of such inconsistencies as mysteries. Paradox and mystery become challenges for the faithful. They become a test of faith. But skeptics, atheists, and agnostics wonder how anyone can begin to accept such verbal word crashing, such confused senses of meaning. How can they accept such verbal, inconsistent, and meaningless nonsense? To understand something about what one cannot understand simply is a contradiction in terms.

Why should we want to believe in mystery? To believe in a mystery is to believe in things that one does not understand. What sort of belief is that, a belief in a mystery that one cannot understand? Religious language for many of the faithful is no more for many skeptics than "verbal abracadabra." Now you see it, now you don't! It's magic. And a belief in magic unbalances the little rational equilibrium we have in facing some of our most serious questions about life, such as, "How can I best live my life?"

As already alluded to, the religious answer to that question always tends to be that without religiously revealed answers there are no serious answers to be had about how we should live out our lives. And thus goes the verbal, merry, merry-go-round about believing in things unknown and unseen. And of course that means faith. And a faith in faith has us believing someone else's faith about faith, and in our accepting that faith, and in calling that faith our own faith. And again in doing so we go through the same old merry, merry-go-round about what it is to have faith. And what kind of faith is it that has faith in a given faith based on someone else's declaration of faith?

People alert to meanings of terms and the meaning of concepts find that logical contradictions and language inconsistencies have the rhetorical force of bringing one up short in our thinking. They block logical thought. They get our attention. Paradoxes are very much like plays on words, puns, or the dramatic statements of ironies. They are attention grabbers. Inconsistencies have the rhetorical force of startling people into abrupt attention to questions at issue.

And it is for this reason a stated blatant inconsistency is an effective rhetorical device for attracting and inviting a critical reader to try to understand what the speaker is saying about a paradoxical subject. And the use of that rhetorical strategy raises the interesting question why the speaker would bring up a paradox as an attention-grabbing strategy in the first place. Why do they use paradoxes simply as rhetorical ploys?

Blatant inconsistencies, then, I suggest, rattle our critical faculties. As in the use of irony, the inconsistency instigates a search for a consistent meaning of what is being said. And that, as we shall see, is also the same force that figurative language has. Figurative language forces us to look for relevant consistencies. We especially find, then, that rhetorical tricks using unstable irony and wry cynical remarks grab folks' attention. Such paradoxical, metaphorical, and ironic ploys then challenge the mind to look at things with greater depth and greater scrutiny. They test our intelligence and our pride. They activate and challenge our wits. They initiate thorough searches through the implications of all those things that when put together produce confusion about verbal matters. Paradoxes are certainly prompts to intellectual inquiry. But on the other hand, we need to protect ourselves from questions that have no answers. Some people with things to sell use such questions to stupefy us into cognitive submission.

A quest for consistency is a test of language use. Inconsistency is how we test the way our language fits with the way we see the world. And irony is one of the best ways to test that fit in the context in which it is strategically uttered. To illustrate that point, let me explore a little bit of subtle irony from the wit of Oscar Wilde and the oft quoted phrase, "a gentleman is never unintentionally rude." Is this ironic sentence praise or condemnation of the behavior of gentlemen? Certainly in one sense it is ironic to say that when gentlemen are rude they are deliberately rude. Wilde's statement in one sense certainly challenges the mind to consider the social class issues involved in the rudeness of gentlemen in the treatment of their seeming inferiors.

One way, then, to try to interpret paradoxes is to treat many of them rhetorically as trick questions that we use to test a given line of thought. Philosophers of religion and theologians utilize paradoxes as a part of their verbal repertoire to throw audiences into a cognitive spin so as to get them to talk about what concerns them most, and that concern is mostly about their religion, and that concern usually is about how to accept personal loss, and especially how to face up to our final farewell and departure in death.

The theologically minded use paradoxical questions to stun minds much as Socrates claimed to do, who expressed his image of himself as a torpedo fish (a sting ray) (Plato, *Meno*). The purpose of Socratic questions in the Platonic *Dialogues* was to throw people into doubt about things that they themselves thought unquestionably true. The Socratic method as a method tested beliefs for their consistency with other beliefs.

And thus people when stunned and with no obviously agreed upon methods for answering questions for which they have no answers, are willing to accept religious messages based upon interpretations that the religious make about their unquestioned religious mythologies. Such paradoxical questions proposed are prompts to considerations of religious "faith-based faith." It is a faith that believes that there are no answers to questions that have secular answers.

When someone asks a question of a person with no possible answer, it should certainly raise the question, as already mentioned: "Why would anyone ask a question that seems to have no answer?" To say the answer is a mystery is to say it has no answer. And the question for a rhetorical critic is, "Why is that question for which there is no answer being asked?" Is the question based upon any faulty presumptions?

We suggest that asking someone about many verbal puzzles or paradoxes can be shown at times to be demonstrably, as I have already said, to be no more than dumb questions based upon false presumptions. It sounds unkind to say to someone that their questions are dumb and stupid. But people who ask such questions are not little children needing their voices to be recognized as being special. One can excuse the young, but such questions are not usually made in unknowledgeable innocence. As questions they knowingly lead us, as known by the very questioner, to endless circling around the meaning of this and that, and then they lead us on into the further questions of meaning of this and that, and then again on to the meaning of this and something else. And the result is that we all end up with the inability to decide upon which meaning anyone should accept in trying to answer such questions. All such questions, if analyzed carefully, can found to be fraught with befuddled meanings and multiple ambiguities.

To illustrate, let us take up for discussion some old philosophical golden nuggets turning on conceptual ambiguities. Take as a first example this question: when a tree falls in a forest does it make any sound? What is sound? Is sound the air compressions that is creating chains of vibrations traveling through air caused by the tree falling? Or is sound something that has to be heard by someone? To be sound, must it be heard? What is the *true* meaning of sound? "What, then, is sound?" How can people ever agree on the meaning of sound in this question when there are different answers? The question seems to demand a single, clear definition. How do we go about defining what it is to be sound? Is the issue nominal, or is sound something definitely *real*?

And there is again that other now-comparable famous discussion of William James about the squirrel that stays on the back of the tree when a man walks around the tree, with the squirrel remaining on the back of the tree; and the squirrel keeps facing the man as he walks around the tree. Does the man walk around the squirrel? Yes, he walks around the area in which the squirrel is located. No, he does not walk around the squirrel, as he never walks around the perimeter of the squirrel's body. What does it truly mean "to walk around the squirrel"? Can we define *really* what it means to walk around?

How do we settle these issues? Do we appeal to what ought to be the correct definition of *sound* and the correct definition of *walk around*? What, then, does it mean to be sound? What does it mean to walk around? These are actually dumb questions if we consider them carefully in the way that they are presumptively being put in this context. For someone to ask these questions is for the questioner to simply ignore the *ambiguity* to be found in the questions that we are trying to answer.

Any qualified speaker of the English language surely knows that these questions are open to two different interpretations. They are based on words to be found in two different realms or frames of discourse. And the ambiguity we find in the question is based on the two senses of what it ordinarily means to be sound and what it ordinarily means to walk around. And both interpreted senses are perfectly intelligible to competent English speakers. Why should any competent speaker ask such ambiguous questions?

Could it be that the person asking such questions is guilty of the faulty presumption of thinking that these terms sound and around have clear precise definable senses. The only plausible explanation, if they think so, is that they are not thinking very carefully. They suffer from an attention deficit disorder, which, if it is not obstinacy, definitely is stupid behavior. Thus, the more likely interpretation of the question about "walking around" in the above case is that the person asking the question actually is not so stupid and knows why the question is being asked. It is a riddle posed to someone who is prone not to think carefully. It is a question put to a supposedly unperceptive, dumb person, and thus it is a doubly dumb trick question. It poses a riddle to a person listening, who might make the careless and faulty presumption that terms like sound and going around have one and only one *true* meaning.

In the above cases one proper reply, we suggest, might be to challenge the motives of the one asking the question. One would simply impugn the questioner's motives in asking a question that one surely knows has no unambiguous answer. Does the questioner truly believe the presumption that there can be an unambiguous answer? How do we know the questioner is not in bad faith? Do we question the questioner's honesty and sincerity? Or, as I am proposing, should we impolitely simply treat such trick questions as dumb questions? Of course my impolite response in calling the questions dumb is in part my own unpardonable nastiness toward people who treat us as stupid. But I as a gentleman would hopefully never want to be deliberately rude.

But probably the most tactful response in confronting the riddle and avoiding the question about bad faith and insincerity, and not giving an *ad hominem* abusive response to the questioner, would be just to throw the questions back on to the person asking the questions. One should just simply ask, "What sense of 'sound' and 'around' do you mean in asking the question? Do you mean by 'sound' the vibration of the air? Or do you mean by 'sound' something that someone hears through their ears? Do you mean walking around the space in which the squirrel is located on the tree? Or do you mean walking around all sides of the squirrel, the ventral side and the dorsal side, and back to the ventral side?" In either case, whatever answer they give, we then can give the correct answer to their question.

From this critical perspective we are entitled to dismiss such questions as simple riddles, as trick or dumb questions. And in any critique of them we can point out that, since the ambiguity in them is irresolvable in the context, the questions are unanswerable in the context in which they are asked. The questions can have no correct answer in a context where sound and around have no stable or fixed definable meanings. And as we have illustrated, there are several interpretations of what is meant by sound and around in the above contexts. And we have done that by definitions that clarify and resolve the ambiguities that we have been exposed by our interpretations.

And all this analysis of around and sound applies equally to talking about saying what we mean by the two terms meaning and mean that we find in my chapter heading "The Meaning of What You Would Like to Mean." There are two senses of meaning in it, the meaning of what we mean to say and the meaning of what we end up actually saying. There is in these two expressions an important contrast in talking about the uses of the term meaning. In sum, there are two senses: "What actually we mean when we say something" and "the intended meaning not yet expressed." To rephrase it, there are two identifiable senses of *meaning*, that is, "meaning to say" and "the meaning in saying it." When we talk about meaning we need to keep these two senses straight in our thinking. And it is our awareness of these differences in senses of a number of other different terms and their synonyms that we need to expand on in coming chapters if we want to come to terms with terms that tend to confuse us about their meaning.

PART II

Theories of Language and Communication

CHAPTER 5

Language Use and Language Usage

We need to constantly remind ourselves that we need to confront ourselves, to think for ourselves, and to analyze or clarify what it is that we are doing and saying; sometimes we even need to analyze and clarify what we are trying to say. We need to confront issues about the meaning of our actions and the meaning of our language uses and usages. How do we go about doing all these things specifically when using language on concrete levels of application where we speak of language use and language usage in the different senses of the use of these two expressions? Doing all these things and understanding what we are doing is a constant analytic juggling act.

One way to do it is to survey what it is that we are doing in *using* language, especially making straight what we are doing in *clarifying* what we are saying. We need to focus on what it is that we are doing when we use language to further our own comprehension of what we think we are saying. And in turn we need to ask what it is that we are doing in helping others to understand what we are trying to say.

Such questions underline the importance of interpretation and definition in furthering any understanding of the meaning of any form or mode of communication, whether it is presentational or stated implicitly, or whether it is said explicitly through words, or even in some instances whether we are communicating without words. We thus present meaning directly or indirectly in all sorts of actions and productions both within and without language. Thus, there is in all this talk about meaning on all levels the appearance of our being enmeshed in the totality of meaning that is involved in everything we say and do. And that observation in a way may be correct. Yet, like all high level abstraction, that observation tends to seem empty.

But let us restrict our discussion here to the meaning of language use and language usage as a first important step in our discussion of the relevant correlatives that I propose to talk about in trying to communicate what it is rhetorically to interpret and to define meaning. In talking about interpreting and defining, we need as a first step to interpret and define what we are *doing to ourselves* in clarifying (*acts of self-clarification*) about what we *say* and *do*. And the next step to take is to define and interpret what we are *doing and saying to others* (*acts facilitating our exchange of meaning*); that is, what we are trying to do in clarifying for them what we want to say to them. We need to know both what it is that we think we are saying and what others understand us to be saying.

But it ought also to be noted that when we especially talk about "definition" and "the meaning of a language," there is a distinct difference between speaking about *use* and speaking about *usage*. It is a fundamental distinction that needs to be made in talking about language. It is fundamental to our understanding of the basic differences between interpreting and defining. Understanding the difference between language use and language usage centers upon the whole problem of trying to interpret, comprehend, and understand what it is that we do and say to other people.

The overall question is, "What is it to say and mean something?" An as a precautionary step, as already suggested, we need to try to escape from many of the circular problems we encounter in talking about meaning, and to do that as I have proposed, we need to expand on the meaning of a number of correlative terms that we can bring into the discussion that distinguishes "use" from "usage." We need to try to discuss the complexity of issues about the meaning of this much richer repertoire of use and usage of a number of related and apparently synonymous and antonymous correlative terms we use to talk about meaning. We need to expand on them to see if the amplification of the meaning of these additional contrasting words does not help make better sense of what we are doing and talking about in talking about language use and language usage.

Let me initiate this amplification and expansion by first introducing a few technical definitions that are definitional proposals.

Language use (=df) is the way we do things with words.

Language use has to do with how we use words to think about our own thinking. We need words to think about our use of words in any act of cognition, identification, or in any act of recognition. We especially need an additional set of words to further our knowledge of words and our knowledge of their uses in sentences. We have to ask ourselves what it is to think that something is knowledge, and then we need to ask ourselves about the differences between the words that we use and their meanings in terms of our already-settled conventional usages of terms in our language. And we need to ask what part usage has had in acquiring any knowledge that we have about the world.

Language usage (=df) is the conventional meanings of the language we speak.

Sometimes our words seem to give us knowledge about real things, and sometimes they seem to give us knowledge about things that are not so real. How do we in talking about reality using words distinguish fact from fiction? There are all sorts of fictive and mythical entities introduced into our lives in the stories that we tell and in the stories that other people tell. We give names to things that now are being fashionably called "virtual reality." Barry Brummett treats this conception of reality in his discussion of *simulation* (Brummett 2003). But is he treating *simulation* as a reality that is descriptive referentially as he equally does for his concept of *representation*? My complaint with this sort of analysis is that it suffers the paradoxes so common in realistic metaphysics. How definably real are simulation and representation? Thus I choose to try to clarify these distinctions by strict definition. I want to do that by talking about them from the perspective of my seeing these activities in terms of fictive conjectures and of trying to see things as real that turn out to be not so real.

Virtual reality depicts realms and concepts found in hypotheses, conjectures, and speculations, and again it depicts objects and people in the realms of a fictive imagination. Virtual reality is often phrased in subjunctive conditionals. As politicians often repeat, "I do not discuss hypotheticals." But what hypocrisy there is in those that use this diversionary political strategy! Politicians use this ploy so as not to answer questions about possible results of their proposed policies. The excuse ignores the presumption that politics is about deliberations about the future, which obviously cannot be discussed except in "hypotheticals."

We imagine virtual models, and we question how conceptually such constructed models can apply to reality. We ask, "Is there any real component or form existing in them that exists out there in reality? Can our hypotheses and models define parts of reality?" Imagination and description thus both play an important part in how we think of a world, whether imaginary or real. We create constructs of meaning with questionable existence. We ask what part they possibly can play out in reality.

What I have emphasized as important in conceptual constructions is not their external reality but their applications that play out in it. It is in applications that we find tests for reality. In other words, what is important is how the terms, concepts, theories, and models that we actually employ play out in our actions in our efforts to control the world. And to speak of reality as if it were something like a stone that we kick suggests that reality is defined by many as what they think is ultimately touchable. Note that in this image of touch there is a sense of what it is to be simultaneous. Reality is being conceived in this case in terms of the engagement found in touching. What more is there in our sense of something being real than that we touch it and we engage it in our efforts to control the world?

These epistemic issues about the language of fiction and about speculative theory and reality raise issues and questions about verbal fiction, about what is sometimes called reification, or in A. N. Whitehead's terms, "misplaced concreteness" (Whitehead 1929, 10). Theory is discourse that amounts at times to no more than speculation. And consequently, there is reality testing in all these questions about what we are actually doing in creating and using hypotheses. Note, then, what we do with hypotheses in testing them in the empirical sciences. Note the absence of reality testing in the pseudo sciences. Pseudo sciences are sciences about mythical entities, such as we find for example in astrology, in phrenology, and in a host of other fads and fetishes such as Dianetics, Scientology, and general semantics.

All this raises questions about the nature of lies and what to many sounds like plain "bullshit" (Frankfurt 2005). And if these "ologies and isms" are not about lies, we ask whether or not they are just reports of myths and fantasies that people use just to entertain us in our ignorance of certain facts of life. In short, a great deal of our language use has to deal with reflecting on the meaning and intentions of what we are saying and asking about. It is about whether or not what is being said is true, whether or not what we hear are lies, whether are not they are just fantasies, or whether or not they simply are narrative mistakes and statements of verbal confusions. "Tell me whether or not what you are saying is so." "How do you know it is so, and why do you think that it is so?" Statements of meanings offer us in our interpretations all sorts of epistemic challenges.

It is important to note that, many of the issues about language use and usage are not simply about truth. They are about things that we think are possibly so, or they are about things about which we have doubts about their being so. Skepticism is not so much a state of mind as a mode of questioning why someone wants to assert something seemingly questionable as true. But importantly, despite our concerns for truth, we do many things with language that have little to do with truth telling. And much of our speculation about definition and interpretation has less to do with truth than with how we frame our thoughts, with what the purposes are that our thoughts serve, and with how we find words for thoughts that fit issues and concerns.

We make judgments about honesty, about public good, and about how about much we care for other people. We offer invitations. We make promises. We propose to join in and cooperate with other people. We even propose how we should talk about matters of mutual concern. To begin planning and setting the stage for discussions of these matters is one good place to start to do these sorts of things. And in one part of any introductory discussion on certain matters is our talk about the meaning of terms and the interpretations of what we are saying. Such talk about grounds for talking is initially just talk about how to talk, and it is not about talk that is talking the world and how to deal with problems in it. Sometimes it takes a lot of talk before we can talk meaningfully about things that we need to talk about. We need sometimes to talk with others about what they want to talk about.

Definitional proposals as stated are statements about such talk that are neither true nor false. To propose is just that, a proposal, and not a statement of fact about our use of words. "Jump in the lake!" is not a true statement but a proposal. Definitional proposals are never truth claims as such. They are prescriptions that we need not accept or use as proposed. We can simply ignore the proposal if we want to do just as G. W. Bush did in denying the definitional proposal that the civil conflict in Iraq was a civil war. It is the same with doctors' prescriptions. We do not need to fill them.

But we cannot always ignore proposals, especially when they are coming from people with whom we have to deal or from people we have to rely on in fulfilling our contractual agreements. We especially cannot ignore definitional proposals made within our own families, disciplines, or trades, or even those made by a president of the United States dealing with a congress passing legislation. Standardized proposals quite often simply define what we call *technical jargon*. It is the language of a discipline or a technology, or even the language of a legal community. Without such language we would not be able to communicate well with the people within our disciplines or within our specialties, or within those communities in which we want to do business.

Language use is not just about information. We simply do many things other than inform people when we use language. We make requests. We give orders. We threaten. Language use has to do with living out our lives with others and communicating with them and reacting to what they say about mutual concerns. Language use thus has to do with many other aims and purposes besides telling people what is true (see Austin 1962).

Using language, then, has to do with the much larger purposes we have when we deal with other people, such as we do in our personal intimacies, in our vocational tasks, in our social involvements, and especially in our politics. Many language uses have to do with the complexities of interacting and bonding. They have to do with how we present ourselves, how we reveal our thoughts, and how we express our opinions. In using language, not only do we express ourselves to ourselves and make some sense about ourselves to ourselves, but we also use language to make sense about why we want to say things to others and in our wanting to relate to them especially as we do in friendships.

We like to reveal our purposes and concerns about how we are relating to people. We confess. We greet. We praise. We apologize. We excuse. We shame.

We agree. And we placate, console, and comfort. These activities are much more than just talking about what is true. They are simply the greater part of our social and interactive behaviors. They are about actions that we need to take to make sense and about actions that ring true to others about what we are saying to gain their trust so as to engage them and to cooperate with them.

The linguistic acts of communication directed to others, appealing and responding, are at heart of what rhetoric is all about. Note the difference between a rhetoric that appears unfortunately directed toward self-justification and a rhetoric that aims at persuading others. One is directed inward, the other outward. But a rhetoric that wants to help others understand what you believe or know is not a rhetoric that speaks necessarily to oneself. It is a rhetoric that we use happily to redirect what we express to ourselves in words that will in turn make sense to others. Self-expression in that case matches with what we say to others. And it is a happy-go-lucky, harmony when self-expression matches what others hear us saying that is in resonance with their aims and purposes.

It has been noted that it is a terrible rhetorical fault to direct only what we have to say to ourselves and fail to say it to our readers. Concern for self-expression simply at times ends up as a cause for rhetorical failure. Often in my own experiences I have heard philosophers read technical papers to general audiences without much concern for their audiences. Can a listener understand material that requires careful, critical reading and scrutinizing interpretations so as to be able to follow it? Can listeners be expected to understand jargon and technical language that is not in their vocabulary?

Such you will find is usually the case in listening to professional papers delivered in philosophy. Professional philosophical audiences have for the most part trouble following the papers addressed to them. And that is why in such sessions it is useful at times, and sometimes almost necessary, to have a commentator summarize for the audience what is being said. And often it takes skill for a commentator to paraphrase to an audience what someone is saying, and that especially is the case in the critical commentaries delivered in professional philosophy.

The great rhetorical sin, then, is to be unaware of one's audience. When a person reflects and writes on things that he or she is interested in only, such writing amounts to no more than writing that is written to one's self. Such a style of writing becomes narcissistic. It can only appeal to those interested in the author. Or it is interesting only to those who are willing to take the pains to interpret the meaning of so much subjective inner, self-expression. A narcissistic and egocentric style of writing simply fails to be aware of a reader's concerns. It is not a style that easily enters into the thoughts and minds of its audience. Such writing requires for it to be understood a maximum of interpretive effort by the reader to determine the author's intentions.

In short many people often write for self-understanding, with little consideration of their reader, who is trying desperately to decipher and understand what is being said. One can see that such writing might be appropriate for a writer who is looking for answers to questions that the writer is concerned to figure out. Self-expression is the first step to take in finding the thoughts that we want to make clear to others and that we want use later for revision. Thought about our own uses of words is at first a solo performance. It looks for solutions in definitions and interpretations. It is a process of self-clarification. It is writing that is a necessary stage when beginning to write to others.

In self-expression, authors put their own thoughts in their own personal frames of judgment and self-assessment. It is as language self-creation. They put their words and their thoughts in analytic frames and engage them in self-critique. In such a stage of writing we need no one outside ourselves to confirm that we are right in our efforts in achieving self-understanding. Self-understanding is not something that can be dictated to us by someone else. It is a part of our personal and intellectual integrity in being able to think for ourselves about ourselves.

This attitude toward inner thoughts and personal understanding is an attitude that seeks independence of mind. But it is an attitude in wanting to communicate with others that ends up fraught with all the dangers that isolated independence and personal and private meanings makes us heir to. Independence of mind in self-cognizance despite its personal achievement can lead to enormous failures in communication.

Wittgenstein, on the other hand, argues (Wittgenstein 1958) against private language, with the presumption that language that does not communicate is not language. In part this is true, but necessarily one sided, as I shall show later. Meaning must in part be a part of our language games, which as we look at them defines usage. That usage cannot be private is in one sense true by definition. But note the dual role of defining in our attempt to make clear both what we mean to ourselves and what we mean to our audiences. And speaking and writing require both self-elucidation and clarification about what is said so we can better communicate our personal and private meanings to someone else. How can we communicate what we are thinking when we are not clear about it to ourselves? Speaking and writing require entering into the vocabulary and the presumptions that others have so that we can see how best to communicate what seems to have meaning for ourselves.

But note the full implications of saying "that the best way to learn something is to teach it." We learn best when we shape what we say clearly to others what we want to understand for ourselves. And when we shape clearly our meaning to others, it helps us better clarify things for ourselves. By expressing thoughts clearly to others, we understand much better what we are saying to ourselves. Expression aimed at others often helps us reconfirm what we think or believe to be our own understandings and cognitive certainties. It is a circle of creation that communicates to others while at the same time we are communicating back to ourselves.

CHAPTER 6

Rhetorical Use and Usage

It must be noted that when we talk about rhetoric, which traditionally has been characterized as the art of persuasion, we need to consider a much wider set of rhetorical aims than the simple notion that rhetoric is just to inform and persuade. We need to examine rhetorical aims besides just persuading and informing. Rhetoric is a much more comprehensive art, especially as one finds it going on in the art of negotiation in politics that aims to bond and interact with others in shaping a community.

Politics, as with morality, aims at shaping mutually accepted commitments. It aims at creating trust. It aims at agreed-upon concerted action toward shared ends and agreed-upon negotiated compromises. Such political rhetoric is more than a rhetoric that aims at persuasion. It is a rhetoric of bonding. It is a rhetoric of *ethos*. It a rhetoric that uses ethical appeals that gives confidence and trust to people seeking to work together and in wanting to share their lives together in mutual understanding.

Today we find in contemporary rhetorical studies that big rhetoric is considered to range across all sorts of communicative behaviors. It is about all sorts of productions that use visual and physical arrangements. It is about the creation and the uses of artifacts, and especially language and literary artifacts, that are said to have eloquence and beauty. Rhetoric concerns itself with all sorts of things that are thought to have meaning. One way of expressing it is to say that rhetoric is the *art of the making of meaning*. In that sense, then, the art of making meaning is big rhetoric. It is an architectonic art. It encompasses both a rhetoric of sight and a rhetoric of sound to achieve intended meaningful and purposeful effects.

Rhetoric in this enlarged sense is both about the shaping meaning, refashioning it, and creating it. It is about the skills necessary to create artful and novel presentations of meaning that are useful in accomplishing our ends in relating to other human beings. It is an artistic rhetoric that reflects on and creates new values and new meanings. It is not just limited to the arts, but it is equally at work in the sciences. It is an art that deals with cultural productions and scientific innovations that can best be communicated by both sight and sound.

Note the question that we often put to artists: "What is the meaning of your work?" And importantly, note that a comparable question is asked of rhetoricians, especially of rhetors about whose work we would like to know what affects they intend to achieve.

Rhetors (=df) are users of rhetoric.

We ask of rhetors, "What is your rhetorical aim and purpose?" Artists and rhetors are asked about their motives and their intentions. They are asked about the artistic means they are using in creating the meaningful artifacts that they produce in both the visual and plastic arts. They are asked about their stylistic efforts to create meaning in compositions of speeches and texts.

Rhetoric in both the visual and musical arts raises comparable questions about the meaning and purpose of their presentations. We use sounds, objects, and behaviors, especially gestures as well as words, to say what we would like to say. And in both art and literature, we want to do and say things in innovative and skillful ways that are creative of meaning. But apart from using words, what is it to say that things or actions have meaning? Can behaviors and artifacts, or even natural objects in themselves apart from words have meaning? If so, how do we come to know and speak about the meaning of natural objects or artifacts?

In asking these seemingly interminable and endless general questions about the meaning of everything, we seem to be equating meaning simply with any awareness or general understanding. Understanding is thought by some realists as knowing the meaning of things. But it is indeed paradoxical to talk about things as having meaning that seem to have no meaning apart from the experiences of human beings. But when we appear to be talking about things having meaning apart from any human understanding, it suggests that there are universals truths that ground the meaning in things separate from awareness and our understanding. How again do we try to escape this perceived duality existing between our concepts and reality? Or can we? Again are we trapped in Wittgenstein's bottle, trying to exit from an unbridgeable dualism?

In reading and writing, we should face up to the uniqueness of the personal engagement we are in at any given moment in time in both our reading and writing. Not facing up to the singularity of these personal events leads us to think our experience of meaning is imitative, repeatable, and not unique. We think that all events can be understood by using language where the meaning of what is said is determined entirely by precedent patterns of fixed language usage. We begin to think of communicating as ritualized and channeled into fixed routines that entirely fit all types of meaningful situations. We mistakenly think of communication as having only recurrent patterns of usage that are endlessly repeatable in like or identical situations.

But from what we know about the generative evolution of meaning through creative use, we can say that any model of communication based on only fixed and determinative meanings of terms does not take into account the creative side of communication. As contexts change, concepts change and terms change their meaning. Something new is introduced in the meaning of words in each and every situation, and novel sets of meanings are always an integral part of each and every different situation.

We should note, then, that each and every situation in which we communicate is a unique experience that differs from every other in some respects, even though differences may only be minor. Meaning is always particular, depending upon the unique perspective of speakers. It is always particular where authors are located in unique locations of space and time. Every act of communication happens in a singular moment of time. It happens for that one time and that time only, and in that time once and for all. Each time I read a poem or write a poem I am confronted with a different situation. You cannot in that sense read the same poem twice.

When we try to come to grips with the fact of the uniqueness of communicative situations, we find that each act of communication is found to exist in a context of novel presumptions about what we are actually doing and saying in that situation. Simply put, every rhetorical situation, despite its being typical in some respects, can be defined as being a novel situation. We cannot just simply interpret what is going on only in terms of past usage of terms in shifting and changing contexts. Reading a poem changes how we read it a second time. Note the problem of seeing old movies and expecting the same experience to be repeated. Note the reluctance to see many theatrical plays twice. We know it will not be the same sort of dramatic experience twice. But on the other hand, often a second seeing reveals meaning not previously grasped, in which case a second seeing may be even much better and turn into a new and happy discovery about what might have been previously missed.

Any act of interpretation has to account for that unique point of existence in time and place in discussing the meaning of what is being said at that very place and point in time. It is for this reason that when we revise our own writing, we keep looking at it each and every time from quite different critical perspectives. We have a sense in revising that we are never quite finished, as we find in each new revised perspective on what we write that things keeps changing. It is thus difficult in revision to ever get a simple sense of closure, as each revision takes on new and reframed perspectives in our reading of texts at different times: "I just read something that makes me think about what I said in a new light." And

I must say that it is continually happening to me now as I continue to revise this book. It is only by having a deadline that I will know I will have ended what I want to say and in part managed to say, at least for that point in time, what I wanted to say.

We should also note that we find within our generative capacity to use words novel patterns, where we give new meanings to words that fit unique contexts and situations. We find that we express in such circumstances novel meanings that at least as far as we know may never have been expressed before. Rhetorical invention, for example, gives us the power to create meaning by finding words that never were put in that particular form and in that particular manner and shape before: "Jolly green monsters eat yellow manure on their canapés, which they sprinkle with red hot and purple candy dots."

Some of the novel meaning we find that is developing in the words that we use personally may not have been part of an original rhetorical intention to say them. Obviously, "red hot" and "candy dots" came to me as an afterthought in thinking about the novelty of my sentence. But how much or how little of our original intention can end up in our words that we finally in the end say? It is an obstacle every writer has to face when he or she cannot find the words to say exactly what he or she wants to say at any given moment. We say our words, and then we find in expressing them new meanings have been generated as we have said them. And after we say them, we now think that we have said something we would have liked to say, even though we did not know quite exactly what to say before we said it.

It is only after the fact of having said our words that they finally meet heartily with our approval. But those words said may not be exactly what we intended to say in the first place. And thus surprisingly, in saying things that are meaningfully new to ourselves, we become enlightened by what we unexpectedly find expressed in our own words. We frequently happily are able to find something new in what we have said that we would like to have said only after we have said it. And thus after we say it, we are satisfied to keep it. We stand by those words that are blessed with our new approval. Hopefully, that approval may be everlasting, but don't depend on it.

As with the old advertising cliché, we run words up the flagpole and hope that we will be lucky enough to discover what it is that we would like to say. Sometimes we have only a mere instinctive sense of what our words might mean, as we are saying them imaginatively in any given rhetorical situation. And in writing we find that we sometimes actually discover something better to say in trying to say things that we wanted to say. We thus are never quite exactly sure what our words will mean until we have finally expressed them in a personal and specific context that is always a unique situation. Our words for the moment may just happen to meet with our temporary, if not permanent, approval. But as life goes on, our opinions are always open to change about the things that we say. How often are we dissatisfied with things that we have written in the past?

It is the power of invention in written composition that enables us to best use the generative capacity of our words to discover new meaning. We find surprisingly in writing, and sometimes not so surprisingly, that our words do not mean exactly what we wanted them to mean. In that case, in writing we revise them or rephrase them. How often to our despair we find that others such as editors are able to say much better what we have all along been trying to say. Recognizing that this is true gives a writer a sense of inadequacy that can be countered only with the thought that what is being said better is, after all, what you originally thought to say in the first place. You then can regain your sense of ownership of your own thought even though someone after reading your words has expressed your thought better than you did.

But fortunately, we do find at other times that we are able to say the things we want to say. But our approval of the words that we write usually follows only after the fact of our writing them down and finally getting them into print. Our understanding comes not before but after we have put our words into print. But it is important that we recognize that in speaking as opposed to writing that we do not have the privilege of deleting our words or editing out the things that we have just said. We do not have time to deliberate carefully on what we are saying. We find that often we have said something different from what we intended to say once we have said it. That is the major problem in impromptu or extemporaneous speaking. We need in such speech to revise what we are saying in the light of the words we have just spoken.

It is important to note that in speaking we hear people often say, "What I have said isn't exactly the way I would like to put it. Let me put it into different words." This is an announcement of a course correction. Rephrasing or interpretive reiteration and a considerable amount of amplification are a natural part of speech making where we cannot edit out the words once spoken. We find as a consequent that often when impromptu or extemporaneous speeches are recorded in print that they are often quite reiterative and redundant in style, and consequently, we often find speeches that fascinated listeners turn out to be quite boring and too reiterative for readers when those same speeches are put into print.

Readers are much more critical than listeners. They have time to be critical, unlike a listener. Listeners have to depend on their short-term memories, unlike readers, who can simply reread what has been momentarily forgotten. Thus, in speech, unlike in writing, we cannot revise our words once said. What we say in speech is already history. We cannot take our words back. They have been said. We can only rephrase them. We can only alter what we have said in speech by qualifying or rephrasing our meaning to adjust it to fit what we were trying to say in the first place.

Consequently, writing style differs from speaking style in that in speaking we often rephrase what we have said. In writing we do not have to rephrase or correct what we have said. We can simply edit it out. In speaking we need also to be more reiterative for emphasis and compensate for the limited uptake of less-attentive listeners who are having trouble hearing exactly what our words mean. Thus, writing style is thus less copious and redundant than extemporaneous styles of speaking.

Our language use thus is of special concern to the rhetorician interested in style and arrangement in written composition. Writing needs something other than the speaker's physical presence to hold a reader's attention. The writer has to create means of holding our interest other than through his or her personal physical presence. One aim of rhetoric is to devise different stylistic means of holding a reader's attention. Consequently, we need rhetorically to devise different types of affective and effective rhetorical appeals and responses to hold an audience's interest in what is going on in the writing. Consequently, we see that it is dangerous to allow some of the elements of a style of speaking to go over into a writing style and vice versa.

The aim of rhetoric is to be practical in politics and enlightening in the enlargement of what we are able to communicate and teach, especially in education. Its aim is to center on the practical aspects of our daily living in communicating with other people. Its aims are for reaching out and affecting audiences with the uses of words that are consonant with their aims and purposes and not just consonant with ours. Practical politics above all aims at seeking such consonant accommodations.

But note that literature sometimes has comparable, practical, enlightenment aims whereby meanings are expressed not just directly but indirectly by a text with cultural and contextual implications. And it should be noted that it is in literature that we find the most creative developments of meaning in our use of language. Literature is the paradigm of creativity in finding new meaning and finding new uses for words in language. The writing of literature is thus appropriately called *creative writing*, in contrast to rhetorical writing, which focuses on rhetorical appeals and responses that are of a more practical bent. In the teaching of composition and writing in English Studies practical writing goes under the common name of *expository writing*. Among those who teach writing in English studies there is a sort of schizophrenia about aims in teaching writing.

Is it creative or expository? Can there be in the teaching of English composition a happy harmony between these two different aims?

The way we "use" language is thus a primary concern of those involved in the study of creative writing. Creative writing involves finding and developing new ways to say things differently. Note the following attempt to say something different about what we have just been saying about creative writing. It is intended to be pretentiously creative and an expository statement about creative writing that actually is lacking in creative word choices:

> Creative writing, in its concern for avoiding the dull, the commonplace, the trite, and the clichéd, as well as the redundancy of everyday platitudinous trivia, becomes literature when it eschews as best it can the "all-too-traveled trails" of conventional and repetitive uses of hackneyed and all-too-bloviated language usage.

How mock ironically literary this concocted platitudinous sentence about creative writing is! It is a parody of much of what we have just said about the qualities of good literary style. The least we can say about "this newly invented statement" in its pompous bad prose style is that it is in all probability a statement that has never been said before in exactly that way in that peculiar sequence of words about that subject matter. The statement illustrates the perennial problems we face in using old words in new ways and in new situations, especially in talking about creative writing.

Language, it should be noted, is indeed generative. And our aim in concocting the above foul fool statement, although the intent was to be humorous, was to make fun of hackneyed usage; nevertheless, the sentence illustrates how language use, even if trite and hackneyed, can still indeed be generative in other ways. Note how "the meaning of the above illustrated statement" indexes the relationship of its expression to our present context of exposition of use and usage. Its full meaning, however, though trite and clichéd, is a function of the present context in which we are now discussing creative use and conventional usage. Its specific meaning is interpreted from the unique context of this book by my discussing the differences between innovative and creative writing and exposition that aims at substantive and illustrative exposition.

And the moral of this little linguistic foreplay in talking about my own little exemplification of innovative meaning or the lack of it shows that the meaning of much of our language use can best be understood primarily by the contextual interpretations that are generated from the presumptions made within rhetorical situations that, metaphysically speaking, are as events ontologically unique.

Understanding does not come from directly parsing the meaning of words used in creative and generative statements. It comes from the full force of all the implications made from the full context of the rhetorical situation. The meaning of our mock statement about literary style has thus has been shaped by the present context. Its meaning is a result of our intentions to be both satirically humorous and to be illustrative about what different things can be said in using the generative powers by using words that are a part of our repertoire of mastered past usage. I have used many often-repeated words in my illustration to produce something ridiculously new in the way we can go about saying things somewhat novel about creativity.

Usage, on the other hand, in contrast to use, I need to repeat, has to do with the meanings of words as historically understood in our present historical situation about our commonly accepted past uses of words that are found legitimated as such by lexicography. Words of standard usage are words or terms by which we can communicate what has been said before repetitively time and time before. Standard language furnishes us with words that possess enough exactitude for functional use from past precedents of use to be able to communicate effectively and efficiently with those who speak within the same cultural and linguistic frame of concepts and words that we are within. It is such frames that enable us to define linguistic usage. Using standard usage enables us to communicate about things previously understood from previously socially conditioned and habituated senses of words. Usage is the meaning of words that have been frequently seen and heard and used by others before and derived and confirmed from interpretations of their repeated uses from observed past experiences.

Usage thus becomes the basic platform of literal and determinate meaning that we use practically in daily talking and writing about our world and also about many of our inner experiences that we have had in the living out of our lives. Language usages are defined from the words we share with others in our bonding and making firm commitments with each other. Language usage is what has precedent use. Those who fail successfully to write and speak precisely with people fully educated with refined distinctions and usages are readily perceived to have language deficiencies. It is all about having words to say exactly what you mean. Such language awareness of precise usage is especially important in law and in the making of contracts.

Refined usage is the language that we use within certain constraints within defined contexts. It is the language that helps us to make clear what we say to one another. We interpret usages in the conventional accepted senses that enable us to give meaning to what we wish to say that is accurate and precise. Usage thus is the common shared meanings of words that are used to be clear about important understandings in certain kinds of defined and recurrent situations. Failure to be able to conform to such patterns of advanced and refined usage is a symptom of language incompetence.

But usage may not be so perfectly clear, as some would like us to believe in our use of usage in many personal situations. We sometimes mistakenly think past usages have the same meaning or sense in each and every context. To think that to be the case can be a very big mistake to make in communicating with others. But usage does give us the great advantage to say what we mean in many common, unexceptionable, acceptable, and repeatable familiar contexts. And too, usage cannot be unduly stretched without the danger of ambiguities when situations of use differ. Usage does not always apply outside conventional channels of meaning that define usage. And boundaries are a difficult and often-undefined border lines that we have to face up to when some people want to use terms differently and we are trying to take a stand on what usage is.

And ordinary usage, in addition to being literal and clear in certain contexts, may also support us in giving us clarifying definitions that may bear on other possible interpretations. Ordinary usage also allows us by definition to expand our knowledge about things in the learning of our language. In a way, defining usage can enlarge on our common understanding of things that are already embodied in part in the meanings of our language usage. Conventional usage thus embodies huge amounts of public knowledge and meaning about how to talk about certain things thought to be real in the world. It is for this reason that studying vocabulary is a form of knowledge acquisition.

It should also be noted that usage as embodying descriptions of things is temporarily static and fixated in meaning. Meaning that is conventional in our everyday, common knowledge becomes reutilized and channeled in the names that we repetitively use for talking about things. Usage thus is above all about what is practical. And usage has a history of dependability and reliability in enabling us to say things that we want to continue to say. Usage gives us the words that help others to understand what they think we are saying.

In sum, then, language use, in contrast to usage, can be creative. Use, unlike our usage, is never static and permanently fixed. It is generative. It creates new meaning through innovative uses by revamping old usages and combining them with new meaning in new and different contexts and situations. It combines old terms with other old terms into new and never-before-used configurations. And consequently, terms as we use them take on new meanings in situations that differ from those once tied to old, established meanings in their once-accepted conventional frames, contexts, and situations.

Language usage evolves through the utilization and acceptance of new evolutionary uses that have been successful in their applications to new and different practical contexts. In that respect language evolves from individual variations that are assimilated into language usage as it evolves into a new culture. It is the same pattern of causal change that exists in Darwinian evolutionary theory.

Individual variation is sedimented by heredity into the evolution of the species. In language, what is passed on to successive generations is usage that has evolved and been refined from someone's innovative personal use.

Uses of language can be multiple and complex. Uses of language from one point of view are rhetorical actions. And you will find that uses are the things that we do with language that are at times resistant to conventional interpretations of the words being used. Uses are thus consequently open to shifts and indeterminacies, ambiguities, imprecision, and inaccuracies of meaning as they move away from the conventional senses of terms that once conventionally have anchored us in the world and that have hooked us up with the practical activities that we need to engage in to be able to function within it.

Language use, by abandoning old trails of usage, gives us the opportunity and freedom to explore and discover what never has been thought or expressed before. Use allows us the freedom through definitional proposals to change the meanings of our words in our language. Use thus through the processes of definition and redefinition enables us to transcend our repertoire of literal usages. Definitional proposals in their use are importantly one mode of language creation and exploration. And definitional reports are at the heart of validating an interpretation of a use that becomes an established usage.

And interpretation is the foundation of any foreign language translation. At times we may find that the complexity of all this shifting back and forth about the meaning of words becomes extremely baffling. And that is why we need the skill of interpretation to sort things out. It is a basic skill necessary for self-definition and any capacity for any self-education.

Having said all this, I now need to expand our discussion of all these condensations of meaning that we have stated about these abstractions that we have used so far in talking about language use, usage, meaning, definition, interpretation, and translation. To help clarify all these ways of talking about defining meaning, I find it necessary to point out all the confusions that we can get into in talking about meaning and definition, especially in communicating in an abstract and overgeneralized fashion, as I so far have been doing. We tend to think of meaning as static. In an important sense it is not. We tend to think of communication as only having recurrent patterns of usage that are endlessly repeatable in different situations. But communication patterns and the meaning of words change.

Later I shall expand on how use and usage both relate to the processes of definition, interpretation, and translation. We shall see that there are different practical levels of application for all these different concepts. We need clear concepts about clarifications to better understand the important processes we engage in when we attempt to make clear what people say either in one's native language, in a formal language, or in a foreign language. In all such cases interpretations differ.

Uses thus allow us to explore what we would like to know about things that are still unknown and even about things yet inconceivable. Use extends the imagination to find words for newly discovered meanings for what we want to say. It empowers us to make newly observed descriptions from our personal perspectives. It empowers us to make new descriptions of meaning from our unique points of view. And importantly, it allows us to note things to others about our experiences that others may not have had before. But innovative uses of language can be subject to error and confusion. Failure to use language usage that fails to distinguish differences can lead to deficiencies in language use. Use in moving away and abandoning conventional usage is especially subject to ambiguity and confusion.

And thus unconventional uses may lead us into making mistaken applications of conventional terms, which creates difficulties for others in interpreting and understanding what we are trying to say. It especially does so when our uses become too innovative and too subjective in their expression. We find in such cases that our language fails to communicate and it isolates us from others. And to be too complicated and to be too innovative in our uses of language makes listening and reading what we have to say incomprehensible and opaque. What we say becomes dense, obscure, and difficult, and as such results in rhetorical and communicative mistakes and failures.

CHAPTER 7

Limits of a Code Theory of Language

The traditional empiricisms of the sciences and the applications of technology and mathematics serve as paradigms for illustrating a code or a representational theory of language. Such a view of a code theory of meaning is modeled by the *semiotics* (science of signs) of C. S. Pierce where meaning is defined by a threefold relationship between *sign, reference*, and *referent*. Meaning is defined by reference. We have much the same theory expounded in Ogden and Richards, *The Meaning of Meaning* (1947) using the semantic triangle of Pierce.

Conceptions of meaning as reference use scientific methods of verification as paradigm illustrations of how meaning applies to our handling the tools of this world and to describing their operations and manipulations in dealing with the things in this world. Note how causal language is the language of control. And consequently the success of the sciences and technology in handling problems has lent credibility to this way of conceiving of meaning in terms of reference. But such a conception of meaning that relates signs to supposedly external processes and the structures of the world (referents) leaves the implication that meaning (reference) is mind dependent and that what goes on outside those meanings is a world independent of that reference. And thus results the whole philosophical problematic that searches for denotative definitions of reality.

As a philosophical preamble to discussing any theory of meaning as reference, a few remarks are in order. What gives rise to this dualism of mind over matter or matter over mind is the theory that minds die and are no longer a part of and become separate from this world. It is the spirit of Platonism that the soul is unlike this world. According to Wordsworth, "The soul that rises with us, our life's star, Hath had elsewhere its setting" (1904, 460). Of course stars come up from the horizon, and they continue to be there in the world on the other side of the world. I do not want to rest my case on discussing meaning on any theory of immanence or any dualism about mind and matter. Nor do I want to discuss meaning as a simulacrum or a representation of reality (Brummett 2003). It is my view that the concept of reality held by epistemic realists is a reification of the term *reality*. As such it leads to misunderstandings in our talk about what is really real or absolutely real, as if such expressions say something more than just speaking about what really is the case. I do not think that philosophically we can explain the relationship between talk and the things we talk about if they are unconnected. It is a dualism that we never seem to be able to bridge. It immerses us in paradox.

But what lends doubts about a dualistic theory of meaning as reference is the belief that our minds are interdependent. Minds in communication are not completely disjunctive and separate from other minds, but instead minds are interactive together within what some deem to be the external world. Minds are in and of this world—as such minds are being in the world (*Dasein*) (Heidegger 1962). Minds are as in Aristotle *anima*, a part of this bodily world bound together socially by communication.

And if mind is conceived as part of the world, as some people who hold naturalistic views conceive it, then meaning becomes a part of the natural evolutionary processes of biological interaction and symbiosis, in which case we cannot conceive of minds independent of their functional connections with the world. It is not necessary to defend this ontology that I speak of with any kind of philosophical dialectics. To see its plausibility it is only necessary to study the psychology of human interaction and brain functions to see that conceptions of mind as independent of external entities explain little or nothing. We need only to note to understand how we and our brains are engaged in a world of shared life and social experience with other people in interacting with what we speak of as the world.

A theory of language based on reference has to distinguish between two types of terms, terms defined by reference, *categorical terms*, and terms defined by how they combine or detach from grammatical structures with embedded reference terms (combination rules and detachment rules in logic). These terms defined by these combination and detachment rules of grammar have been traditionally called *syncategorical terms*. Syncategorical terms logically operate in various ways on the categorical terms. Their meaning is in their syntactical functions in relating logically to attachment or detachment operations upon the configurations of categorical terms.

Syncategorical terms therefore are defined by these grammatical functions. In other words, in communicating we use referential terms to predicate something about other referential terms; that is, we make statements about them, such as about the denoted attributes or the character of the actions predicated about in using them. To make these statements relate to each other, we need to understand their logical grammar. It is a traditional conception in grammar that a sentence as an assertion says that something is said of something. Or as a question it asks whether something is said of something.

In a referential theory of language, signs are tokens, placeholders, or stand-ins for a reference to a referent. Terms defined by reference are used in making statements that are logical propositions. Unlike in logic, where propositions are *statements that are either said to be true or false or indeterminate*, in forensics or debate we speak in terms of a different contrast, and we regard propositions differently as *points of argument*. Propositions in speech communications are either about reported facts or about proposals for actions, that is, *propositions of fact* or *propositions of value*. We argue for or against a proposition.

Terms, then, either synthesize other terms or symbolize referents. Synthesizing terms or syncategorical terms are called *syntactical terms*. And *logical syntax* or *linguistic grammar* as such studies the synthesizing of terms and how they bind together and relate to referential terms. And *semantics* is in sum a study of reference. Terms thus have either syntactical meaning or semantic meaning. And in the terms of formal semantics, meaning is defined by rules of reference or semantic rules. A formal semantics is a rule-driven semantics in which rules or definitions are rigidly defined.

Note that new meanings in a referential theory can be created by definitional proposals, especially by using descriptions and references to designate things, or by operational or causal theories of reference. Such have been the efforts made in defining many scientific concepts operationally (*operational definitions*).

In operational definitions we begin with protocol statements about how observations generate the meanings of words, such as historically has been the case in defining scientific measurements. In such cases we start with root senses using primitive protocols to define new terms or empirical or conceptual variables, and then in turn we use these newly defined terms again and again for defining other terms, thus shaping large systems of definitional frameworks.

Thus, we increasingly introduce by this method of introduction much more complex terms that are based on interlocking and combining definitions within new definitions. All these logical transformations using logical definitions make the terms of any technical language into a whole that is a complex formal system or rule-driven enterprise. It becomes a scaffolding of definitions. All statements in it are said to be analytic, that is, true by definition.

But those who believe that meaning is solely created by reference and semantic protocols in this described way have problems with descriptive accounts of language creativity as it takes place in everyday language use. Such a logical or syntactic way of defining terms does not accurately describe how the meaning of terms has changed within the evolution of language. Creative and imaginative uses of our words historically have given terms new and different meanings in new and different contexts. In the development of language new meanings have been discovered in the novel and innovative phrasing of our words, in which meanings obviously evolve and differ in their interpretations as they vary in the contexts of their uses. Words take on new senses as they are applied, refined, and extended to fit analogous but different situations and contexts.

Poets take great pride in creating new meanings with their novel uses of words. What we mean in speaking figuratively generates new forms of conceptualization that we become consciously aware of when we begin to interpret them. Interpretation attempts to define what is said and what is implied differently in our use of rhetorical figures, such as metaphor, simile, metonymy, synecdoche, and even such figures as oxymoron and personification.

What then is figurative language? It is not a concept with a precise literal meaning. The use of rhetorical figures I want to show obviously complicates how we talk about meaning. Figurative language at the present time is considered foremost a vague and very controversial topic. But it is a topic that has been around for a long time, even before there were poets to impress us with their sonorous, ornamented use of language that even after ages continues to impress us. Historically, then, people used figurative language long before writing, as it seems to be so obviously a natural form of thought that came into being with the first speakers of language. Even before anyone was consciously aware of what figures are, they existed in the normal patterns of speech. Figurative language is a part of the natural language process that must have originally played an important role in the very development and early evolution of languages.

Figurative use is inherently a part of the functioning brain, a part of the brain that harbors and uses presumption. Presumption is dependent upon the residues we find in our long-term memory, which is a combination and synthesis of those images and incidents contained in both semantic memory and episodic memory. Why the brain naturally takes to metaphors appears thus to be a fundamental part of human nature and the way we think the world works. Figurative language creates structures in the brain that, because of their biological formation in the synapses of the brain, help shape our thinking, and thus cognition is in part metaphorical and in part a result of synecdoche because of how the brain functions in distinguishing new aspects of experience that help make new and novel connections.

The overwhelming presence of metaphor and synecdoche in our thinking has led many to think that human cognition has its very beginning in metaphor and synecdoche. These are important issues, as they tend to prompt one-sided conceptions of how meaning is created for uses through metaphorical adaptations. And any semantic theory must take issue with the literal-figurative dichotomy of plain speech because, as we shall see, literal and figurative features are interactive in cognition.

What we can say historically is that poetry as a genre of writing goes back to our primitive roots in a singing and oral culture. It goes back long before the very beginnings of civilization. It goes back long before the mnemonic uses of script. There was poetry and a sense of metaphor long before any development of speech was transcribed into written prose. It came about before the making of books and before print literacy became a cultural phenomenon, and it came about before print literacy produced a popular human enlightenment that helped develop modern intellectual frames of mind.

Before printing there was little popular demand or need for universal literacy, socially or politically, as cognition and memory rested on mastery of oral languages. Before that stage in human enlightenment of print literacy, people communicated simply by talking or reading aloud from printed scripts as aids to memory. In a way printed scripts were the teleprompters of their day. And consequently people found little need for dictionaries, and the meaning of words were explained usually in contexts where words were being used differently.

At this point in our discussion we simply want to note in discussing the meaning of meaning that many things in life were at this time just unknowable. And the term *everything* as a universal becomes an inclusive stand-in. It becomes an all-inclusive category. The category everything includes the fictions of our imagination, our paradoxes, our negations, and even those things unnamed that are said to even lie beyond our most fanciful flights of imagination. Everything as a category, as a placeholder, applies to just everything imaginable and even the things yet unimaginable, even to those things that we can never imagine. As such the category everything can have no defined reference using a referential theory of meaning. But everything is a category many want to call God. It is the category of infinite possibility. And note on the other hand, *nothing* as a category in contrast does not even include itself.

What we can say in summation in discussing the limits of language is that we shall know many new things in the future that we cannot know now, nor even in the least way begin to anticipate knowing. Those things not created as yet are beyond the meaning of our present usages of words. At present they are the "yet unnamed unknowable." To know what we are going to create is to have in part already created the idea that will be used in creating it. I was shocked at the question in the recent presidential debates asking how the candidates would deal with things that they do not know. Note how such a question is loaded with paradox.

To think that the founding fathers, for instance, could have foreseen the likes of the twenty-first century and to think that they could have foreseen the challenges that we have now to interpretations of the United States Constitution were simply out of the question at that point in history. How could the founders in their wildest imagination possibly have anticipated the creative emergence of the complexity of contemporary economic, social, business, and financial institutions? Cartels, hedge funds, computer files, nuclear weapons, television commercials, and cinema were unthinkable and unknown to our constitutional forebears.

How could our founding fathers have imagined our present-day political and legal systems that have developed from the historical foundations of the system of government that they defined? How could they have foreseen the kinds of laws created about the offices of government that have since been created? Our founding fathers in their original instauration of a system of constitutional law could not have had expectations of what now are defined in law, such as corporations, nonprofit groups, and legal systems. Nor could they have conceived any of the newly envisioned different types and branches of bureaucratic government in place using regulatory powers.

Just how could any of their supposed wisdom have established a system of law and government that could be directly applicable in the twenty-first century to what we now have as institutions that started up with individual ingenuity and were defined into law? Note how even now people have trouble defining derivatives. Obviously, there can be silly questions about what the founding fathers meant by their words in the Constitution. But many today for political motives still keep insisting on asking them. It seems obvious that the Constitution is an ongoing contract that has been revised by states, their representatives, and officers of the federal government in the forever-changing processes of governing and being governed. The important question, then, is, who interprets the meaning of written and even unwritten contracts that have been developed within the framework of the law? And note the presumptions behind the use of precedents in common law and how they integrate with constitutional law. Note how the use of precedents often collides with those powers derived from the Constitution.

How have the many abstract concepts formulated in the Constitution come to have their present-day practical applications in the present regulatory statutes that have evolved into new laws and new forms of government that *define* our society today? Note here in this context in talking about the Constitution, we have used another and a different and distinct sense of *what it is to define*. Loosely, in talking about defining in this general sense, we mean giving shape or order to the things that we want to talk about. We can define a perspective. We can define a frame that encompasses what we are talking about. We can define the way we want people to look at things. Define in this sense is to give a determinative structure within a given frame that we can use to organize our groups and coordinate our actions.

We certainly are not talking about the meaning of words when we speak of defining law and the types of organizations we have in society. Here define means "establishing the limits and the conditions for something to exist." The United States Constitution, both written and undefined, defines the limits of laws and the functions of our government. Those limits are constantly being revised and redefined with new judicial interpretations. But note, then, the looseness or vagueness of those defined limits that we say exist in the Constitution. And historically they have out of practical necessity been *refined or redefined* by numerous court decisions.

Note, then, the controversy over what the words in the Constitution mean. Did the founders have *an intent* in inscribing in it their meaning? Have words in the Constitution been redefined in judicial precedents? In viewing the operations of the courts, do we want to say, at least in part, that legal rights and responsibilities were created and defined by past precedents established by the courts and that the process continues on into the future by adding new precedents to what has already been constituted as law? Or should we maintain that judicial interpretations of the Constitution should begin with what the words mean in our language today as defined in their applications to present-day behaviors and deeds?

It is worthy of note that these verbal conundrums about law and government are some of the most important questions in politics today. Note the conflict between notions of interpretation and defining when it comes to issues in law. And note the comparable significance of covenants, old and new, in the history of religion, and in the historical formation of secular governing bodies. They are the frames in which many people judge their relationships to both God and country.

How do we distinguish between the different issues that can be raised about definition and interpretation as explanations of meaning? It is the major issue that arises about any question that we have about meaning. Is it, as John Dewey in his *Logic and the Theory of Inquiry* suggests, that the first step in solving any problem is first *to define it*? But in a modification of Dewey, I suggest that it would be better first *to interpret* what we think the problems and issues are prefatory to any beginning attempts at defining them.

At this point I want to repeat a phrase of my introductory semantic axiom. "We *interpret* to determine *language use*, and *we define* to determine *language usage*." Here again, in what I have to say I am, as I have said, been expanding on the meaning of the terms in my basic semiotic axiom. In a paradigmatic sense interpretive summaries and commentaries are paradigms of language use. Paradigmatically, dictionaries define language usage. These are complex issues, as I have already said about meaning that to talk about them requires further expansion, elaboration, and specification.

But it is important at this point, as a point of clarification of my expanded meaning, to note the difference between *giving a definition* and saying that *something has a definition*. Defining is in one sense is *an act*. It is doing something. It is an act we make in response to needs for clarification. But in another sense giving a definition is *a formulation*. It is what we have produced. It is a formula of words. Definition in this sense is something we can produce or even create. And a definition as a formulation is a product of the act of defining. Defining is something we do in producing a formula or a code. Defining is a form of talk, and thus we first talk, and then we walk the talk that we talked about. Definition thus importantly becomes our ground for initiating actions out of our aims and intentions.

We may define, but we may not be successful in defining what it is that we are trying to do in defining. We can define, but in the process we may fail to create a successful formulation applicable to whatever it is that we are trying to define. What we may have produced is an unsuccessful definition. Sometimes our talking just gets us nowhere. Our act, our definition, can end up, alas, being no definition at all. We have not succeeded in providing what one might consider an adequate or applicable formulation. As an act it is not *satisfying*. Defining, in the terms generally used by J. L. Austin, is an act that can be plagued with what he understates by calling them *infelicities*.

There are thus two different senses of what it is to be a definition. It is an act, and secondly it is a successful making of an applicable product framed in words useful in clarifying what is being talked about. On the one hand, when we have formulated a definition, we may have provided someone with an incorrect grammatical or a mistaken logical form of a definition. Its very faulty formal grammar nullifies it as a logical definition. It does not have the proper logical structure or form of a definition. Logical definitions define what can be put in the placeholders or the blanks in the syntactical structures that we use for talking about things. Logical definitions may fail in making these insertions into sentences correctly.

And sometimes we find our definitions have no direct applications or causal reference to things. Though it has the proper grammatical form of being a logical definition, yet it has no direct application to experiences engaged in. In other words, definitions may not be successful, and in that respect they may be thought not to be definitions at all. Therefore, it is important to note the distinction between *trying to define* and *defining* in the sense of providing *a grammatical or a logical form of a definition* and finally to note the next step in defining of going one step further when the *act of defining is a successful performance*. In this last sense it is a communicative achievement.

Here are some examples of failures, selected from my early education as a kid, where the defining terms are obscure, or again they are about nonexistent things. In elementary school I was told, "A sentence is a complete thought." How is a thought complete? I have a thought of a dog. The thought is complete, but it is not a sentence. And another example from high school biology, "Protoplasm is a simple life substance." What is it about a simple life substance that explains anything? How do we verify such vague expressions that have no denotation? "Protoplasm" becomes a name for a mystery explaining nothing about the contents and functions of a living cell.

In the last analysis, note that what it is to be a definition depends upon how we view language in its applications. We can view it either from *the point of view of a user* or from *the point of view of the language used*. Language users do things with language such as thinking and cooperating in doing things with other people. And definitions help us in carrying out these mutually complementary tasks by saying and interpreting what is being said. Sometimes definitions propose. Sometimes they report. Either way, they relate rhetorically to how we use language clearly in dealing with other people.

Definitional proposals are *prescriptions*. Note that a doctor's prescription is an instruction to a pharmacist. It is never true or false. But a definitional report is about language use and usage. A report is *true or false about a use or a usage*. Reports of usage are about the facts about patterns of recurrent uses of words. Note that definitional proposals help us communicate better. Note that reports can help us understand better what is meant by the terms being used in what is being said. They are all about clarity in our applications of terms. Instead of approaching the subject of meaning and definition through looking at language use in terms of established usage, we suggest that we should first look to see how the terms meaning and definition function, not as prescribing or reporting correct usage but as looking to see how the terms interpretation and definition make our messages clear and how they help us keep straight what we mean to do and say.

And then second we should take a step back and look at language from the point of view of the listener or the reader. We should look to see how our words are being used to clarify what it is being said to the reader. And we should ask whether or not what someone is saying successfully achieves a level of mutual understanding between a speaker and a hearer, or between a writer and a reader about what is being said by the words used.

There are thus questions about meaning as it relates to interpretation and definition. One is about what are we doing in clarifying what we think we say.

What is it that we are trying to do in trying to make sense about what we are trying to say to others? And the others are the questions that the listener or reader asks in trying to interpret what is being said. They are questions about whether or not the speaker or author has successfully communicated what he or she has been trying to do or say. Definition and interpretation are thus complementary activities in determining meaning in two different perspectives, one trying to do something and the other in achieving an aim.

But some still want to claim that language is limited in meaning to only what our terms or words refer to. Words mean only the coded meaning assigned to them. This may be true in technical language but not in natural language use. Just focusing on technical terms leads to the conception of language as simply a code for designated referents. Thus, technical language is the primary exemplification of what it is to be a code theory of language. Such a point of view of language leads to the controversy over whether language is a cage, which seems to be implied by the *Tractatus* (Wittgenstein 1922). We cannot talk outside the frames of our referential terms.

And this restriction leads to his other famous remark, "Whereof one cannot speak, therefore one must be silent" (Wittgenstein 1922, 189). These claims of Wittgenstein in his *Tractatus* suggest the implication that our conscious awareness of things in this world is limited to a narrow circumscribed circle defined by the references made by the words that we speak. Our words define what we can talk about. In a way this view may be surely right in certain contexts, but it is right only in the narrow sense where the meaning of words is defined by references to things, where "the meaning is a reference." I maintain in opposition to this overstatement about meaning that reference and code are only in part the way language functions in most social and political contexts.

We take it that the Platonic (Socratic) and the Old Testament presumption about names is that to name something is to name what is already known without that name. Knowledge is preverbal. It is referential. But, as we interpret the Koran, when Allah gives man names, he also gives Adam knowledge at the same time about what is being named. For Allah to teach Adam the names of things would have been for Allah to have given Adam knowledge simultaneously with the giving of those names. It would have been for Allah to speak with Adam in Allah's language, for if Adam did not know Allah's language, how could Allah have told Adam about the names of things? Language is learned through language.

In other words, when Allah showed Adam what he was talking about, Allah had to describe and define things to Adam in Allah's language, which in turn became Adam's language. It was the description by Allah of the things named in Allah's language that was knowledge. There is a fascinating subtext to this story. Allah in giving Adam knowledge that the angels did not as yet have from Allah precipitated the angels' envy and their consequent revolt. What a different reason for the revolt of the angels than that found in John Milton in *Paradise Lost* or even Anatole France, *La Revolte des Anges*.

For Allah to name things, Allah had to give Adam distinctions by which he could describe and comprehend the complexity of the interrelations of things that he did not understand about things. Acquisition of language in this way is a form of knowledge acquisition. But to remove Allah from the scene of language creation would have made little difference historically to a theory that our knowledge acquisition comes through our language use and usage. Without Allah's role in the formation of language, we still can substitute instead an ongoing evolutionary process in the development of language. We can imagine language simply evolving from itself and not coming into being from any external imposition of names on things that is understood apart from that language such as we do in a theory of reference.

Such a view of language acquisition such as through Allah's language says that we live in a language. But to use again Ludwig Wittgenstein's metaphor and to interpret it differently, language is still a kind of cage. To use Rudolph Carnap's general terminology to make a comparable point, we cannot escape being in a metalanguage to talk about a language. We always have to frame language by using a language.

> A *metalanguage* (=df) is a language we use to talk about another language.

And to name we have to describe what we name from inside our cage or inside our metalanguage. In English when we talk about the meanings of other languages, whether formal or foreign vernacular languages, English becomes our metalanguage. And if we need to talk about our own language English, we still can use English as our metalanguage. But these metaphors are somewhat misleading, in that we can escape our so-called language cage by creating new languages with new meanings just as we can in developing newly invented logical or formal languages. But yet we still need a language to take this interpretive step to get out of our language. We are in a sense being pulled up by our own bootstraps. We do it by interpreting the novelty of what we are saying as our terms apply differently in different contexts.

And of course this physical impossibility described in the metaphor of lifting ourselves up by our own bootstraps also suggests analogously that there is something wrong with our analogy. And the claim that we use language to extend our use of language to new things suggests that it is a paradox to say so, and to say that we extend language usage by novel language use is conceptually a contradiction, for how do we use usage to define use? But as we move further along in working through these issues about the complexities of meaning and the creation of new language uses, especially about the uses of figurative language, I want to put the issues about interpretation and definition in a dramatically new and different light. In order to do this, I need to explain these issues by new definitions and by new analogies.

So far, hopefully, then, we can agree on this much. We cannot escape being in a metalanguage in talking about interpretation and definition. Metalanguage is the language we use to interpret another language. And to name or describe what we interpret or define is done from inside our cage or from inside our metalanguage. In interpreting and defining, it is especially important to note that we can use one or another language to talk about still another altogether different language. And it is important to add that not only can we use our own language to translate another language into our language, but we can talk about our own language, and we can talk about the emergence in it of new senses of words developing within uses of our own language.

We need to take seriously the evidence of language change produced by linguists. We want, then, in contrast to say that the creative and imaginative use of some of our words is what gives our words their meanings. And this creative process is not referential. We want to emphasize that new meaning can be discovered in novel uses and innovatively phrased figurative expressions. But nevertheless this does not deny, as we have pointed out, that new meanings can be created by definitional proposals, especially by using descriptions and references that define and precise usages. Such is the main way the theory of meaning as reference describes how language is being shaped in the language of the sciences and technology.

Technical language is just one way we give meanings that add to our repertoire of usage. It is this theory of reference extrapolated over all language that explains why some people look at language reductively as a code. They see it best illustrated when they observe how language is translated into computer language codes. In that transformational process, language is being literally translated, going from one language code to another. It is just transcription by using a code book. It simply is rewriting one code into another code.

But those who believe that meaning is solely created by reference or by code have problems with the use of vague terms rhetorically. Vague language can be used deliberately. It can be used mistakenly. Vagueness also may be the act of not saying enough. Vagueness can be attributed to a lack of precision in terms. It can be cured by defining terms precisely. But the function of codes, on the other hand, is to eliminate ambiguity. When we analyze the problems of ambiguity and vagueness, we should find that it is unsurprising that terms that are vague or ambiguous in some contexts are not vague or ambiguous in others, which thus seems counterintuitive to what a code theory of language would indicate.

Who is rich and who is poor? Note the recent controversy in the recent election as who is in the middle class. Note too the comparable difficulty in speaking of someone as middle aged. We do not stipulate by reference about who is middle aged. Precisely at what age do we speak of someone as middle aged? It is a term that has developed its meaning in a context of cultural use. And it can be vague and ambiguous in certain contexts. We certainly know that someone eight or eighty is not middle aged. But when do people begin or stop being middle aged? Note that people today live longer, and especially now with the average age increasing with new advances in medicine.

Our concept of middle age is changing. The average life span in 1945 was in the sixties, and now in the new millennium it is in the eighties and rising. We have thus begun lately as a result of these changes in longevity to alter our meaning of the term *middle age*. Younger people want to remain younger when they age. And the middle-aged people want to avoid being thought old. And thus we find that the extensions and development of new meanings of words such as middle age have developed from new cultural circumstances that require revised rough approximations to fit our cultural images of ourselves. Note the following bit of dialogue from an aging woman: "I do not think of myself as old, though I am now going through my change of life. Just because I no longer can have babies, I don't think of myself as yet old. I still feel in the prime of my life. I feel middle aged."

Ambiguity and vagueness have practical uses in communicating with other people, especially in advocacy. And this is especially true about purposeful ambiguity and vagueness when we want to be tactful and not to be too personal in dealing with untrustworthy people. It is worthy of note that reminding and noting, as I have been doing in my own text, have practical rhetorical purposes in argument. It is a style of indirect argument that I have consistently adopted in discussing the rhetorical uses of interpretation and definition.

But again I want to remind you that we use the term *argument* in different senses. I want to point out that in English the senses of what it is to be an argument are manifold. Arguments can be quarrels. Arguments can be rhetorical appeals. Arguments can be logically deductive arguments. And arguments can also be logically inductive arguments. Logical arguments are explicit in fully annotated proofs. But in contrast, arguments can be implicit by indirection and simply based upon mutually held assumptions. "Are you arguing with me? Why, then, are you telling me that?" Note that ironically, my argument here about what is an argument has been put forth indirectly by reminders.

Not only are arguments in part indirect, but they are said to be elliptical and enthymematic. The following is a technical definition of enthymeme in the language of both informal logic and rhetoric:

> *Enthymemes* (=df) are truncated arguments with some sentences understood.

We can make rhetorical appeals by reminders that call attention to things (terms and premises understood). These things are not normally noted about argument, as they are taken for granted. When many people make their arguments, they often fail to clearly note the meaning of the terms they use and the presumptions behind their use. Arguments quite often occur in a context of numerous, unacknowledged presumptions. Some people sometimes dislike calling their appeals arguments, but their appeal may often be interpreted as doing just that.

My own reminders are, for the most part, reports to you and are not direct arguments about what I think we understand about the processes of definition and interpretation. Hopefully, some of these distinctions as reminders will clarify some of the roles that definition and interpretation play in understanding the meaning of what we say and what others say and think we say. But to make my indirect appeal (argument) that that is the case, I need to discuss further the distinctions that we need to make to be rhetorically straight about talking about definition and interpretation. And to do that I need to change my frame of reference to talk about the number of different roles that we play rhetorically in interpreting and defining.

CHAPTER 8

Definitional Proposals and Definitional Reports

It is has been my contention all along that we have to deal with language in language. There are two fundamental rhetorical processes for talking about meaning using other words. One is to initiate new meaning. The other is to report about what meaning has been sanctioned technically and lexically, and to report on what are the meaning of words judged to be used as current usage (Urdang 2008).

But to talk further about reports of usage and in talking about definition we need to deal with some of the problems of creating language. Importantly, what is first, foremost, and important in talking about meaning is that it can be created. And consequently, we need to remind ourselves how language use ends up creating new uses of terms for new projects and new situations.

New words for the most part are created from and work out from a system or frame of old words. And the new words and the new uses of old words come to represent new thoughts and new meanings that can be reliably depended upon in our actions and our understandings of each other. Thus, dictionaries function not only to define what current uses have become accepted and established usage, but they also are used to report past usage in our heritage that has been preserved in written texts and that has shaped our cultural legacy. Reports of old word uses preserved in print are needed to interpret the records of written passages in preserved texts. Reports of meaning in dictionaries are not only about meanings of words used in current practice, but they are also reports of uses by readers that interpret works of writers no longer with us.

As has already been pointed out, the development of technical language through definitional proposals is just one way a person has in coming to terms with another persons' terms. For example, if we want to talk about something that has not been talked about before, we might want to lump that cluster of thoughts together under a new term. We then can introduce our new term to someone who will not adversely object to our defining new terms so that we can reach a mutual understanding about the matters of mutual concern that normally would be expressed in old terms.

And we introduce new terms with the assumption that there is a need for a new term to deal with the complexity we have in talking about and dealing with complicated and difficult matters. Note that neologism as a fault happens when people see that there is no need for a new term where an old term will do. Why give a new name for something that we already have a name for? But if we mean by neologism simply a new proposed name that we want to introduce to talk about things that we have difficulty in talking about, there is no reason then to think of *neologism* as a pejorative term.

To illustrate an introduction of a new term (neologism), I have an idea about a new development in the way we drive automobiles. I want to give a name for some new technical modifications of cars. For example, let me call a "wraploop" an automobile that rotates in circles with lateral but without any forward or backward movement. I stipulate by definition:

> A *wraploop* (=df) is an automobile that rotates in a circle and can move sideways without any forward or backward movement.

I do not know if there is such an automobile. I suspect there is. Probably some one has invented one by now. At least I have a concept of one that might have been created by automotive engineers. Moreover, I am fairly certain that if an automotive engineer designed and constructed such a vehicle, he or she would want to make his or her own definitional proposals for labeling their new invention. If they did, their proposals would be neither true nor false. And my own definitional proposal to define wraploops would most likely be ignored by them as the privilege of naming rights belongs to them. It should be their verbal child. Someone else in that case would have earned the privilege by their own enterprise and initiative to name the car that they had patented. Rightfully it would be their novel invention.

Definitional proposals contrast with definitional reports that are always, if accurate, true or false about usage. If such an invention were to come about, and if a name were accepted or patented, then it would be true or false about the usage of what the term wraploop would mean. For example, it might turn up that the accepted name for the vehicle described might not be wraploop at all, but possibly something like a "parkimeasymobile." Questions, then, about definitional reports are empirical questions that can be confirmed by the observation of users. Such definitions, then, would be reports of what the "standardizers" of our uses of language as usage would propose. We find after such acceptances of proposals that many such reports find their way into dictionaries.

And it becomes true or false that a word has a definition of its meaning in a dictionary of accepted usage.

A definitional proposal as a recommendation is either acceptable or unacceptable. A definitional proposal as a proposal once converted into a report of usage becomes true or false by generalized acceptance of its use. Thus, some definitions are true or false, and some are not. It depends upon the rhetorical function of a definition, as either a report or a proposal, as to how we think of it as having any truth value when it is used to talk about things. A definitional proposal is a proposal for acceptance, but once accepted, it is true or false that it has been accepted. A definitional report thus defines what is named and accepted nominally as a correct usage.

Note the caveat here that the use of technical language needs legitimatization. Legitimatization is a matter of both social and political politics. It has to be accepted and standardized, especially within a discipline or a specialty. But we need to distinguish a language that is made up of a mix of technical language and a language whose terms have evolved from use in contexts that have become usage without any formal proposals, that is, natural language. Natural language is created from the normal processes of meaning transference that take place when contexts affect meaning shifts when situations differ, and especially when rhetorical figures develop and sediment themselves by repeated use into new literal usages. Let us distinguish this language mix of terms evolving from both rhetorical figures in the natural languages and technical language. Let us call this mix ordinary language.

> *Ordinary language* (=df) is the merger of technical language into the mix of literal terms that have evolved historically in the context of natural language use.
>
> *Natural language* (=df) is language coming from the mix of adaptations from the different modes by which we transfer senses of terms that are found in ordinary use.

Natural language is the language that has evolved in new and novel contexts that has become usage. The process by which novel uses of figures of speech become usage I propose to call the *literalization of figurative uses*. A major way this is done, as I shall show, is through repetitive use of tropes and figures in certain contexts of language use. Imitation and repetition of figures deadens their contextual implications. Connotations of words and their emotive associations, their emotive freight, diminish as a result of their literalization. Figurative expressions lose their rich and associative meanings and leave us with simple senses of words once communicated historically using figures of speech. Once this happens, it can be said, using my proposed jargon, that these rhetorical figures have been *literalized*. Once literalized, terms are now amenable to definitions.

Importantly, in reading we should attend to the author's textual stipulations of definitions, such as I have been doing, and we should charitably grant the writer the right to define words as he or she so pleases within the context of his or her written text. We especially have to do it if we want to hear an author out. Definitional proposals are quite often made just only for a brief moment of time as we read them in the context of a given text. In sciences and mathematics we call such definitions *stipulations*. Here is an illustrative example of a stipulation I found in Monroe C. Beardsley (1950, 214): "When I speak of 'hard-edge abstractionist paintings' here, I refer to nonrepresentational paintings featuring clear geometric designs in which areas are marked by contrasting hues and separated by straight lines."

What is important about such stipulative definitions in specific contexts by authors is that there can be no quarrel with an author's privilege or prerogative to do so. Such momentary stipulations merely enrich the meaning of what is said for the purposes of the text. We can only quarrel with the author's rhetoric in introducing stipulations that might be confusing, but we cannot argue against him or her if he or she wishes to define terms for his or her own purposes of clarification.

The purpose of such stipulations is to facilitate communication and comprehension. In that stipulations may confuse someone when we make them, we all the more need to be certain in using them that stipulations be precise and clear about the meaning of what we are trying to say. Our assigning meaning to terms usually converts them into placeholders for other, more complex expressions, thus simplifying uptake in our reading where we do not need to repeat the words of complex expressions in thinking about them in the sentences in which they are embedded. They are much like synecdoche in being images for larger images. Stipulations again are much like pronouns. They become terms of reference to names and words in a context.

Definitional proposals may have just a very short life expectancy in a given text. Many are used just to serve for a moment as placeholders for a complex expression, to hold it briefly in our attention in our short-term memories. For example, in math we might say, for the purposes of simplification in a proof, "Let us call the complex algebraic expression v (t-13) by the letter p." Many definitions like that of p may be proposed for just the length of a text or just as shorthand as placeholders in a short mathematical proof.

We are also certain that many of the definitional proposals that we have been introducing in this book will certainly die away after you read them, as you may never find many of these proposed terms ever used again by anyone else. Usually only the gist of what has been said in any long passage is remembered. And the words used in passages of writing are for the most part usually immediately forgotten after they have been read. Thus, momentary stipulations die with the decay of details in a passage just as we forget much of what we have just read.

The memory of the exact wording in written texts is mostly lost, and the words are then immediately forgotten after we read them. Long-term memory is not photographic memory. What we remember in long-term memory for the most part is a mere gist of the meaning. The gist is usually recalled in mere paraphrases of what has been said. Who can honestly say without tedious bouts of memorization that they have a long-term memory for any substantial amount of the exact words of material that they have heard or read? Note the difficulty required to memorize any extensive amount of poetry. It just requires hard work. Note the importance of writing notes about quotes in doing research.

I do not expect our personal usage of some of my terms in this book to extend beyond my text. However, some of my proposals presented in this book have been used by other authors. They are not mine. But I expect too that many of these will be forgotten. Many of these terms of others that I have used are not as yet common currency in our reading, either in rhetorical studies or informal logic. Insofar as they are terms that have not found their way as yet into most logic and rhetoric texts, they are sanctioned only by a limited body of literature. They are to a great extent, then, uncommon usage.

Such specialized usage for such terms as I am proposing, then, has not entered into ordinary language usage, nor is such usage universally accepted by either members of the Informal Logic Association or the members of the Rhetoric Society of America, of which I have been a member. Although the two named organizations do not have a formal constitutional authority to standardize technical language for their disciplines, many other specialties and disciplines do have such authorities for formal standardization. They have organizational procedures for sanctioning usage in their specialties and disciplines. Two such examples are the American Psychological Association and the American Chemical Society. Both standardize the technical jargon for their professions. I wish to call special attention to the diagnostic jargon of the American Psychiatric Association (2000). Not only are mental disorders defined by fiat, they are coded for efficiency in diagnostics.

Technical language arises from the need to talk about the complex details that go into the complex affairs, patterns, arrangements, and assemblages found in the different disciplines and specialties. And ordinary language is open ended about accepting much technical language that is practically useful in everyday living. Slowly, useful technical definitions are absorbed into ordinary use and usage. But how do we draw the line that defines the openness of ordinary language to a great deal of technical language? What is accepted lexically as usage has no precise criterion. Need is the only motive we have for any general acceptance. Acceptance is simply a matter of frequency. Note here my sense of define as defining a boundary. Language acceptance as a social act has no boundaries. Who are the gatekeepers to say that a technical term has moved into ordinary discourse? Commonly, it is the dictionary makers who are the deciders, who make the decision as to what counts as ordinary accepted usage (Urdang 2008).

Most technical language about skills and crafts does not find its way into the unabridged dictionary. Many such words are in supply and tech manuals and not in dictionaries. Note the number of words from biology and chemistry, however, that do make it, but a biologist and a chemist also do have many words in their vocabularies that do not find their place in dictionaries. How many species of plants and animals have been named? Most of these names are not found in dictionaries. I once tried to find names for the common weeds in southern Illinois. They were just a mere part of the local rural vocabulary. It was only the old-time farmers who were the authorities. And as time passed, their verbal wisdom was in general being slowly ignored. Most of the newer generation had forgotten the names of common weeds.

When we turn to mathematics, it is interesting to note too when counting words that the series of natural numbers is infinitely generative. And what about proper names? Do we include them in our vocabulary? What about place names? I was fascinated that Tonti, the name of a famous French explorer, is the name of a crossroads in Marion County, Illinois. How many such names for the most part are unrecorded (Crystal 2008)? I recall hearing Harlow Shapley, the astronomer, remarking on a TV talk show that at the Harvard University astronomy department, the graduate students had the privilege of finding new galaxies in the myriads of them out there and naming them after themselves. That sort of naming has a short life with insiders, as is the case with many of the new atomic particles. Are proper names, then, a part of our total vocabulary? Just think of all the place names on the surface of the earth. At a junction near my hometown there was a store called Slap Out. The store got its name from the owner, who, when he did not have something, would say, "I am plum slap out." Place names are subject to changing histories (see Crystal 2008b).

Note the meaning of a great deal of slang. It is language of a limited group that has usually a short life span and sometimes disappears with a generation and is not accepted lexically as acceptable in dictionaries. Yet slang is language often used that forcefully draws attention to its shock and novelty. But notably, some slang when it becomes effective gets respectable. But much slang, on the other hand, has words that some people like to forget in that it has a disrespectable and a sordid past often said to be politically incorrect. Many profanities and obscenities, out of fear of the language police (in the English studies sense), do not find their way into dictionaries.

In canvassing our vocabularies and their origins just think of all the names of all the mechanical parts on all of the machinery and equipment in the world. It is no wonder we run out of names sometimes and have to resort to numbers for identification. Think of all the names of people in the world. Thus, the naming and labeling of all the kinds of things and the naming of all their aspects and all their complexities in all the disciplines is an open and endless, never-ending cataloguing task.

The notion that we have either large or small vocabularies is especially relative to our uses of technical language, our vocations, our culture, and our specialties, and it is in no way limited to the vocabulary words that we find listed in an unabridged dictionary. All this inability to determine our word use potential tends to confirm the generative character of how we create and propose names to be added to our vocabularies so as to function smoothly in any group or society.

Dictionaries do not propose definitions, they report them. What they report is that a word has historically been found to have been used to mean such and such with limited frequency in some contexts (that is, interpreted to mean such and such). But dictionaries give us very little clue as to the wide number of implications that can be drawn from a metaphor. They have difficulties in drawing a line between what is literal and figurative. Interpretive inferences about metaphors range across a range or gamut of presumptions that are needed to interpret fully what is being said in the use of rhetorical figures. The discussion of the full range of interpretive issues about indirection and inferential meaning generated by figurative language requires that we look at inferential theories of communication and their illustrations and explanations.

Interpretive theory, methods, and their applications for studying meaning (=df) is called *hermeneutics*. But for the most part, definitions in dictionaries are not then logical definitions at all. Rather, dictionaries give us words that are *useful in interpreting* the uses of words in specified contexts. After all, their explanations of word use are interpretations that lexicographers make in compiling lexical definitions. It is much easier to use a dictionary to interpret what we read than it is to use a dictionary to help find words to use in writing and speaking. For that we need *thesauruses* and *dictionaries of synonyms* for suggestions. Skills of writing and speaking are acquired by experience, not by the use of dictionaries (Urdang 2008).

To have confidence in using a word in writing we need to master usage in a context of use. We need an enrichment of many terms by the historical information that surrounds a word's use. Importantly, we learn usages from others.

We need to master usage in a context by hearing or reading other people using words if we are to communicate with other competent users of a language. Note how this is confirmed in the way we master or learn to use foreign languages. Language learning requires engaging and using the language in the context of its use with other speakers of that language.

Precise and refined use of language is not adequately captured in dictionaries. Dictionaries only illustrate and report usage by samples of usage, and in doing so they do not give us the full spectrum of many subtle forms of both sophisticated and practical refined usages. Dictionaries simply report the usage of the language in certain contexts. They give us samples of the complex variations that they find in historical usage. Dictionaries only collectively and selectively report usages over the spectrum of time in which the historical usage has occurred. What they report on is merely a selection of samples of language use.

By the very fact that dictionaries are foundationally historical in their reports of usage, dictionaries have difficulty in remaining current in their reports of usage. Moreover, dictionaries, being essentially conservative, are reluctant to pass from their interpretation of some uses of words to sanctioning them as usages. Some people have a holier-than-thou attitude about people who use unsanctioned uses of words not found in dictionaries. Of course, rhetorically speaking, we need to go along with such people in the use of dictionary-sanctioned language. We need to do it if we are going to get them to respect us and if we are going to rhetorically appeal to them to trust us.

In sum, dictionaries thus only collectively and selectively report usages over the historical period in which the usage has occurred. As stated, some usages become obsolete. Some usages become exceedingly rare. By the very fact that dictionaries are foundationally historical in their reports of usage, dictionaries have difficulty focusing on and remaining current in their reports of present-day changing uses that they might question and deem to be usage. What is usage takes time to observe, as it requires repeated observation of the frequency of a pattern of use. In other words, dictionaries always take samples of usage from a selected span of observations in a limited span of time.

Moreover, dictionaries are essentially conservative. In one way, they are guardians of precedents (see again Urdang 2008). And they are fully aware that reporting usage tends to sanction their interpretations of usage, which by its nature is always past tense. Some people have a holier-than-thou attitude about people, especially untutored people, who use unsanctioned uses not in the dictionary. They define their intellectual integrity by their own sense of language refinement. And how they do frown on neologisms! But note how the use of the term neologism as mentioned is used ambiguously. In some contexts what is meant is that a neologism is simply a new use of a term. In others neologism is looked upon as a fault in the use of language.

Of course, rhetorically speaking, we need to go along with people in our use of dictionary-sanctioned language. It is the "in thing" in language respectability. When in Rome, do as the Romans do. It is good public policy for those who have no power to change anything but who need to blend in and compromise with the people who want to maintain their self-styled, prideful propriety. We especially have to do it if we want other people to buy the little, pricey pig that we have in our poke that we have up for sale at the marked-down price of $99.99. It is the price we pay for merchandizing.

Whitehead in *Modes of Thought* (1938, 173) discusses *the fallacy of the perfect dictionary*, which is the mistake of thinking that terms in everyday language usage can be defined precisely. The development of abridged dictionaries requires abridgment. Abridgment is not just a condensation process. It is also an elimination process. The vernacular dictionaries have evolved from historical studies of usage of terms that begin to develop new senses as they were extended into new contexts and situations.

The historical evolution of languages is an obvious fact of history in both language diversifications and language unification. Both directions of language change, the disappearance of usages and the introduction of new usages, have occurred throughout history. In times when societies are fragmenting, such as after the decline of empires or after the detachment of strong viable societies from their parent societies, their languages change when they begin to move apart. We see language groups becoming isolated, out of touch with the parent language, and as a result their common tongue changes little by little into dialects that at times are no longer comprehensible to the language societies from which they have evolved. Note the variations in language spoken across many nations. Some nations have dialects incomprehensible to each other in different sections of their countries.

On the other hand, we have seen great empires and nations develop around the lingua francas of political, military, commercial, or religious hegemonies that possess an ethnic or linguistic identity or grouping. Aramaic in ancient times was the lingua franca of the Middle East, coming from Persia. Arabic, which replaced it in the Middle East, was the language of the Koran. Swahili became the commercial lingua franca of the East African coast. Swahili is an amalgam of Bantu and Arabic.

Spanish naval power dominated the Caribbean, Central America, and Latin America, especially when the power of the Spanish Armada was at its peak. The power of Athens was naval power. The power of Venice was naval power. The power of Portugal was naval power. The imperial languages especially spread around the world during the age of discovery in the fourteenth through the sixteenth centuries. In the eighteenth and nineteenth centuries English spread as the lingua franca of commerce, and as England became an economic power the English language spread around the globe. English now especially has become the dominant language of international commerce with the new American commercial hegemony and with globalization after World War II.

We see, then, in the history of the world that many of these great imperial languages not only developed commercial languages, but they have also developed literary languages. Different linguistic cultures have sought to define themselves by a national literature. They have developed classical canons of their literature, which in turn have become the basis of their language education in schools. The basis of literature in education in the schools has stabilized many a vernacular language. As such, there is, then, in all the great imperial languages a tendency toward stabilization and standardization that centers on the traditions of their literature.

A corollary to this realization that a language is always contemporary in its usage is that the etymology of a word does not help us know or report how a given word is used at the present time. Etymology only helps us understand how the word has changed. We may revive historical usages through resurrecting etymologies, but that is only possible to the degree that we can rekindle the sense of the historical usage in a contemporary audience.

The root sense of a word, as studied in historical philology, does, however, play an important role in language usage insofar as the root senses of the word are often easily perceptible by contemporary audiences, as is perceived in the uses of prefixes and suffixes (Urdang 1975, 1986, 1998). For example, the root senses of Anglo-Saxon roots are embedded and play an important role in figures and tropes, unlike Latin and Greek roots that are today losing their historical sense in the everyday usage of terms. Latin, and especially Greek, roots no longer plays an active role in the vernacular since the recent dramatic decline of classical education in the schools.

Nevertheless, still, figurative uses of words play a part in the utilization of etymologies. Metaphors are especially involved in vernacular languages in the transfer of uses from one context to another. Often metaphor affected dramatic shifts in the history of the language, and quite often those processes can be reversed. This resuscitation of usage happens when we find a need to revive an old obsolete usage or an etymological derived usage for either practical or aesthetic reasons. And this is the reason that the terms and distinctions made in classical literature can be seen to be so refreshingly new at times to those presently embedded in contemporary concepts and distinctions. Many classical scholars feed on such resurrected novelties.

Usage is thus our stable starting point of what it is to be literal. It is the language that embodies the knowledge that is embedded in our language, which we can use to speak clearly to members of our speech community. It is the language that embodies the wisdom of our culture. Usage has thus to do with linguistic convention and traditional assumptions about the fixity of the meanings of the words that we use in our everyday speech. In talking about usage, we do not treat words from the point of their wealth of implications, connotations, or associations. Instead, we think of usage as token stand-ins, as code words, or as representations of meanings that we have been used in the past to talk literally about our world and to talk about the contents of its realities, and especially about some of the descriptions we have to talk about in discussing the inner and emotional feelings of our personal lives. Usage in sum is the acculturation of fixed and established ways of language use that shapes our linguistic community as it moves within fixed patterns of language usage and within its refined changes going on into the future.

Language usage essentially, then, is conservative. It presumes standards of correctness. Not only does usage refer to the way that others have acceptably and understandably spoken before, but it also refers to how our language gives us literal meanings of the terms that we can use to be clear about what we wish to say. It is the base that gives language preservationists the privilege of preaching correctness. It gives us conventional and standardized meanings. It allows us to introduce and to precise the stipulations of the meaning that we give to our terms. It is the reservoir of standardized terms that we think we can easily understand and act on.

Usage, then, is about the words and terms that we can easily catalogue. It allows us to collect and put words into our dictionaries. We index usage and put it into alphabetically ordered lists in our standard dictionaries that we can use to confirm the correctness of our accepted interpretations of our uses of words as confirmed by lexical authorities. And we see usage is often sanction by those privileged enough to join the self-appointed language police, as we see it done by people such as William Safire, who every Sunday in the *New York Times Magazine* has told us the correct usage of our words. And it is much the same sort of language policing that we find in *Fowler's Dictionary of Modern English Usage*. *Fowler's* is a book established as a model for correctness for words, especially those words that are found and deemed respectable in written texts that have an approved social status. "Act vb. In the sense behave like, the word, once used as freely as play, has contracted a slangy or vulgarly colloquial tone, & is now more appropriate in such expressions as act the giddy goat than in act the philosopher" (1926, 7).

Usage thus allows the linguistic prescriptivists to assign the meanings of the words that are used to privilege the propriety and the social respectability of those who play a leading part in shaping an elite or a privileged community. Words in effect grant status to the so-called and self-styled respectable speakers in their language community. It is no accident that language for many is a mark of status. It distinguishes the illiterate and vulgar from the respectable, the self-selected elite, who in turn give license to the language of an elite. Note the way that high-toned and hortatory language is used likewise to fake intellectual pretensions.

There is another form of prescription of correctness that allows those who think they know to set the standards of correctness of words for their technical disciplines. It allows specialists to define the terms of their specialties so as better to communicate with accuracy and precision about measurements, descriptions, dimensions, and sizes in talking about the tools, machine parts, and commercial objects of business, vocational, and commercial interests. And the physicist thus defines speed as velocity precisely whereby all sorts of descriptions of movement can be better distinguished and defined, such as initial velocity, average velocity, final velocity, and instantaneous velocity. The physicist can thus talk about "speed" and "movement" in terms that are precise descriptions that eliminate all ambiguities that we run into when we want to talk about motion in using such literal terms as "slow," "fast," speed," and "movement."

Usage thus has much to do about what is thought to be literal. It is the language use that can be standardized and refined to give us determinate and precise meanings. Those concerned with usage essentially seek to establish codes of meaning. Thus, in interpreting and reporting what we mean, we need to confront our use of terms with terms that have been established, defined, or sanctioned as having describable stable usages. Stable usage is thus the foundation for all our important communications, especially as we see it happen so desirably in the language of the law.

An interesting context to examine definitional proposals is to be found in the development of codes that take place within trades and industries. Building and safety codes in many cases become public law. Other professional codes that have been proposed and adopted within groups and organizations too have sanctions that are enforced by law. Such codes can be national as well as local. What is important about such codes is their standardization and definition. Codes are defined. And any statement reporting their acceptance and recognition by various authorities or legal entities is a definitional report. They can be a part of any institution, such as the honor code at West Point. Note that military codes are sanctioned by military law. And ethical codes of the legal profession are a part of the rules of the court system.

However, many standardized codes of ethics, as in many professions such as business, medicine, psychology, or journalism, are lax. They are little more than words for moral sanctions of blame and shame and calls for ostracism. But again, some professions do have codes within regulatory law to enforce many of their behaviors. What all this codification and standardization illustrates is the complexity of the variety of both logical and rhetorical definitions that have a role in constituting and approving the norms and laws that regulate behavior in any society.

It should be noted that dictionaries in their reports of usage give us very little clue to the wide number of implications that can be drawn from any metaphor. Such interpretive inferences range across a range or gamut of new associations that are contextually implied by any metaphorical use of a term. The discussion of the full range of interpretive issues about indirection and inferential meaning, especially as generated by figurative language, requires an in-depth discussion of *figurative language* as an umbrella term. And likewise, the term *definition* requires an in-depth discussion of how definition equally depends upon our conception of interpretation as another umbrella term that embodies under the single term many different senses of its various uses.

But for the most part, then, definitions in dictionaries are not logical definitions at all. Rather, dictionaries in their reports of usage give us words as pointed out that are found *useful in interpreting* the uses of words in specific contexts. Unless we have some strict notions of correctness, our uses of terms may extend beyond those limited illustrations of use that are to be found in dictionaries. To have confidence in using a word in writing, we need to master usage in a context of use, usage that requires that our language use be saturated fully by the uses coming from a significant number of other competent language users in our speech community.

Precise and refined use of language as pointed out is not always adequately captured in dictionaries. Dictionaries only illustrate usage by samples of usage, and in doing so they do not give us the full spectrum of the usages found in a speech community. Dictionaries simply report the usage of the language in certain contexts, and especially they report uses in literary contexts. They only give us samples of the complex variations of use that are found in samples of historical use. And they then show us that to understand usage we need to see how historical use requires interpretation if we are to arrive at that judgment made from the many citations that lexicographers used to say about what is usage.

The senses of what it is to be an interpretation is determined by the aggregated set of historical uses of the terms interpretation and definition that have developed and gathered from samples and examples over time throughout the history of the English Language. The evolving process that leads to multiple senses of terms can thus be labeled as umbrella terms, whose uses are shaped by aggregations of a number of related senses. Such a reversal of treatment in talking about interpretation and definition by talking about umbrella terms, as I am proposing, reframes how we can cognitively best come to terms with the terms interpretation and definition. And that contention and its justification, I again maintain, requires amplification and expansion of what we mean when, as I am doing in this text, we talk about the meaning of terms by continuing to reframe our discussion along with still other different semantic frames or other *terministic screens* (see Winterowd 1985, 145–77).

CHAPTER 9

An Inferential Theory of Language

What is important in developing a realistic perception of language change is to acknowledge that the meaning of words are always contemporary and that what words mean is always open to change. And in our awareness of this change we should also recognize the role of imitation in maintaining usage. And we should also recognize too how usage relates both to memory and to being a part of a language community with a system of signs technically called our *sociolect*. Note how we educate usage by drilling and repeating words. And the confirmation of that adequacy of our use of conventional usages for certain circles in societies motivates the conservatism of the *prescriptivists* about our language usage. It is such conservatism that underpins our sense of language correctness. Repetition thus is the basis of our notion of usage.

But note that I do not want to say that we interpret usage, as I stated in my basic semiotic axiom; rather, I want to say that we interpret use in order to define usage. To repeat my basic mantra, *we interpret use; we define usage*. And if in interpreting use we find that use is conventionally repeated by others, we should then conclude that our use is usage. And a standard of usage is confirmed and legitimated by lexicographers putting usage into lexical definitions into their dictionaries.

Each of us thus has a repertoire of usage, our *personal idiolect*. We importantly perfect our idiolect in both our formal education and in our efforts at self-education. All of us have in our idiolects an ever-changing and reshaping set of words that that we use to speak and to write with. Our repertoire of written usage among those with formal education is much larger than our spoken usage primarily because a bookish vocabulary does not easily flow into our everyday speaking patterns. Written usage multiplies endlessly in the context of the historical accumulation of so many written texts. I find in my own writing that I often use words that I have never spoken before. To use them properly presumes that I think my audience has them in their reading vocabulary as well as I do. The written or reading usage of a sociolect is called the *grapholect* (Hirsch 1981).

Part of our language development and education, then, is about enlarging our basic repertoire of usage. Our speaking use and usage are consequently in large part determined by the local community or the area that we live in. Our personal idiolect is a product of our family and our community of close face-to-face encounters, and especially it is acquired from the local schools that we attend. We speak of this local or regional use and usage as our *dialect*.

Some sociolects contain hegemonic cultural and elite dialects. Such dialects are what prescriptivists choose to call good English, Spanish, Italian, Japanese, Chinese, or German. Prescriptivists, through gatekeepers or their language police, create mechanisms to put the hegemonic dialect forward as the correct standard of the sociolect. Importantly, they sanction the properties of the grapholect, its spelling and its grammar.

Historically there seems to be an obvious correlation within different language communities, where we find that the standardized grapholect inhibits language evolution and radical changes in language usage. Note how dictionaries, such as Webster's, have been a conservative obstacle, slowing changes in the usages, especially in the spelling of the grapholect. Note the conservative absurdities in ritualistic spelling bees. Normally, we learn to spell with our fingers as we type or spell in the way we write in cursive script. And now spell checkers on word processors are making spelling and grammatical rules even more conservative still.

Interpretation is, as suggested, an umbrella term. But when it applies to language use, we need to recognize that interpretation of how language is used relates importantly to the content of what is being said as well as to what is indirectly being said. Interpretation of the meaning of what is being said indirectly always presumes an inferential theory of language. Such a view of language is presumed, where language is doing and implying something in a context of presumptions and signaled intentions. It is understood from what is going on in a communicative situation.

On the other hand, usage goes hand and in hand, as we have illustrated, with a code theory of language, and especially it applies to any notion of a rule-driven semantics, with its definitional rigidities promulgated by standardizers. Codes are codes by definition. Rather than think of these theories as theories, as I eschew notions of theory in talking about language change, I prefer to think of accounts of language change not as theories that are generalized explanations but as descriptions of how meaning is both assigned and grows in an evolutionary fashion in the advance, progress, and growth of a linguistic culture.

Note that in English studies they speak of "the defined meaning," or in other words, "defining words." In English studies "defined meaning" is called "the denotation." But this notion of denotation is quite unlike the logician's notion of denotation, which is defined by an "ostensive reference." What English studies calls a denotative definition in logical studies is spoken of as a "connotative definition." Either way, such definitions, a "denotative definition" in English studies or a "connotative definition" in logic, are based on a representational theory of language or on a code theory of meaning of a word that defines by using words. They are definitions that are expressed in words.

But also in English studies they speak of the "connotations of words." Connotations in English jargon are the "associated meaning" or the "emotive senses" that attach themselves to our use of words. Here we see that connotations have their sources in what we think to be inferentially associated with the use of the word. Connotations as spoken of in English studies have their sources in our presumptive background knowledge of the things that are defined in denotative definitions. Connotations in English studies are comparable in a way to what Aristotle called the *accidental properties* of things. They are the properties of things that we associate with other things often shared by those things.

But also certain associations are made or implied in talking about certain things. When we speak of "murder," the full canopy of criminal justice descends on the term, and the penalties of such a crime by punitive executions are called into play. Certain associations are implied from our background knowledge and the experiences we have about murder as a crime. Such terms as murder are sometimes spoken of as *loaded terms* because of the wealth of implications that follow from their usage. Note the implications of saying that abortion is murder. These inferences about associated meanings are determined by the contextual implications we make in saying things. Instead of direct perceptual properties, what is suggested by the use of a term becomes the focus of interpretation.

The complexities of such inferences about connotations, associations, and contextual implications make it possible for interpretations to go on and on, and in some cases where matters are complex, they seem to want to never end. That possible infinite expansion on possible interpretations is why interpretations at times are always thought open ended and never coming to an end in any final, defined, terminating conclusion. The sense of closure we desire in a definition is entirely lacking in such inferential interpretations.

An inferential theory of communication that attempts to account for the grounds of interpretation is well defined, explained, and illustrated in Dan Sperber and Deidre Wilson's *Relevance; Communication, and Cognition* (1986). Presumption is the key term in any topic that concerns either interpretation or rhetorical criticism. And presumption, as in Sperber and Wilson, is the basis of what I have to say that is important about interpretation, and presumption is the concept that puts us straight about a great deal of our talk about interpretation.

But first and above all, rhetorical criticism and interpretation as a tool of critical thinking are used to expose *unwarranted presumption*, which to my mind is the greatest defect that is found in our argumentative and communicative practices. Unwarranted presumption is the fatal flaw of all a priori–based ideologies. Presumption is at the heart of what constitutes prejudice. It is the flaw in people who think they know too much. Thus my notion of presumption frames the issues for much of what I want to say about interpretation, rhetorical mistakes, and rhetorical ploys.

Presumption, then, is the foundation of understanding what people are talking about. Interpretation, as well as rhetorical criticism, above all increases our awareness of presumption, especially the mistaken ones that people commonly make about other people. It above all exposes ignorance. It is a part of our living in our wells of ignorance, where we are uninformed and where we are grossly mistaken about many things about us and about what goes on around us. Examining presumptions is especially a key to any criticism that tries to avoid misunderstandings with other people about what we say and do in talking with each other.

Sperber and Wilson's general view is that we should look at communication, not just as transferring messages to a receiver by coded language, signals, or symbols (the code theory of language), but rather that we should *also* view communication as an interaction between people doing things, where the actions going on are interpreted by the participants in a context of presumption and signaled intentions.

In summary the key issue for Sperber and Wilson is that communication begins with a *manifest assumption* (*presumption*) *of an intent* on the part of someone to communicate. What is important in communication is what is *manifestly relevant* about communicative intentions. It is this communicative assumption (*presumption*) that determines whether what is presented *ostensively (referentially)*, either by language or actions is maximally relevant to this communicative intent. Being *maximally relevant* is thus Sperber and Wilson's key to relevant and reliable interpretation.

If you tell me that so-and-so shot his wife, why are you telling me that? The hearer of any ostensive reference interprets the relevance of the intentions to communicate from his or her own cognitive environment and knowledge background, which includes the presumptive cognitive awareness of the knowledge background of the speaker. The relevance is that the communicative intent has to be understood from what is maximally relevant in the mutual cognitive understandings of both the speaker and hearer (*background presumptions*). It is in the perceiving and inferring of what follows from this relevance, from the mutually held assumptions that the speaker maximally communicates to the hearer. Note the importance of relevance in unmasking assumption (*presumption*).

Many years ago the subtlety of communicating by presumption and background knowledge was dramatically impressed upon me by a simple little event, but it was for me at the time a dramatic incident. I keep repeating this story in that it is so exemplary of the role of presumption in communication. It was one of those "Aha!" experiences that made me suddenly aware of how we communicate a great deal without saying very much, and in this very case by not saying anything at all.

What happened has been for me a paradigm of communicative indirection and an exemplar of contextual implication (*conservational implicatures*). The incident occurred in a dormitory recreational room at the University of Oklahoma at Norman. I was attending a summer institute for high school teachers in the history and philosophy of science sponsored by the National Science Foundation.

A preteen, or maybe just barely a teen, a mathematical prodigy, was housed in the dormitory with a large number of high school science teachers attending a number of other National Science Foundation summer institutes. A small group of teachers to whom I was talking was gathered together chatting away in a friendly conversation. Some of the teachers from other National Science Foundation programs were taking advanced courses in physics and mathematics, and they had this spectacular young grade school prodigy in their classes. I had heard them talk about how brilliant he was. They were in awe of him, and they treated him with deferential respect, as they seemed altogether humiliated by the little grade school genius making them feel just plain stupid.

That Saturday afternoon the teachers and the prodigy were gathered together on the first floor of the dormitory with the TV on in the background. There was a baseball game going on in the background on TV. I was talking to the teachers about baseball and baseball players. The little prodigy stood there in our midst. I jokingly made an ironic remark to them about a baseball player. To be funny I grossly exaggerated some of his statistics. It was obvious to everyone that what I was saying was not true.

The young prodigy however interrupted me to tell me that I was wrong and corrected me about the accuracy of my statistics. At the moment I was astounded that the small boy would be so presumptuous to correct me, a dignified philosopher committed to the truth. After all, it is the usual expectation that kids do not correct consenting, dignified adults. Suddenly I saw the eyes of the teachers quickly glance at each other seeking mutual acknowledgment. And I sensed a sigh of relief among those teachers. I saw in their relaxed smiles what they were communicating to each other in those quick exchanges of glances.

Without saying a word, those teachers communicated to me and to each other that the boy was at that moment just an unsophisticated, naïve, young kid. They communicated that the boy was not able to detect an obvious bit of ironic, byplay or horseplay in my mocking them with my erroneous statements about some baseball statistics. They had finally found something to feel superior about in relating to that young kid.

And as I did not reply to the boy, the kid appeared puzzled by my silence. Silence in the meanwhile descended over everybody. By the expression on the kid's face everyone could see that the boy did not realize what was happening around him in that situation. He had been removed from his prodigy pedestal. He was out of it. It was obvious that the boy had a lot of growing up to do to participate in adult, or should I say not-so-adult, conversation. He was still an immature boy. He was a duck out of water. He could not handle the presumptions, or the contextual implications of a remark that was little more than an ironic, playful bit of baseball chatter.

Despite no words being spoken, a great deal of communication took place in that situation simply by mere glances and the quick little exchange of smiles. How one looks at what went on in that little innocent and interesting drama depends a great deal upon how you interpret the background assumptions (presumptions) in that situation. Analyzing, interpreting, and explaining what took place in those glances and smiles are what a great deal of rhetorical criticism is all about.

The most interesting factors that played out in the incident were the background knowledge (cognitive environment) and the presumptions (mutually held assumptions) existing in the minds of those teachers. Those glances and smiles communicated *an intent* to communicate. What they meant was determined by their *relevance* to the presumptions playing out in the incident. What was said by those glances and smiles led to the responses (judgments) that those teachers were making in that situation about the young boy, which every one of those teachers mutually understood from their mutual glances and their quick vanishing smiles.

The glances confirmed how each teacher had interpreted the boy's questioning my statement about my inflated baseball statistics. Each acknowledged their perception of the awkward arrogance as well as ignorance of the boy trying to correct someone about a jocose lie. Those glances simply mirrored each other's thoughts about the situation and the actions of the boy. Each made the other aware why they were glancing at each other (a communicative intention). And the little twitch of a smile that they made acknowledged why they understood (what was *relevant* from the mutually held assumptions).

But also one could tell from the quick suppression of those smiles that the teachers did not want to hurt the boy's feelings. They were all too kind in hiding from him what they were thinking. The young boy, who had been so damned sure of himself when he challenged my statistics, failed to see the reactions of the teachers who were standing directly behind him.

The young boy, not sophisticated enough socially to sense what was happening, appeared puzzled about the silent reaction. He kept looking around to see what had created the silence. We can be sure by now that the boy, who is now old, learned later lessons about presumptions and irony on other different and other awkward occasions that he surely needed to experience to grow up.

What was crucial, then, in understanding this silent communicative exchange was the knowledge background and the presumptions of the teachers involved. The young kid had been bothering the high school teachers a great deal, for some were heard confessing their embarrassment in his doing so much better than they were doing in their classes. Egos were certainly involved. The teachers were heard discussing the problem among themselves.

It took no more than glances given these background presumptions for each of them to confirm (to trigger) to the other the relevance of the boy's actions to the issues that were bothering them. They had no trouble in interpreting that the remark made by me was as no more than a bit of teasing, playful, and verbal byplay in making fun of a particular baseball player. The boy's failure to understand the attempt at humor simply appeared to be naïve in the eyes of those teachers.

Those first glances of those teachers were no more than a question looking for a response as to whether others were thinking the same thing. And the fact that they were all as a group glancing at each other with relaxed smiles confirmed that they were. Each had their answer to their question in the other's smiles. What those glances said was that the prodigy was just an immature kid. He was not very smart when he misinterpreted a feeble attempt at humor as a serious statement of information about some stupid baseball statistics.

This incident has come to be for me a paradigm illustrating the inferential theory of communication of Sperber and Wilson. I choose to use this example of indirect communication and not the one used by Sperber and Wilson throughout their book, because interpretation in this case requires an awareness of the very rich background of presumption that this situation contained. Every story, fictive or not, needs background assumptions if the actions of the characters are to be interpreted, so I believe this story had a richness of assumptions that make it possible to interpret the complexity of what went on in that actual situation.

Note that in the theater, dramas have to set the scene and background about what is happening for the audience to be able to understand the presumptions that characters have in the action going on onstage. Again the same applies to the novel, where there is much more opportunity than in the theater for the author to set the scene and the background of characters so as to be able to generate better the knowledge background that creates all the presumptions necessary for the reader to understand the action going on in the story. It is such complex back grounding that makes it difficult to interpret and infer the meaning of the dialogue in a Henry James novel.

And obviously, an inferential theory of meaning helps us understand the difficulties we have in dealing with strangers. All this explains why in making judgments and decisions about other people, a little knowledge becomes a dangerous thing. Judgments about people can prove disastrous, if not unjust and immoral, when behaviors are made from interpretations based upon flimsy evidence about another person's awareness of a situation and upon the paucity of their background knowledge. Prejudice is based upon these kinds of false presumptions about the facts in a situation. Prejudice is always a case of *unwarranted presumption*, and it is in my view the greatest human fallacy of them all. It is a fallacy born out of ignorance that is compounded by human arrogance based upon comparisons and the presumption that one knows more than is actually known.

CHAPTER 10

Figurative and Literal Language

Note that the interpretation of a metaphor begins with the literal senses of its terms. "John is a snake in the grass." The literal sense stands atop a secondary meaning that the metaphor actually implicitly expresses. Metaphors like ironies have a semantic twist. They say one thing that differs from the meaning of what we literally mean by the words that shape the figure of speech.

When we say, "John is a lion," we state that he is a lion, but we presume that John is not a lion. And that contradictory twist of saying something that is not the case triggers a switch of what we mean in calling John a lion. We presume that the person using the metaphor does not believe that the literal interpretation on the face of it is true: John is no lion. But then the question arises, what does someone mean by saying something not true? And thus follows the recognition that something else must be implied by speaking with such contrariety and opposition to the literal meaning of the sentence. By speaking falsely, we seem to want to say something other than the literal sense of the meaning of what was said. We know metaphors, then, by the contextual implications of saying things that are neither categorically possible nor factually true.

Meaning switches are pervasive in communications. It happens in all sorts of ways other than with metaphors. It happens in the use of subjunctive counterfactuals (Yoos 1975). It happens in puns. It happens in fiction. It happens in irony. It involves shifts of perspectives on the way we look at things. Sometimes it occurs in such category shifts as in personifications. And as a result of such category shifts, questions arise about the implications that follow from the interpretive accounts of why these categorical shifts are being made. Shifts of meaning occur in all uses of various rhetorical figures such as irony, metaphor, oxymoron, synecdoche, metonymy, personification, meiosis, hyperbole, simile, and even allegory. It is noteworthy in our attempts to define figures that the usual way we define them is by how we interpret them (Yoos 1971).

The first basic point that should be noted about figurative language is based on their surface literality. It starts with the use of literal terms. We start with the terms such as "snake in the grass." But John is not such a crawling creature. But the literal terms of "snake in the grass" provide a stable foundation from which we extend and interpret the meanings of the figure of speech, which in turn we interpret from the presumptions we have about the human behaviors that are like that of snakes. They are hidden and dangerous, and even treacherous.

Metaphors, for example, use a reservoir of words taken from usages that are used literally and unambiguously in certain other contexts to say precisely what we do mean to say. And if that literal meaning of what we say is not true or impossible, or a distortion, or an exaggeration, the awareness that it is a "truth controverting-statement" made by the speaker or author shifts our attention to things that might be implied by anyone controverting deliberately the truth of any statement. It leads us to look at things in new and different ways. And given the context of the statement, the presumptions of the context immediately suggest what is maximally relevant among the associated connections to the conventional literal denotations of the terms used.

Metaphor brings to our attention, in a condensed and a focused way, things difficult to summarize or express in our use of literal senses of words. What is meant has no conventional usage. Rhetorically metaphors flatter a reader's sensibility and sensitivity. They create a sense of intimacy and a congruent meeting of minds having common beliefs and assumptions. They suggest to readers that the author stands together with them in harmony about a common background of mutually held sets of understandings and presumptions. Metaphors bind authors and readers together in shared feelings and in familiar held agreements. If a metaphor is to be understood, the minds of the author and reader need to meet in a bond of mutual associations and shared understandings. Author and reader, speaker and listener, as has been said, do an emotional dance together. It is this intimacy of meaning that makes the use of metaphors ever so very personal and cultural in a sense of their bonding together people in the common ways of their lives.

Basically using Wittgenstein's way of phrasing it, "A metaphor is a way of 'seeing something *as*." Or again as he phrases it, "It is seeing plus a thought." Or again it might be said to be a way "of thinking of something *as*," "a concept *plus* a thought" (1958, 193–213). There are, I wish to point out, both *perceptual* and *conceptual* metaphors. But more needs to be said and expanded on about these different kinds of metaphors, as there are important problems about what I term conceptual metaphors. They are not easily detected. They are more easily missed, as they easily slide between figurative language and literal language unnoticed even when we examine them carefully both literally and analytically. Conceptual metaphors are the chief cause of our use of empty and vacuous concepts. What seems figurative is taken quite mistakenly to be literal, thus multiplying ambiguity.

It is the power of our imaginations that gives us the power to see things from new perspectives. Metaphor is one of the mind's ways of escaping its literal foothold on reality and releasing itself from logical constraints of literal terms for speculation and conjecture. Metaphors allow the mind to escape reality and create is own reality, a reality that is creative and full of new meaning. Thus the imagination, through the use of rhetorical figures, allows us to create new conceptions. Although many of these imaginative conceptions are about things outside this world, yet they still maybe found to be in part of and in a way coherent with our literal world of meaning. We are able to extend our literal conception of the world and become by our interpretations of figures a newly integrated part of it, especially when these figurative creations can be revised, applied, and used for control of the things that we say and do.

Figures allow us to bring back into this world meaning that we create in our imaginative worlds. It allows us to bring figurative meaning back and drag it down to earth and share it with what we think of as having literal meaning. It allows our metaphors to be concrete in meaning and to settle their new meanings back into the safety of our common-sense literality, where the practical work of the world is being done.

But some figures raise the question of whether or not they are ever in touch with reality. Note how figurative most religious language is in trying express the inexpressible in literal words. Does such language return to reality even though it is found to be literal in tone and sentiment and is expressed in the most appealing language based and grounded in our resonant emotions? "God is my refuge!" "He is my Lord and my shepherd!" Note these words used in such figurative expressions in praising God seem to have the simplest of literal referents. There is a seemingly very literal base of felt understanding in these highly symbolic and figurative expressions of religious sentiments that people are willing to live by.

Metaphors access feeling in ways that many literal terms cannot. Thus, we see the primacy of metaphor in talking about religious experiences where the most sublime meets the pedestrian and the plebeian and the sacred merges with the profane. And what is so important in religions is how stories and myths are grounded in the everyday way we live out our hopes and how they placate the fears in our lives. Language usage thus gives us our word base that allows us to express thoughts of even the ethereal and the sublime. The literal anchors religious reflections by means of metaphor with heartfelt sentiment and myth. Religious language has the emotive force of prompting meanings about faiths and religious experiences that are the integral parts of the lives of so many people who have heartfelt emotions that are found in family intimacies and in love and care.

But is there any clear sense of what it is to be literal? Is there any clear sense of what it is to be figurative? These two questions go hand in hand. Literal and figurative appear to be correlatives in certain senses in the uses of these two terms. Both terms seem to be involved in the definition of the other. Figurative language is not literal, and equally literal language is not figurative. Either way, literal is often thought opposite to figurative, and vice versa, thus again creating a vicious circle about which term is the negative term and which one is not. Which term is prior in the definition of the other?

Literality is one of the obvious surface traits of metaphors. And when metaphors downgrade their figurative meaning, they seem to be becoming more and more literal in ordinary ways of speaking. And when metaphors are said to be dead, which means metaphorically in one sense that they are not alive literally, and in that sense they become notoriously literal about what they mean. But when we equate a code theory of language with literal ways of speaking, we are helpless to understand the mysterious ways that coded symbols shift meanings away from their code-book definitions when used wildly figuratively.

In rhetoric there are all sorts of figurative devices we can use to say things that were otherwise thought unsayable. But many of these figurative devices work as stated by changing our perspectives and by helping us reframe the way we look at things by calling our attention to things not noticed before. They get us to look at things in fresh and new and different ways. Schemes and tropes in rhetoric are figurative devices that transform grammar and rules of predication and alter perspectives in the ways that we fundamentally look at things.

An interesting way of regarding rhetorical figures, especially metaphors, is suggested by Monroe C. Beardsley's (1958) controversion theory of metaphor and oxymoron. Beardsley's controversion theory, especially in his analysis of oxymorons, points to some of the subtleties in the interpretation of seeming contrary attributions made in ordinary speech. As Beardsley claims, we see in ordinary usage that the conjunctive use of terms in using opposing and contrary senses has the effect of causing a semantic shift in the meaning of terms (141–44).

Take Beardsley's example (141) of the oxymoron *nasty-nice*. It would appear that no one could be nasty and nice at the same time. But, if one gives credit to a speaker of knowing better than to assert what are obviously contrary attributes to the same subject, we must give that person the benefit of doubt of knowing better than saying something that is contradictory. We then take it that the senses of the terms used are different. There is a semantic shift from the common or ordinary accepted meaning or the literal meaning of the terms.

We may say with nasty-nice that the likely shifts would either be that that the person was really nice and appeared nasty on the surface or that person appeared nice on the surface and was really nasty underneath. Either interpretation of nasty-nice apart from a context seems plausible, although the latter interpretation is the more frequently heard expression. Usually, though, presumptions will help determine which interpretation is chosen. Note that we might, for instance, in interpreting the expression with the altruistic Christian presumption, mean that everyone is deep down nice and the nastiness on the surface is just another a way of being nice, such as sometimes a grouchy and an old loveable, insulting curmudgeon appears nice to some folks.

And note how analogous this interpretation is to the familiar expression used in talking about "Minnesota nice." Governor Tim Pawlenty of Minnesota spoke of how the collapse of the Interstate 35W bridge over the Mississippi brought out the meaning of goodness in "Minnesota nice" in the way the locals rescued the victims who were in shock in their fallen cars when the bridge came tumbling down into the river. "Minnesota nice" can be interpreted many ways among Minnesotans, and some interpretations are not so approbative in the way the governor as a politician meant to flatter and pander to the Minnesota electorate. Note in this respect the interpretation of "nice" is context dependent, with presumptions about how "Minnesota nice" might not be so nice after all. For some who use the expression, it implies that Minnesotans are stifling, cloying, and naive. Note, then, the importance of how the interpretation of a semantic twist depends on the wealth of background assumptions presupposed by any interpretation, as explained by an inferential theory of interpretation in a given cultural context such as found in Minnesota.

But note the puzzlement generated when we speak of a figurative expression as being literally the case. We should expect, if Beardsley's contention is correct, that a semantic shift is triggered by the obvious contrariety of the attributes and their implications in the context. But note that if we say, "He is literally a jackass," we try to understand what it means to say that a person can be literally a jackass without being a jackass. In this case there is the transformation of both the meaning of the term literal and the implications of calling someone a jackass. Both are doubly figurative transfers. First, there are two senses of being a jackass, one literal and one metaphorical. And second, there are two sense of being literal. And then we need to ask, how can a figure of speech be literally figuratively true? (Yoos 1968).

Let us explore theses twists on the term *literal*. Take as an example the figurative expression "to literally to eat one's words." The term "literally" here in this case seems an obvious candidate for a semantic shift that is metaphorical. If this be the case, we are using the term *literally* in more than one sense, and that opens up the question at issue about what the meaning is of literal in a context when you speak of a figure of speech such as eating one's word to be literally true. In this case we seem to mean figuratively that it is *figuratively true* that he literally had to eat his words. How strange! How do we escape such trick questions when we cannot shake the sense that literal is opposite to figurative in meaning? Let me give it another interpretive try.

What metaphors do is allow us to see things from shifting perspectives. As Wittgenstein puts it, we *see things as,* or we *see things plus a thought* (1958). Metaphors are perceptual when we use imagery in our metaphors. But sometimes metaphors, as already stated, are conceptual. When conceptual our thought does not have an image in it, but nevertheless we are still trying to conceive of something *as* literal that cannot be taken literally. There may be a shift categorically. Note that when we say that an action is "literally psychological terrorism," we are thinking of terrorism as psychological abuse and not literally as physical abuse. There is a transfer in the meaning of abuse.

Note how the term *terrorism* has in recent years been figuratively extended to all sorts of behaviors. We see all sorts of acts in terms of "a concept of terrorism" that has its literal origins in actions that use physical violence. But today we use the expression terrorism in both local and international politics as an umbrella term for many types of actions that are said to be inciting terror on a horrendous scale. Note the seeming redundancy of the phrase "terror and horror."

But we can ask how can there be a form of nonphysical violence when the presumption is that violence is thought categorically to be physical? Epithets concerning terrorism are strikingly transformative about what we mean by violence and terrorism, especially when we see acts of threatening from the view of different concepts, such as thinking of abuse as verbal use of "hate terms" such as profanity, obscenities, curses, and extreme forms of belittlement. All such provocations may be interpreted by some presumptively as terroristic threats.

One way of looking at metaphors, then, is that they generate new perspectives on the way we look at things. And what gives meaning to metaphors is the contextual implications that metaphors have, given the presumptions that a speaker and audience have that are generating implications mutually understood. Thus, metaphors require a community of discourse of people with common cultural backgrounds and presumptions to make them meaningful. We always need a rhetorical context to define our presumptions. And we attempt through metaphor to transcend the conventional and literal meaning of language usage. And we use synecdoche or metonymy as selective bits of meaning to allude to larger contexts and wholes about commonly understood things. We use synecdoche to allude to encompassing complexities that surround the bits and parts of things that we are talking about.

Note in the following example of the use of figurative language: "Our military *arm* is the *weapon* we have for guaranteeing our national security." The condensed imagery in this combination of synecdoche and metaphor bring into play all sorts of presumptions about the knowledge that we have about the situation and the use of military force. It alludes to what is being said to the larger wholes of meaning contained in presumptions about arms, military, weapons, and national security. Metaphor and synecdoche help construct meaning by alluding to presumptions about what we know about the images we conjure up and by alluding to the experiences we have had that are suggested by them. These presumptions come from both our semantic and episodic memories. Metaphor and synecdoche are two interestingly different but comparable figures of speech. Both rely on contrasting imagery and relationships. Both are dependent on allusions to experiences that we have had. Metaphor and synecdoche help us look at things quite differently as a result of their different kinds of allusions to related or comparable images and the experiences we have had of things.

In using live and effective metaphors and synecdoche we should note that there is a sudden shock of recognition that things being perceived are perceived afresh and anew. It is the suddenness and the reversal that shifts our perspective about the way we look at or how we regard things. The shift or twist allows us to examine all the surrounding allusions and suggestions. Reversals are the stock and trade of the dramatic arts. Sudden reversals shock our expectations by reversing the grand order we have in looking at things in our conventional ways.

Metaphors thus enable us to note qualities and states of things never noted before or not even considered before. And synecdoche, on the other hand, helps us to allude to all sorts of presumptive knowledge we have about the larger context of things that we are talking about. Synecdoche thus acts as a stimulus for reminders. But sadly, once we begin to repeat our metaphors, and equally our synecdoche, these figures soon diminish their powers of allusion and denotation. They are, as we say, becoming dead from the loss of their powers of allusion and suggestion, which is why we speak of them as figuratively stale or metaphorically as dead. Comparably the same happens in synecdoche. They no longer are lively in providing us with contrasting perspectives and thus tend toward becoming literal.

How much of our language usage is littered with dead metaphors and synecdoche? And this has led many to the conclusion that the original sources of the meaning of terms has been in synecdoche and metaphor. All terms and words are said by some to become no more than literal sediments of things once lively expressed in synecdoche and metaphor. Like twice-told jokes, synecdoche and metaphors are said to have lost their zip when repeated. They become trite and clichéd. They are "routinized" by overrepetition, and eventually they turn into dead deposits of literal meaning that have become absorbed into what we think of as our common literal meaning of words or our ordinary literal usage.

Note how our awareness of the metaphor "I am sitting on top of the world" has vanished into an almost literal expression of a sense of triumph that was once expressed metaphorically in a once-grand megalomaniacal statement of a sense of glorious achievement. To express our sense of triumph we do not much think of ourselves as sitting up on the North Pole (another figure of speech that has become a proper name for a place). Note that Eskimos had no conception of such a place. Such a conception of a place requires conceptions of the world that were not in their reference systems.

But to speak of a metaphor as dead now has the literal sense that what was once a metaphorical term is now a literal one. But nevertheless, a *dead metaphor* was a metaphor in the history of its past use. But there is a problem whether the term *dead metaphor* is now literally a literal term, that is, meaning literally a term that once was used metaphorically that has become literal. Or should we say that it still is a metaphor and that it is not quite dead, and that it still has a breath of life in it and it has not quite attained yet a literal meaning? Such seems the slippery slope from metaphor to literality.

Let me point out that there is an unwarranted presumption by some people that literal and figurative are logically complementary terms; that is, if an expression is not figurative it must be literal. But note some terms, though literal, may still have, as they say, trailing clouds of etymologies. In other words, they are metaphors that are half dead. We can speak of a term as literal even though it carries still many of the associations that still relate to its past figurative use. I propose to call such terms *quasi-literal* to call attention to the transition from complementary to contrary terms.

Sitting on top of the world still has lingering images of geographical supremacy hanging around its literal meaning of triumph. But it requires something more to know that *sincere* at one time meant "without wax." Since the term has no longer any image of wax trailing behind it, *sincere* is a dead metaphor literally. And sitting on top of the world is quasi-literal as we still have those lingering images of the North Pole, especially now that the Russians want to put their flag on it.

And note, then, that I have introduced quasi-literal as a proposed technical term, which makes literal and figurative by my definition no longer complementary terms, but still they are contrary, as there is a middle sense of literal that is not exactly literal in every respect and that is no longer figurative in every respect. Note that I might have proposed to call quasi-literal terms also quasi-figurative terms by definition, but if I had introduced quasi-literal and quasi-figurative without stipulation and used them without proposing them, I could not have said these two terms were identical in meaning if I simply talked about them using ordinary language usage.

Noting and reminding rhetorically are two of the primary modes of communicating that allude to a common ground of experience. In noting certain features of language, we see how figurative language gives focus and attention to new semantic ways of clarifying and interpreting our meaning. But if you have already noted this to be true in your own experience, my noting then becomes simply reminding. Reminding is just one way of noting. Reminding is bringing to mind what you already have noted before so that you will again note it be the case again once that you have been reminded.

We use figures to give surprise and freshness to the things that we say. Freshness is a quality we notice when we are choking on the stale air of the commonly used expressions that surrounds our conventional usage. The surprise that comes from using figures comes with denouement and the discoveries that result from the unexpected perspectives generated by the figures. Figures have in them the stuff of theater and drama. And when what we say deviates from the direct and routine, it gets our attention. It is the dominant quality found in commercial advertising.

As I stated in the beginning redundancy keeps something in focus for an extended time so as to keep triggering the implications it has for the topic at hand. Redundancy of a figure gives us even more and more processing time to fully grasp its figurative meaning. This is the instrumental value of extended metaphors. In rhetoric as stated before, by using figures we achieve perspective reversals by using different rhetorical devices: by using syntactical anomalies, by semantic anomalies, by devices that trigger surprise references, by unexpected allusions, and especially by introducing newly reframed perspectives. Figures provide us with new contrasts and new comparisons by playing with ambivalent and shifting references.

Thus, it is the case that such rhetorical devices as simile, metaphor, and synecdoche alter our attention away from the ordinary and the routine perspectives that we usually have on things. They do it by bringing to our attention new foci and fresh perspectives that are surprisingly thought way out and far out from our usual ways of looking on things. They take us off the old, tired paths that we normally take to look upon things. It is this sort of shifting that has justified what has come to be known in critical thinking as lateral thinking. The uses of literal terms are thus prone to dull our attention to what might be considered ordinary. But figures, on the other hand, refresh our way of looking at the ordinary if we want rhetorically to stress their importance, as they say in the business jargon of self-adulation, "of thinking outside the box."

We might consider ourselves as just ordinary, but we can refresh our way of looking at ourselves by looking at ourselves as someone else. Portrait painters such as Rembrandt almost as a genre have painted self-portraits of themselves as other people. They see themselves as other. Ironically, in the 2008 election campaign, we had the odd reversal of Tina Fey mimicking Sarah Palin and even Sarah Palin seeing herself as Tina Fey. What a double entendre! Each seeing herself as the other. Note the difference in the implications of this dramatic reversal.

And from my own perspective, looking at myself I want to say, "Oh would some power give me the gift to see myself as Charlie McCarthy, a wooden dummy head, giving voice to the preachings of all those liberal Internet blogs." How I would hate myself if I thought of myself as such a wooden-headed liberal preacher. Such is the way metaphors work. They allow others to see things as something else. They allow us to see ourselves as someone else. And they allow us to take stock of ourselves from fresh perspectives.

Would we not want to call, then, such self-portraits painted as someone else visual metaphors? Would calling them visual metaphors be a verbal metaphor? Or a conceptual metaphor? If we did, would not the term metaphor be a generic concept that could be instantiated in the way sounds are listened to even as we listen to music? Is program music musical metaphor? Note how musical programs function comparably to titles in our looking at paintings (Yoos 1966). Titles control and direct perception in the way that we hear music as it does for the way we look at paintings. We hear tones as images of clouds, festivals, seasons, and landscapes. Note when we speak of a monument or a piece of architecture as a metaphor, are we speaking metaphorically? Could monuments and buildings be literally metaphors in a conceptual sense? Note that Santiago Calatrava, the architect, refers to a building he completed in Sweden as *turning human torso*.

The best example I have seen of a visual metaphor was on David Letterman's nightly show on TV. He had his visiting "zoo friend" bring his odd assortment of unusual animals onto the program. One night it was a two-headed turtle. It was crawling slowly on Letterman's desk. And each head of the turtle seemed to want to crawl in opposite directions. David Letterman remarked, "It is like marriage."

Rhetorical figures are traditionally divided up into schemes and tropes. *Schemes* mostly depend for their effectiveness on alterations in syntax by repetition, by shifting or clarifying references, and by altering presumptions and using ellipses, diversions, and other forms of omission. Such rhetorical strategies are important in helping us understand the elements of eloquence and literary style that bring meaning into full force and focus and give us clarity about new ways of understanding. They give us new refinements of meaning.

But *tropes* are figures that create new uses of terms by semantic change, by shifts and twists of meaning, and by divided reference that connote different senses of the terms. They often deal with rhetorical condensations and expansions of meaning. The most interesting of the tropes I find are metaphor and synecdoche. Both figures deal with the shifting meanings of words by calling something "something" that it is not. Tropes are the stuff of literary style. They make the most of common experiences to express new points of view that the writer can presumptively share with his or her reader.

When we define all the tropes or figures we see that their definitions often border on each other. Note how poetic imagery quickly turns to metaphor. We suggest finally that when we are speaking of tropes and figures we are calling attention to processes that deviate from straightforward and normal ways of saying that something is the case. These figurative labels flag for us and point out to us the sorts of meaningful deviations from literal usage that prove useful for finding and creating new meaning rhetorically.

The naming and defining of the tropes labels the ways we usually interpret these deviations from direct ways of literal speaking. And in many cases, then, what we call tropes are often defined by our modes of interpretation. And as a result, our mode of interpretation is sometimes the only way we know what is being named by these figurative labels. There is nothing essential to be found in the definitions of figures. We simply come to know figures of speech in the long run in most cases, if we examine their usual definitions, by the ways we go about interpreting them.

PART III

*Interpretation and Definition as
Historically Developed Concepts*

CHAPTER 11

Interpretation and *Definition* as Umbrella Terms

Definition and interpretations are roughly about a set of heterogeneous set of communicative actions that aim at clarity about things that we say, do, and perceive. Both activities aim at accuracy and precision in achieving understanding of what is being said and then in turn from what is being said generate meanings that can be acted upon. Interpretations and definitions are the central communicative actions needed for all thought and action. They are basic for all communications for mutual understanding and for any cognition.

This common aim of clarification of trying to make sense is shared by these two interactive yet contrasting rhetorical modes. I find that we have no definite conception or clarity however about what it is to clarify except in trying to make judgments that simply make better sense about what is being said. Making sense is the first, and in many ways the final, judgment we make in facing the world and facing up to the tribulations that we find in it.

But any talk about clarity in the ways we make sense to ourselves and others is a metaphor. As a metaphor it indirectly describes the physical processes of making a medium through which light travels free from image distortion. Note that glass can be translucent but not clear. Clear glass is free from any image distortion. Note how these distinctions about clear glass are certified technically by definition and scaled by glassmakers. They are important distinctions for optics. And new distinctions about clarity are needed as glass technology becomes more and more reflective, refractive, screened, colored, and filtered if we are to be able to talk about image clarity. Comparably, interpretation and defining look to the limitations that we need to overcome to eliminate any extraneous corruption of the senses we find in our perceptions and in our thinking. Interpretation and definition in communicating, then, are like the adjustments we make in our eyeglasses and in our uses of telescopes and binoculars so as to see the world better.

The terms *definition* and *interpretation*, as we talk about clarity of meaning, however, do relate to a number of comparable and complex rhetorical processes whereby we render what we are talking about as more or less perspicuous, such as naming, identifying, specifying, describing, explaining, classifying, outlining, summarizing, paraphrasing, and translating. All these listed processes, many of them correlative, aid in clarifying by bringing our meaning of terms into clear definition. Not only is this true of description, but it is especially so when we engage in narrative framing, such as we do in providing synopses of stories and scenarios of dramatic representations. We can give definitions through narrative as well as by exposition. All the above-listed rhetorical acts aid in clarifying and rendering certain pieces of writing perspicuous to our understanding so as to make them applicable in our life adjustments.

But note that *clear* and *perspicuous* are comparative adjectives. What is said to be the clearest may still lack a modicum of clarity. Note that despite Richard Nixon's firm affirmation of "Let me make myself perfectly clear," nothing he said, despite his best efforts and those of his speechwriters, made what he said perfectly clear. And note that being clear is something that the speaker is not the judge of in communications. Others end up in being the judge of that.

How odd to say something is perfectly perspicuous! It is odd, for in one way of speaking, to say that what is said is clear and perspicuous is sufficient unto the day thereof, and nothing more needs to be added in the way of clarification. Clear in that context is not a comparative adjective. It is about sufficiency, and very much again like things that are said to be perfect, as perfect things they cannot be more perfect. Perfectly clear adds nothing simply to just being just clear.

Rather than following up further on these semantic twists and turns on these somewhat misleading light and telescope metaphors about clarity, I want to describe interpretation and definition as umbrella terms. As umbrella terms they do not permit any clear definition of their meaning. But again, is not speaking of them as umbrella term as I am doing just using another metaphor? But, speaking metaphorically, umbrella terms do have a way of aggregating comparable and useful patterns in talking about complexity that are amenable to certain variable descriptions within the parameters of limited sets and ranges of defined patterns. But we can never give these kinds of limited patterns and their combinations any definite descriptions with any precision in identifying pattern recognition. Umbrella terms are about things more or less alike, with a great deal of variability in their differences and contrasts.

But in talking about discourse interpretation and definition as umbrella terms, we are thus naming overlapping rhetorical and logical functions that make for different kinds of clarification in our thoughts and actions in communicating.

In one sense *analysis* is a name we give for our uses of interpretation and definition as rhetorical modes whereby in our analysis we use distinctions to make clarifications. Especially in analysis we use distinctions to make definitions that help us clarify meaning.

And in another sense, hermeneutics is another technical name that we give to the various ways we give phenomenological descriptions or deconstructive reductions, as European philosophers have done in interpreting and clarifying. And it is important to note that analytic philosophy and hermeneutics are separate names historically used for two quite different, seemingly opposed but conceptually related, traditions in contemporary philosophy aiming at clarification. And too, they are names like interpretation and definition that are equally umbrella terms for two different approaches to studying language. They are when differentiated just as multilayered as are two sides to the same coin.

But it is my hope here, though, to show that by reframing the two terms definition and interpretation within newly reframed conceptions and redefined modes of rhetoric, we can cast a great deal of new light on the common problems of meaning dealt with by these opposed contemporary philosophical traditions that aim at clarification. In a way, both traditions are different sides of an overall approach to sense and meaning that approaches the problems of meaning on different levels of interpretation. Interpretation, like most umbrella terms, is multilayered, ranging over many different patterns. And in a way, I want to show that we can bring what we mean by both interpretation and definition together as clarifying modes by showing how they interact with each other. In doing so, we can see how the semantic interaction named by the two terms plays out in our understanding of the use of different models or frames used by hermeneuticists and semiologists in any analysis of meaning.

The various rhetorical and logical modes of interpretation and definition adapt differently to rhetorical situations depending on what our rhetorical aims, ends, and purposes are in that situation. Sometimes we want or need to know the meaning of certain words. Sometimes we want to know the precise meaning of sentences. Sometimes we want to know the overall meaning of texts. And sometimes we want to know about the meaning of paradoxical questions that we seem to be asking that we have no answers for.

Sometimes we want to choose words to say accurately and precisely what we want to mean. Sometimes we simply want to know what was meant by our various uses of words that we find puzzling in our listening and reading. And sometimes we want to know the various applications of terms reported in dictionaries about conventional language usage. And sometimes we need to know exactly what we have said and what follows from our having said it. And as I hope to show in our addressing all these issues, definition and interpretation are related notions that work together to help us make the best rhetorical choices on how best to communicate our aims and purposes in communicating.

Our first question, then, is to ask, what are the many things that go on in the name of interpretation? As we already pointed out, interpretation is certainly a term with a gamut of uses. It is a term that spreads across a spectrum of cognitive activities. Interpretation is a basic term in the psychology of perception. How do our senses interpret what we hear and see? Again we see that the term is adapted to talk about all sorts of levels of responses: to actions, responses to listening, responses to writing, and even the responses we make both in the creation and the appreciation of the arts.

Interpretation is especially important in determining what is going on in the literary arts. And interpretations of word uses are what lexicographers do in describing word usage. Lexicographers in their defining, we need to note, both interpret and report uses of words that they consider and judge to be conventional and acceptable usage. We trust lexicographers. We treat them as experts at doing their interpretive and defining tasks for us. But the problem for lexicographers is that their judgments rest upon the experiences of language uses of those very users of dictionaries who are seeking their advice.

But talk about defining, unlike interpretation on the other hand, is much more than about the meaning of words. Defining is one way of providing objective understanding of all sorts of notions, such as concepts, processes, algorithms, and even our understanding of what are thought to be real properties of our everyday things. We define locations, boundaries, and limits. We define laws, rules, procedures, locations, standards, and models. We define terms in mathematics, and especially we define the technical terms in the technologies and in the sciences. We define policy. We define aims and purposes. We define benchmarks. We define intentions. Definition is especially a way of determining exactly where we stand on contractual matters, as in legal transactions. Definition is the way we have of assuring certitude about exactly where we stand when we communicate back and forth with each other with mutual understanding and confidence about the meanings of the words we are using and then together applying them as we interact with other people.

And from another perspective, definition is inherent and foundational to logic and mathematics. Definition leads to what is definitive, definite, and determinate in creating points of agreement with other people. Definition leads to reliable terms whereby we can act with predictability and confidence. It leads to the creation of terms that others can depend on and in turn can use and act on, especially by formulating words that can be put into promises and contractual obligations.

All these roughly described processes and functions of defining and interpretation need to be clarified for us to better be able to talk straight about them, especially in the application of the strategies and tactics we have in using these rhetorical modes to make clear what we are trying to say. Defining and interpreting thus are very important forms of linguistic and social verbal interaction. They are fundamental in defining our language games. They are the foundation of what we ultimately consider our knowledge about the world and especially the knowledge we have about ourselves.

If the terms definition and interpretation do not admit of any definite definition or any precise determinate determinations, how, then, can we be straight in talking about what we do in their name? Am I here again in asking this question posing another one of those tautological and empty questions? Is our prosperity prosperous? Are definitions always definite? Are definitions always determinate? And also, Are not all interpretations equally determinative as definitions? I seem here again repeating myself, going in verbal circles, mouthing tautologies, and circling through mere "synonymous synonyms" of definition and interpretation. How repetitive can I get?

To take another tack and to take another turn at questioning these seemingly indeterminate questions, it is interesting to note that some, in talking about definition and interpretation, want to talk about the "true meaning" of what is being said. But isn't that phrase "true meaning" simply again just another empty redundancy? What difference is there between the "meaning of a sentence" and "the true meaning of a sentence"? A second term seems to be adding nothing to the first term in these expressions. Are these phrases not just identical in meaning?

Or, comparably, take again the phrase "straight and true"; is this compound set of terms again just another empty redundancy? Isn't it the case that a true line is a straight line? Isn't a straight line definite and determinate in its direction? On the other hand, is there not an important qualification being added to *straight* by adding to it the term *true*? Note that straight is usually defined as the shortest distance between two points. And we can measure the shortest distance by an inelastic string with no stretch to it, which by definition is the least distance. Presumably, a string stretched tight just like a chalk line covers the shortest distance.

But how, then, do we determine that something is true? For an aim to be true, it must be directed at a point. What is the relationship between the shortest distance and the direction that aims toward that point? Are straight and true simply a redundancy? Has any meaning been added in conjoining the two? If so, what do we need to add to make a straight line true? And again, to repeat, are we not just verbally circling when we add true to straight? How do we knife through this paradox if straight and true are not strictly synonymous?

But there are contexts I want to show where this is not so. Straight and true are not strictly synonymous in navigation and in firing a gun. A true course and true heading are not the same. And our aim in shooting a gun is not a straight line to the target. Our headings in navigation are foremost a matter of a correct aim, which is not always a straight line, and this is especially so when we are taking the shortest distance, which on the earth's surface is a great circle on the earth's sphere. There we move straight to a given point of latitude and longitude by constantly changing direction when navigating the shortest distance between two points on the surface of the earth's sphere.

And likewise, we might analogously say something comparable about rhetoric. We aim in rhetoric to make a point. Aim and point are separable in thought as we write. For example, my aim here is to inform you. But my aim is not always identical with the point that I want to make in fulfilling that aim. In rhetoric, when we are straightforward, there is no unnecessary indirection in what we say. We come straight out and make the point. We aim to persuade, and we do it by making a point. But importantly, in rhetoric we should note that in speaking and writing we can rhetorically *describe our aim* and we can rhetorically *describe the point* that we intend to aim at. Getting someone's meaning or interpreting what they mean apparently seems to be doing two different things, *defining an aim* and *defining the point* aimed at. In composing we find that they are often quite separate.

My aim is to clarify the meaning of interpretation and definition. The point that I am making is that there is no definition of these terms but only an illumination of how we use various terms to clarify certain of their uses. They are rhetorical processes, named interpretation and definition, that are indeed complex and require much in the way of clarity about them by expansion and elaboration on what they name if I am to make clear my point about their uses. Definitely, in what I am doing here what I mean by aim and point differ.

But are these rhetorical ways of talking about interpretation and talking about aim and point nothing more again than loose conceptual metaphors about navigation? Should we be using metaphors to talk about interpretation and defining in order to come to terms with what seem to be nothing more than figurative expressions that are not exactly clear? Note the following seemingly defining metaphors: "Democracy is standing in line." "War is hell." How informative are these metaphors? They definitely are full of interesting allusions and interesting implications. But they are never precise in talking about democracy and war. Can we be at all precise in using metaphors such as my one about navigation to define distinctions about modes, aims, and points made in using rhetoric?

What value, then, is there in using metaphor to clarify the meaning of a term when the metaphor used itself requires clarification? Metaphorical definitions do not precise the meaning of our terms. They are simply adding an additional burden of interpretation that is required to clarify what is being said. Metaphors, as many seem to agree, are not the best way to give straight answers. They can give only suggestive answers about clarification, and for that reason they are serviceable only as steps to further steps that need further clarification. Is there any hope of being clear in this use of this prolonged method of slow-boat interpretive clarification through multiple uses of metaphors to come to terms with the terms definition and interpretation?

Let's try to take a further step and explicate somewhat further on our metaphor about navigation. Bearings in radar navigation have two measurements, range and direction. In navigation one determines one's present position by taking a bearing, an angular measurement referenced from true north. And then to fix one's location, one needs to measure the range, the distance to a known location. Locations are always, then, defined by reference to fixed coordinates based upon a relationship to another fixed point of reference. And such a fixed point of reference on the earth's surface is framed by the intersection of the Greenwich meridian and the equator that defines the zero points of the coordinate system of maps and defines locations specified by latitude and longitude.

And comparably, in reading a text we have something similar happening. We literally in reading and in interpretation establish the author's aim as defined by reference to the belief systems of an audience. The author's aim is carried out in a context of audience presumption. And effective rhetoric is all about relating frames of reference that an author has to the defined reference frames in the fixed beliefs and attitudes of the audience. And from this we can conclude that rhetorical aims are defined and interpreted within a context of presumptions made by both the author and the audience.

Both author and audience in order to understand each other require a mutual understanding of the context of the rhetorical situation that they both find themselves in while communicating with each other. In every way rhetorical aims and purposes are defined and interpreted in particular situations defined by authors and audiences who are fully aware and understand the presumptions that each other has in their shared context.

I propose, then, in general that we think of definition and interpretation as umbrella terms that label the different modes of rhetoric that we use to try to rectify, correct, and overcome communicative constraints that limit our understanding of what we think our words mean within the overlapping frames of reference between two people communicating. Simply in relating to others there is a need to be clear about the meaning of the words we act and rely upon. Mutually acceptable meaning, then, is the basis of mutual understanding in any type of harmonized synchronous action between individuals.

To show how better to come to terms with the terms definition and interpretation, I propose, then, at this point to treat them, as I have said, as umbrella terms and not as definable logical terms. As umbrella terms they seem to have no common generic sense. And as umbrella terms they are essentially indefinable without any unique acceptable, prescriptive determination of words that stand for either term. As umbrella terms they label a whole host of rhetorical modes and a number of logical distinctions that in general aim at clarification and understanding.

But how, then, do we clarify the meaning of these rhetorical modes and logical distinctions, as they are constantly subject to innovation and modification in the development of a literate culture? For that reason the term interpretation has no distinct and precisely distinguishable distinctions that would permit it to have a definition. All we have to describe umbrella terms is the history of rhetorical development that describes the evolution of these rhetorical modes of clarification. They have been developed as our intellectual culture has evolved, making it more likely that we have, as time passes, a language that enables us more and more to come to terms with each other.

To take another tack to what I mean, then, by calling definition and interpretation umbrella terms, let me somewhat expand on the meaning of these two different terms by exploring the implications of umbrella term as a metaphor. Umbrella terms, as I propose to describe them, are terms that have no generic covering or no unifying condition of application. Sometimes in the uses of umbrellas there is literally not sufficient space under them for others to be shielded from the rain or the sun.

The same applies to umbrella terms that are generated by historical events and contexts. They are terms that aggregate distinct and different activities linked by a certain networking of properties of which no one property is held in common that might be presumed useful to define their usage. Umbrella terms such as, for example, those covering historical styles fail to cover all the related characteristic of styles of a given period. What is baroque or rococo ranges across widely different sets of stylistic features that do not yield certainty about such stylistic concepts.

We invite strangers and innovators to stand under our large and commodious verbal umbrellas. We invite them to frame our way of looking at things under a single conceptual umbrage that we roughly, but do not definitively, adumbrate. In other words, umbrella terms do not admit of logical definitions.

They cover a number of relative comparable patterns of common interrelated features and traits that often morph easily into other related concepts.

As Ludwig Wittgenstein distinguishes and illustrates by reminders, certain terms have no generic definition. Most often they name historical concepts. They are terms that collate and collect elements defined by what Wittgenstein called "family resemblances" (1958). They are only united by an umbra, a uniting shadow that simply at times can only be expressed by historical terms, such as names of styles, political movements, social classes, and political parties. Many evolve as aggregate patterns from metaphors. And for that reason many terms such as "the Renaissance" and "the Enlightenment" are in fact nothing more than dead metaphors

Note, then, that many such terms, as metaphors do, mark a coming together of events, just as does an umbrella term. They mark a convention of events of those seeking common umbrage by common association. An umbrella term, just as Wittgenstein's term family resemblance, is a metaphor that calls attention to a historical and hereditary set of family traits. Families have histories. They have genetic and social patterns that have a history.

Umbrella terms are terms that thus have no unique description about their usage. Umbrella terms simply aggregate elements that are related by a set of interlocking analogous properties that they share under their aggregated name. They have no common organizing description. What makes umbrella terms interesting is that they apply to cross-sections of intimately related and associated experiences that when taken as a whole point to shared analogies existing between very complex sets of phenomena. They identify patterns that we use to separate large aggregates from other equally indefinable sets of related aggregates with comparable analogous patterns.

Note that the term *liberalism* as a label covers historically many views held by adherents who have dramatically at times differed about their political convictions. Consequently, there are all sorts of controversy about who is a liberal and who is not. What do libertarians, economic liberals, social liberals, equalitarian liberals, and even socialists and leftist Marxists have in common in speaking of themselves as "liberal"? But there are threads within these differences and within their historical origins that weave liberals together despite the somewhat dramatic and opposing views about who is or not thought to be liberal.

Each type of liberal often thinks of himself or herself as paradigmatically a true liberal. Just as there is no such thing as true baroque or classical Greek, there is no true concept of a liberal. The term liberal for liberals becomes as a result a term of self-approbation about their own political club. And it is for this reason that conservatives at the present time try to define liberal as a term in such a way as to demean or degrade the term liberal as a political label.

Conservatives with this sort of stereotyping try to confuse people by defining liberal so as to make the term's use pejorative.

Note that lately conservatives have been speaking of "the L word," as if the term were a dirty epithet. They wish to convert the term to a word of opprobrium by definition. Note how calling a person "a leftist" is emotively a loaded term. "Liberal are leftists." Being left is extreme, and that is bad. But are all liberals leftists? And after all, did not liberals do much the same for conservatives for decades prior to 1970 to demean their political opposition, equating conservatives with reactionaries or right-wing extremists?

Comparably, conservatives differ widely without again any defining set of essential attributes. They are prudential, traditional, religious, economic, and even pragmatic, or even utilitarian. Many who call themselves conservatives thus do not have that much in common. Thus, among those who label themselves conservatives there exist deep divisions, with little in common, as seems to be the case with many so-called liberals. Again the term conservative, like liberal, is an umbrella term (Yoos 2008).

Note too that political parties have been umbrella organizations. Although they issue platforms and manifestos, they never are seriously defined by any given set of fixed principles. Note how specious party platforms can be. They act very much like fly paper. They are fly bait for voters. For the most part political platforms are merely empty statements of platitudes.

It is for this rhetorical reason we are justified in seeing other party platforms and manifestos as also not standing on any abiding and defined set of moral or political principles. Parties, despite their claims to be doing so, notoriously do not give well-defined, precise, and unified statements of what they stand for. Ironically, each accuses the other of having no principles, as if principles are what define a party.

Rather than using defining principles *to define* political parties as party platforms do, we should see parties as defined by people with common historical affinities of attitude, custom, and beliefs who seek to act together under a common political label or under *an umbrella term*. As such, political parties as umbrella organizations are heterogeneous and not homogeneous entities. It is difficult to name many mixtures of similar patterns except by defining what makes them into aggregates with comparable analogous patterns. The best we can do in politics is to describe historical patterns and affinities that turn parties into such nominal aggregates.

Note in geology "aggregates" consists of historically fused, sedimented stones and particles that are cemented together. They are cemented rock of fused small stones that create quarry stone in different varieties of colors and patterns. Note the differences in the patterns in limestone and granite. Just as there are Vermont and New Hampshire Democrats and Republicans, there are Vermont and New Hampshire quarry stones. And equally, there are quite different varieties of politics and quarry stones coming from North and South Carolina. Aggregates vary significantly historically and geologically, with no defining precision to determine their precise nature. They are umbrella terms for aggregate patterns historically developed that are useful for making comparisons for different colored and textured architectural facades. Each different aggregate pattern has a different historical and regional narrative.

Definition, as I am suggesting, is a whole set of activities knitted together without any binding set of essential characteristics, but they are, as Wittgenstein (1958) says of games, bound together as a group by a set of family resemblances. And that raises the question, how can umbrella terms be functional if they are not amenable to any strict definition? Wittgenstein's notion of family resemblance is certainly a metaphor. But how shall we interpret his metaphor? Is there some literal sense embedded in our talk about family resemblances?

The least we can say about this is that there is no strict definition of what constitutes a family resemblance. There are simply hereditary and cultural similar features that we aggregate together. Family resemblances link a group of people *historically* together. What is interesting are the genealogical interconnections that bind families by physical and character traits. In looking at family resemblances, we find that families do have likenesses, but nothing is essential about those likenesses. Families are bound together by some notions of heredity, by a history, by the legality of family names, and by the bonds of *matrimony* that bind them together.

Note that "matrimony" is not called "patrimony" despite the fact that marriages in much of Western Society are patriarchal. Likewise, we might say the same notion of patriarchy applies to definitions. Someone fathers them. As an activity definitions are related often to a seeming linguistic authority that sanctions and in turn is sanctioned by other authorities. All rests on what is authorized socially in what is called by those rhetoricians who speak of the terms of our language as "socially constructed discourse."

And note that families, as some people try to define them, are bonded together not by commonalities but by links of resemblances sanctioned by legal constraints about marriages and by different hereditary patterns produced by DNA. Families notoriously, we should note, speak with some of the same phonic and intonated speech patterns as others in the family have. How often are we mistaken about mothers and daughters speaking on the telephone?

But again families have intergenerational differences and conflicts that make living in families sometimes difficult and that often make it difficult for members to escape from each other. Noteworthy families are bonded by many different asymmetrical and symmetrical relationships. Consequently, what defines families has made the concept of a family a controversial issue in politics. Thus, the concept of family resemblance ends up being the antithesis of what any definition of concept needs to be in order to be perfectly clear.

But, as already mentioned, some people talk of definitions as some kind of explanation. Explanations and definitions seem tied together. But are definitions really explanations? And if so, how are they so? And then a further question arises as to how we can really ever know what it is "to define" in any precise sense what it is to be called an explanation? Do definitions as explanations ultimately give meanings to words with any final exactitude or certitude? Explanations, we find, differ depending on what we are asked to explain. Note the differences between explanations of how, why, when, where, what, and who did what to whom. Each is a different kind of explanation with a different logical format and a different mode of verification. As such, explanation as well as argument are very much like interpretation and definition: both end up as umbrella terms.

Just as explanations and arguments are interrelated, so are interpretations and definitions. This raises the question about how they are related. Is it meaning that defines definitions? Or is it the other way around, that definitions are what defines meaning? Or again we might ask, do definitions just help us discover the meanings of our word uses? Or are definitions simply ways of assisting us in making ourselves understood? Or last, is definition, as I have suggested, an umbrella term that labels a number of distinct but related rhetorical activities and among them are the use of what logicians define as logical definitions?

To repeat myself again, Richard Nixon in his obfuscations often would say, "Let me make myself perfectly clear." But as my old teacher A. E. Berndtson would have said about Nixon's request, "Nixon was not the judge of that." But the least we can say that to be clear, but not so perfectly clear, is that family resemblance as an umbrella term can give us only a partial clarification of the terms interpretation and definition. But to be more clear about their use and their meaning, I suggest, we now need to look at interpretation and definition as correlatives terms, where the meaning of one term finds its meaning defined in terms of the other. Correlatives shift the discussion to a whole new semantic frame centering not on resemblances but on *contrasts*. It is in such correlative frames that we see how language use can be seen to be personal and creative.

CHAPTER 12

Interpretation and *Definition* as Correlative Terms

One way, then, of looking at questions about the sources of meaning is to regard the terms interpretation and definition, not just as umbrella terms but as correlatives. Here again we are confronted with other semantic problems about clarification and definitional precision. *Correlatives* are terms whose definitions involve the definition of each other.

Not only are definitions of correlatives puzzlingly self-reflexive, but they also raise the question whether the definition of one term in terms of another is not just another circular definition. If that is the case, we would end up again in a hopeless head-biting-tail circle about where to stop, wondering about which term, interpretation or definition, is the primitive term.

Note sometimes we look at *health* and *sickness* as correlatives. Someone suggested that the National Institute of Health should be called the National Institute for Diseases. But note the complexity of viewing these two terms as correlatives. How do we distinguish between disease and sickness? To be diseased is to be sick, but can we be sick without a disease? Note the vague borderline between these terms. And when it comes to correlatives, which term would be the primary or the positive term, health or disease or sickness? What is a lack of sickness? What is a lack of health?

Note, then, the shift we make when we make health the primary term and when health issues are centered on wellness and not on illness or disease. Note how all these terms seem interrelated, requiring distinctions about one term to define or to be precise about the other. And that raises the question about the relationship between being healthy and being unhealthy. As pointed out in logic, a term and it negation are called *complements*. Such terms in logic are called complementary terms; that is, if we predicate one of something, than it would be false to predicate the other of the same thing. Asserting one term of a subject makes its complement false. Asserting the complement to be true of a subject would make the other term, of which it is a complement, false when applied to that very same subject.

But note that in this case we might want to say that someone is neither healthy or unhealthy. In that case being healthy seems to require more than being just not unhealthy. How well do we have to be to be well? What are the positive symptoms of health? When we talk about symptoms, we usually are talking about what is unhealthy. Note the etymology of the term sign. Signs etymologically were symptoms. Symptoms were signs of diseases.

But can we define health as a mere deficiency of disease? It seems easier to define disease in positive attributes (positive descriptive terms) and not in terms of a lack of symptoms of wellness. But note that symptoms of disease tend to be pejorative signs, but as descriptions they are logically and positively descriptive and amenable to logical definitions. But it seems odd, though, to define health as a deficiency of disease. Certainly, we see readily observable aspects of disease in trying to avoid disease. Avoidance and prevention of disease thus in this case becomes the focus of the actions on whatever it is that keeps us healthy. But note that prevention and cure are both equally important in maintaining health and eliminating diseases.

But then, on the other hand, there are all those bodily, good-making physiological functions and physical adjustment activities that help define physical health. Fitness can be defined by standardized fitness tests. Should we then be looking at health primarily from the point of prevention? But again, being free from disease does not make us healthy. More is required in the way of exercise and diet to make a body healthy.

And the ability to adjust to problems, again, is what makes us mentally healthy. The same parallel problems also apply, then, in talking about mental health. We see the problems of trying to diagnose problems in mental health in terms of mental disease. Mental disease is a term that indicates a pejorative pathology that leads to problems about social alienation. It is a stigma in politics to have sought treatment for mental health. Consequently, note how some mental health clinics, to avoid the pejorative connotations, are described in terms of "behavioral health."

We see again similar nominal problems in trying to diagnose problems of mental health in terms of neurological functions and psychological adaptability to problems. Obviously, we need to evaluate clearly our conceptions of mental health and disease with a new set of categories, such as in terms of talk about maintenance and prevention, for as the old aphorism goes, an ounce of prevention is worth a pound of cure. The same applies to mental health.

Correlatives considered as complementary terms or contrary terms using binary frames tend to be simplistic. They tend to oversimplify our perspectives on this world. But importantly, still, we do tend to see correlatives in terms of one another. And it is important to note that we often as a result tend to see contrasting terms as correlative terms. We focus on a difference or a contrast that distinguishes one term from the other. And if we have a clear concept of the contrast, that helps us in part to clarify the meaning of correlative terms.

Note that such terms as freedom and responsibility, necessary and contingent, cause and effect, and means and ends are considered as correlative terms. A definition of one seems to entail the definition of the other. All are terms that seem to describe the important considerations that we have in dealing with our choices and our ability to prevent things from happening or making things happen in the world.

And all equally are at the heart of choosing what we want to do and say. Each entails the definition of the other. If you are free to do something, you have no responsibility to do it. If something is necessary, it is not contingent. If you have a cause, you have an effect. And if something is a means, there must be an end for which it is a means. And in a parallel manner, as I have suggested before, if we define something, we must find the correct interpretation of what we are defining. Note, then, that just as a cause is a step to an effect, an interpretation is a step to a definition.

Note the lexical history of talking about correlatives. There are correlative conjunctions. There are correlative verbs or verbals, correlative adjectives, and correlative nouns. For instance, if we use the term *either*, there is a presumption of an *or*. If there is to be a *both*, there is a presumption of an *and* to follow. The same holds for conjunctive adverbs, which create the grammar of coherence that holds an extended piece of discourse together. If we say "consequently" in introducing a conclusion in a logical proof, there must have been a previous logical sentence given as a reason. The same holds for "therefore." There must have been a previous premise or premises for the announced conclusion.

Correlative nouns and adjectives have similar parallel distinctions. If there is a "right" there presumptively must be a "duty" to justify that right. And it is presumptively the same when we talk about "false": there must be something thought "true." Many philosophical problems turn on justifying the priority of one of these terms over the other. In both epistemology and ethics we find that one term is being sought as a ground for the other. And it is worthy of note that this priority that is sought is important in the understanding of the meaning of correlative terms.

Without going into any enormous amount of discussion on these issues, we see the discussion of the priority of cause in talking about effect in David Hume (1739). We see that in the discussion of rights and duty within the law the priority of duty, for example, in the legal writing of jurist Oliver Wendell Holmes, Jr. And as for the priority of determining what is true by disconfirmation, there is the work of Karl Popper. And as for as the question of priority of ends over means, there is the work of Aristotle and John Dewey.

In treating interpretation and definition as correlatives, I find some very interesting analogies with the other correlatives. I propose, then, to look at what seems prior in the contrasts between two correlative terms and then look to other related correlative terms that in turn are related to them as correlative terms. Especially, we see a certain amount or degree of parallel synonymy in contrasting correlatives. Note that when we speak of responsibilities, obligations, duties, and debt, we presume that there is someone or something that we are responsible to or for, that there is someone who expects that we fulfill our obligations, our duty, or that we repay our debt. In each case there is a correlative presumption.

When we talk about definition as a correlative term, we find that definition is something *opposite* and *contrastive* with what we do in the name of interpretation. With definition we are seeking more certainty about what we are talking about, and that requires that we interpret what we are saying. Definition is all about determination. It is about formulation. It is seeking something definite. It has to do with protocols and rules or distinctions that keep things straight. It is about specifications of meaning. It is all about laying down terms that we can stand on. Definitions are words that we can rely upon in concrete and particular applications. Definitions need to be pragmatically sound for if we are to carry out transactions with other people and thus they are needed to give us guidance in dealing with the material elements of this world. They lay down the foundations for application and control.

If you are free to do something, you have no responsibility to do it. If something is necessary, it is not contingent. If you have a cause, you have an effect. And if something is a means, there must be an end for which it is a means. In each case the preceding term takes priority and defines the other correlative term. And equally, before we can define something, someone must find the correct interpretation of the thing we are defining. Just as a cause is a step to an effect, an interpretation is a step toward definition. "Interpretation" thus becomes when we seek clarity of meaning the priority term when we are discussing definition.

My recommendation, then, is that we look carefully at the priority of interpretation over definition. And much of this book is an attempt to show and illustrate that priority. But importantly, at this point in the discussion we want still to insist that there is no essential definition of how we use these two terms. In this respect I am only reporting on our usage of these terms as they have historically evolved in our use of the English language.

At this point, for me to reject essentialist views is to challenge the presumptions of a great deal of classical philosophy that are still residual in the philosophical community. But what I have to say runs counter to the essentialism thought to be found in Plato and Aristotle. As we proceed to unpack the complexity of these issues, I hope to show that essentialism is only a limit and not a precise point that we see in the stable conditions of the world. The world that I perceive has so much built-in change and instability in it. And my perception of that change undermines all expectations about the rigid fixity of so many of our concepts and any thoughts of permanence of the referents found in our scientific models. What we perceive as knowledge is altering and changing. Scientific models are always open to additional amendments and reversals of perspectives.

But to keep our analysis of contrasting terms straight we need much more precise language (i.e., technical terms) to talk about contrasting terms. In Aristotelian logic, for example, we can distinguish different types of terms that require rigid definitions to make them distinct and precise and enable us to talk about both the logical notions of *contradiction* and *contrariety*. First, *negative terms* are to be contrasted with *negations of sentences*. "The town is inhospitable" is a predication of a negative term. It is to be contrasted with saying "The town is not hospitable," or again with the sentence "It is not the case that the town is hospitable." The last two are negative sentences: the former is a negative predication, and the latter is a negation of a sentence. All three sentences are logical equivalents; that is, they have the same truth value in logic.

In the above examples of *hospitable* and *inhospitable*, the logic of the negation of the term hospitable makes inhospitable a negative term or a complementary term. But here again we are confronted with a logical problem, as with health and illness. Is there a middle ground where the town may be neither hospitable nor inhospitable, where the town is simply indifferent in the way it treats strangers? What I have introduced is the problem of distinguishing complementary terms in logic from contrary terms. *Contrary terms*, such as hot and cold, cannot be asserted as both true of the same thing, but they may be false when what is talked about is neither hot nor cold.

But note that in talking about *morality*, we have a number of terms that reflect some distinct differences in the use of their negative prefixes with sentence negations. In these instances terms have complicated uses, so that we have trouble labeling them as complementary or contrary. For example, if an action is *moral*, it follows that it is not *nonmoral*. But if an action is moral, it does not follow that it is not *immoral*, for some actions thought moral can be opposed to what is a nonmoral action where there is no moral issue involved in the action.

Immoral actions are actions, however, that might be categorized as actions that might be moral ones generically. Moral actions and immoral actions, then, both belong to the supercategory of moral actions, in which case an immoral action can be called a moral action that meets with our moral disapproval. But such talk becomes confusing if we want to talk about such a strange category as *immoral moral* actions. In this case the expression turns into an oxymoron. Note the way modifiers slant when we speak of *a moral immoral* action. Is capital punishment an immoral moral action? Can we murder someone in the name of justice and still be moral? Can justified assassinations or legalized executions be moral?

But there are added difficulties in speaking of an action as *amoral*. In speaking about a lack of moral sense in acting as being amoral, we might just want to take an amoral way of acting as immoral. But that raises confusion. We have in talking about someone being amoral a sense opposed to what it is to be moral, with someone acting in the sense of nonmoral, which seems to be one sense of what it is to be acting in an amoral way. When actions, however, are nonmoral, they are neither moral nor immoral in, which case moral and immoral become contrary terms and not complementary terms, as when we talk about actions being neither moral nor immoral. They are, then, simply nonmoral.

And then again, these distinctions made above are sometimes made in talking about persons. One can be moral, immoral, or amoral. Note in this case we might consider these terms as not just contraries or complements but as correlatives. When we define moral by definition, can we define what is amoral of someone by their lack of moral inclinations? But note the difficulty of defining amoral if we do not have some conception of what it is to be moral. What these examples illustrate is the importance of the way we define terms in terms of other terms, such as we do in defining complementary and contrary terms. We are equally doing the same sorts of oppositions in defining correlatives. Our negations and distinctions, then, are all important in the way we define correlatives.

We need further clarifications to see the basis for many of the distinctions that exist between correlative terms that are not being defined logically. We need to do this to make sense of the fact that one term is involved in the definition of the other. Interpretation and definition are not logically opposed as terms. But what then is the basis of the opposition between these correlative terms if it is not logical? To answer that, we need further frameworks of rhetoric to clarify how we use other terms to come to terms with terms, especially in our uses of correlative terms. We need to break the vicious circle about correlative terms by exploring their close synonyms and their contrasts with their antonyms that add to the complexity of how these terms are frequently used.

It is in the examination of this complexity that we need to try to find words to interpret and define the right thing to say to make our meanings clear. I do not want to go into a lengthy examination of synonyms and antonyms here to show how we can generate different senses of how we can use words with new distinctions to make what we say clear. Here I am only trying to show how roughly this correlative frame of terms works as we find contrasting distinctions between them.

But to see that done more systematically I do want to refer to my *Reframing Rhetoric* in my chapter entitled "Difficulties in Dealing with Presumption." There I examined in some depth the complexity of the synonyms of assumption and presumption analytically and contrastively. "To sort out the ambiguities in talking about presumptions, I [found] it useful to see how the notion of presumption conflicts, overlaps, and for the most part is thought synonymous with a number of other related terms, such as 'presupposition,' 'postulation,' 'assumption,' and 'supposition.'" And I went on to say, "In a blank noncontextualized sense, all these five terms appear to be exact synonyms. It is an error of empty abstraction to think of these terms as strictly synonymous apart from their contextual usages, even though they are frequently treated as synonymous in many cases in nontechnical contexts"

I then appealed to Wittgenstein's dictum about how concepts differ in different language games. Or, to rephrase it, how the meaning of our concepts change meaning in different contexts of application. And with that reminder, I carefully examined "the verbs from which these nominalized five terms (that are above mentioned) are derived." And what followed in that chapter is an example of the contrastive analysis that I am recommending. What followed as a result was a lengthy examination of "a wide spectrum of differing contextual usages of *presume, presuppose, postulate, assume,* and *suppose*" (2007, 239–44).

All I want to do here in this context, then, is to illustrate the wealth of distinctions that one can find, as I did in *Reframing Rhetoric*, where we can discover by our examination the wealth of contrasts that goes on between synonyms and antonyms as correlatives. And such examinations of the contrasts between synonyms and between the senses of antonyms as a starting point are to be found in dictionaries of synonyms or in *Roget's Thesaurus* (see also Urdang 1975).

Let me, then, sketch a brief model here to illustrate the complexity of the contrasts that are generated by a select list of synonyms. I will simply use the model I am introducing by using it to tally contrasts for a brief, select group of just five synonyms that are analogous in meaning. And I will do likewise the same for a group of five antonyms that also are analogous in meaning. What I want to demonstrate is the number of multiple contrasts that are generated by these comparisons and contrasts. Figure 12.1 illustrates the total contrasts

Synonyms	1	2	3	4	5
Antonyms	1	2	3	4	5
Tally of Synonym Contrasts with Antonyms	5	5	5	5	5
	Total 25				
Synonym Contrasts Tally	4	3	2	1	
	Total 10				
Antonym Contrasts Tally	4	3	2	1	
	Total 10				
Total Contrast Tallies	25 + 10 + 10 = 45				

Figure 12.1. Model of Contrasts (Between Synonyms and Antonyms)

generated by five synonym and five antonyms. As you will see from the figure, the total amounts to forty-five contrasts where we will find places or *loci* for distinguishing different senses of meaning.

And using that model of correlative contrasts, I also present in figure 12.2 a select set of five synonyms and antonyms that illustrate the application of the model in figure 12.1 to show how there are contrasts between these synonyms and these antonyms of the term *defined*, and there are also contrasts between all the synonyms and between some of the antonyms of *defined* that will vary with different selected contexts. Such is the matrix of language contrasts that aids us in saying things with new and different distinctions that enable us to be original and creative about what we personally have to say in the unique, personal contexts in which we communicate.

Such multiplication of contrasting meaning illustrates the power of correlatives to generate new distinctions and new meanings to express clearly what we want to say in specific situations. Such generation of new distinctions is just one more dimension of the generative capacity of language to say things that have never been said before with those words in other contexts. And that is the aim

		Five Synonyms		
Definite	Determined	Definitive	Settled	Decided
		Five Antonyms		
Obscure	Unclear	Ambiguous	Equivocal	Questionable

Figure 12.2. An Application of Model of Contrasts

of most writers: to make a case for something that has never been put exactly into those words before, words that are their own and not words with meanings purloined from some other writer. Correlative terms permit us to say new things by altering our usage to fit our changed circumstances. They, like figurative language, are at the heart of great deal of language refinement.

CHAPTER 13

Contrasts between Definitions and Interpretations

But how do definitions and interpretations contrastingly differ? To proceed to talk about differences, we need to make a distinction between *seeing something as similar* and *seeing something as different*. And when we try to specify the difference, we ask in what respect two things are similar or they are different. The first sort of "seeing as" is based on comparative descriptions. The second sort of "seeing as" is based on finding contrasts. Contrasting descriptions require distinctions or properties that are applicable to one term and not to the other.

Definitions, in one sense of the term, are roughly descriptions or explanations of the meaning of words. But interpretations are in a way much the same sort of thing, but there is a difference. Interpretations are without any of that sense of a fixed sense of final determination that we expect from definitions. But on the other hand, definitions have much in common with what it is to be an interpretation. Definitions are formed on the basis of interpretations; that is, definitions are interpretations of uses of language that have been determined or judged to be usage by experts interpreting language use and usage.

To expand on the issue of what a definition is, we might ask the question, what is the nature of a definition? Or again, we might ask, what is the nature of an interpretation? But are interpretations and definitions the sorts of things that really have natures? But to pursue this question requires further discussion and argument about what sorts of things can be said to have natures.

On the nature of things (*De Rerum Naturae*) by Lucretius is at the center of one of those age-old philosophical controversies that have been lingering around since antiquity; it still especially hangs on in modern physics. Beneath this talk about the nature of things lie many of the dangers about asking for definitions. However, I want to postpone that important discussion about defining the nature of things until later, when we discuss real definitions. The reality of real definitions is a very contentious thing, with a long history in philosophy.

Interpretation as a term in one sense differs from the sense of what it is *to paraphrase*, despite the fact that a paraphrase is in a way an interpretation of what is expressed by the words being paraphrased. To say that there is only "one possible interpretation" of a sentence, we would have to say that the only possible interpretation would necessarily by definition be a paraphrase. Both interpretations and paraphrases are thus expressions in words that differ from the original words used. But there is, then, the added presumption that a paraphrase is a correct, an adequate, or maybe "the only valid interpretation," especially if we can show that two valid interpretations end up meaning exactly the same thing. Of course, we assume that a paraphrase is equal in meaning to what it interprets, and it is possible there may be other interpretations equal in meaning to the paraphrase and what it interprets.

But to speak of an interpretation, on the other hand, is to regard it as the opposite of a paraphrase; for when we speak of an interpretation, there is the presumption that what is said is open to other possible interpretations. When we speak of something as an interpretation, we leave open the question whether or not there are other equally valid or justified interpretations. For example, an ambiguous sentence is open to two or more possible valid interpretations. But when we speak of paraphrases, we do not think of validity. We think of some sort of identity of meaning. We speak of a paraphrase as being an accurate or precise statement of what is said. But *accuracy* and *precision* are not the terms we use in talking about interpretations. Interpretations are valid, likely, or plausible, while definitions, like paraphrases, if good, can be said to be practically adequate or precise and even accurate enough about what is said.

One thing for certain, when we raise questions about the meaning of what it is to be an interpretation, issues are never logically definable by any simple, determinative descriptions of what the interpreted statement or expression is saying. But that is not how we talk about definitions. We assume that definitions are logically and precisely determinate. And we find that many definitions are conventionally prescriptively determinate by consensual acts of legitimatization. They are determinate as accepted in the standardizations made by recognized authorities considered as experts about the standards of correctness of everyday word usage.

But also we sometimes find that our definitions may be faulty, illogical, and inapplicable and that they fail to do their tasks. And at other times definitions can be both logically simple and fulfill their rhetorical tasks in précising the meaning of our terms. What is important in talking about interpretations and definitions is to see the rhetorical differences in their uses in addressing different sorts of questions and problems about meaning. And such questions, as we hope to show, can be answered by analyzing the many different rhetorical uses of definition and interpretation in different sorts of contexts that are using different rhetorical modes. These uses can be diverse, elaborate, and complex.

But it is important to note here that the task of interpretations in explaining meaning can go on endlessly. The search for the full implications and the meaning of what is said in many cases never seems to be complete with any decisive mark for closure. What someone says is always dependent on contexts and perspectives rich with endless implications. Interpretation is always dependent on the variety of descriptions that one can make about what is possibly meant by someone saying something in the complexity of complicated rhetorical situations.

Written discourse, too, it should be noted, is an open-ended invitation to an open-ended number of audiences with all their different possible presumptions about what appear to be the changing knowledge of language usage and the different knowledge backgrounds that they can bring to the table as individual readers. We see this infinite search for meaning going on continuously among scholars searching for the meaning of the texts of some of our great historical authors.

Take just two examples, Plato and Shakespeare. Platonic interpretive criticism has been going on for well over two millennia. Interpretive criticism of Plato's works has been piling up high and deep in our libraries. And Shakespearean interpretive criticism is a worthy competitor, and probably given the verbal virtuosity and the humanity of Shakespeare, it will probably never end as long as civilization endures. And what has always surprised me is that critical interpretations end up using many more words than are found in the written text that is being critiqued. We see this in the critical commentary (*explication de texte*) generated in discussing the meaning of many short lyrical poems.

The extent to which interpretation is wide open is a part of the historical circumstances and varying cultures within which human utterances are produced and recorded. Conceptual powers, given their generative nature and the differences in culture, are unbounded, with no limits to what people will use to interpret and conceptualize what someone says; this is especially the case when a text is stripped from its original context and reconceptualized in a host of fictive interpretive conjectures.

Both interpretation and definition are decisively interactive as rhetorical tasks. In many ways the terms definition and interpretation cannot be precisely separated, as both terms involve each other and are entangled together when we talk about clarification. And to repeat, each term is an umbrella term covering many related and comparable clarifying activities. By umbrella terms, again, I mean terms that are names for many closely related conceptions that have no common essential characteristics linking them together. As said, umbrella terms are historical. They cluster around overlapping objects of interest, and they tend to create patterns of connected interest with other similar patterns of connected interest. Such is how the terms definition and interpretation interact with each other as we explore issues about their meaning. Both terms at times name rhetorical tools that network and overlap in the processes of clarification when we try to seek some sort of universal understanding of what we or others mean.

Rhetorical and communication skills involve using the tools of the arts of speaking, listening, reading, and writing. These arts as (qua) arts are open ended, distinct, and interrelated. Speaking well is not easy to master. Listening well, again, is not easy either. Ask any psychotherapist how difficult it is to listen. Note how important awareness and self-awareness are to psychologists and psychiatrists. Reading well is especially not easy, as most in the scholarly disciplines in the humanities will attest. It certainly can be hard work. And writing above all is not an easy task either. Why else has writing become for many a profession? Not many do it quite well. Writing in certain types of genre can be terribly difficult and hard work that requires a great deal of verbal mastery and transformative skill.

Simple literacy, it needs to be pointed out, is never adequate enough to communicate complex thoughts. Advanced literacy is one of the prerequisites for working in academia. There the need for it cannot be too much emphasized, for one key to success in academia is the very high levels of defining and interpretive skills that are prerequisites for analysis and critique. And most of all, advanced literacy and critical skills are prized achievements for those who want to have any personal or intellectual pride in knowing about what is going on in their own lives and knowing about the world around them.

Interpretation and definition in the end are about comprehension and understanding. And comprehension is always a matter of how much is being understood. And since that is always a matter of degree, we can never be fully certain that we ever fully understand in the end an author's meaning and intentions. The question is not whether we simply understand, but how much interpretation and definition working together help us better understand what we think that we understand.

CHAPTER 14

Nominal, Conceptual, and Real Definitions

Requests for definitions that are logical and grammatical in form seem to be of three sorts. They seem to doing one of three things. They are responses to requests for defining real things, that is, *real definitions*. They are responses for requests about the definition of our concepts, that is, *conceptual definitions*. They are responses for requests about the senses or the meanings of words that we use, that is, *nominal definitions*.

It is a mistake in defining to confuse these three uses of definitions with each other when we define things. To use an ideal concept or a norm to define a real thing is to give a *persuasive definition* (Stevenson 1944). To give a real definition for the request for a definition of a concept is to *reify a concept*. Both errors, giving persuasive definitions or reifying concepts, are among the most common mistakes made in thought and argument. Both mistakes, persuasive definitions and reifications, turn on the errors of projecting thoughts, values, attitudes, and feeling into reality.

Such common rhetorical mistakes lead to a great deal of frustration about words and the meaning of words. They lead to the conviction by many that a great deal of argument about the referents of names is simply arbitrarily nominal and hopelessly subjective. Such disputes end up being words about words. But even more disturbing is that some people deliberately or in ignorance use reifications and persuasive definitions to confuse others who are very vulnerable to such shifts and verbal confusions about what our thoughts and concepts stand for.

It is quite common today in philosophical discussions to hear philosophers seeking a definition of a concept. But what is it to define a concept? Sometimes they speak of developing a concept, sometimes they talk about constructing concepts, and sometimes they even speak of creating a concept. Concepts are said to be ideas or elements of thought that we can use to shape or fashion our thinking. The questions about such constructions are, For what purposes? What is involved in concept creation? Some say the purpose is for creating new knowledge. But can we actually create knowledge? Some think that knowledge can only be discovered. Others think that definitions are about ideal notions and of eternal, ideal forms that are at the basis of the absolute order of things. They are for them the real and true objects of knowledge that are either discovered or recovered, as in Plato, by reminiscences from past heavenly experience.

One problem in any theory of knowledge is, How do our concepts relate to terms? Do our terms simply stand for concepts? And are our concepts thus the way we discover knowledge. What is the proper order of discovery? Do we first look at names? Or do we first look at our concepts? Or, is the source of our knowledge in our perceptions or in our observation of things thought to be found in nature? And which comes first in our order of knowledge, our thoughts of our concepts or our thoughts of our terms that we use to express them? Or, in the end are these simply misplaced and misleading questions about what concepts mean and stand for?

For Wittgenstein (1958) language flux is tied to shifting notions and conceptions. Our conceptions are attached to words in our language games, or they are in play with words that shift within different contexts. But that does not tell us anything about the connections between words and ideas. In our conceptions about both our words and about our ideas, the fundamental questions to ask are, which is the necessary condition for the other? And how do we relate definitions of terms to definitions of concepts? In Wittgenstein the fixity is in the term and not in the concepts that change as the language games change (1972).

But note how often we speak of terms as if they were concepts and vice versa. *Concept* and *term* seem interchangeable in our talk about notions and terms. This suggests that for some purposes, whether we are defining words, concepts, or things, it doesn't really much matter. In speaking, at times, there seems little difference. When we are able to come to terms with terms, are our agreements about them equally both verbal and conceptual? And when we come to terms with terms, are we directly dealing with reality? In that case, is there any real difference between words standing for concepts and words standing for real things?

We seem to be dealing with virtually synonymous language on all three levels when we talk about terms and concepts and what they stand for. Conspicuously, when we define both terms and concepts and the reality of what they stand often, we use the *same patterns of defining terms* to accomplish these three tasks. Is there, then, any difference between the three types of definitions in practice? Looking at nominal and conceptual definitions, are we not simply defining different sides of the same coin?

But note that when Wittgenstein spoke of concepts changing, he noted that the terms or words were not changing: *"Wenn sich die Sprachspiele ändern,*

ändern sich die Begriffe, und mit den Begriffen die Bedeutungen der Wörter [When language-games change, then there is a change in concepts, and with the concepts the meaning of the words change]."

With Wittgenstein there comes about a change in the meaning of a concept that attaches itself to a word. And in addition, some people speak of socially constructed concepts that they attach to words. Some others, as mentioned, speak of the creation of concepts. Some speak of concepts as if we even have concepts without words, and at times it is thought that we are able creatively to put those "verbal-less thoughts" into words.

All these separations in thought suggest that concepts are independent of the words, and this appears to be true insofar as we have the same concept but phrased in different words in foreign languages. This reason for the separation of words and the thoughts they stand for is comparable to the thoughts logicians have when they maintain that we can have the same proposition expressed in different languages. Propositions are expressed by sentences, but sentences expressing the same propositions differ in the words expressing them in French, German, or Russian.

But just as our concept of a concept suggests that we cannot think without concepts, so it seems that we are not able to think rationally without concepts, for reasons seem to demand concepts. And as Immanuel Kant points out, "Without sensibility no object would be given to us; and without understanding no object would be thought. Thoughts without content are empty; intuitions without concepts are blind" (or concepts without percepts are empty, and our percepts without concepts are blind; 1781, 107). Thus, it is Kant's rationalist view that we have to have both concepts and percepts together to have knowledge.

But the problem with such a contention is, Are the terms *concept* and *percept* univocal terms? Do these terms have more than one sense? That is, are they multivocal? Note also the difference in use between the term concept and conception and percept and perception. Concepts and percepts in their conception—are they static? But conception does not always end up in fixed and determinate concepts. Our conceptions may go astray.

Yet independent of context we seem to think there is little difference between having a concept and having a conception. But again, many philosophers seek in their common intuitive arguments to show that certain definitions of concepts are inadequate. They do so by showing that a defined concept fails to capture the full meaning of that concept. What defeats the definitions of concepts are exceptions or counterexamples in their applications. Such arguments about the defects in concepts show that our definitions of them do not always adequately describe what is being intuitively grasped by those who think that they have a full grasp of what a concept means or stands for.

How do we adequately define religion as a concept? Can we ever define a concept of religion? What is our idea of religion? Note that in this case we ought not to speak of a concept of religion as we do of objects as having essential properties, for concepts or ideas do not have properties. We only predicate properties to things. We can have concepts of things with properties, but in thinking of concepts, we are shifting from ideas about things to the concept of the thing that has the attributes and properties. We are simply shifting properties and attributes from things to an idea about properties or attributes of things.

When we think of defining things, there is a shift in our focus about ideas and our concepts about what we are defining. Are we then defining a reference or a referent? In defining the referents, we are defining something thought real, or even possibly real in the sense of an existing unreal real or a virtual or fictive reality. Hamlet is part of the reality of Shakespeare's plays. Even imaginary things can be defined thus by real definitions. What is important to recognize is that we are constantly shifting back and forth, going from definitions of things to definitions of concepts, and finally to definitions of things, and then reversing ourselves back again to concepts and back to the words that seeks to represent them.

Ultimately, does it, as it has been already asked, make much difference if we simply focus on the definitions themselves, their defining terms, instead of thinking of what sorts of things they are definitions about? But there are differences nevertheless in how we speak about defining words, concepts, or things. We should not, for instance, think of "the senses of a concept," for words only seem to have different senses. Certain real things are not to be distinguished by senses of words, but the senses are the avenues involved in any sense perception of real things. And only things have different properties or attributes, but it is not the case with words and concepts that they have properties or attributes. What sense does it have to say that words and concepts have properties?

Thus, we see that conceptual definitions appear to relate to mental entities that can be formed or shaped by mental or rational beings. We can shape our ideas. We can alter them dramatically and even drastically. How much, then, are concepts subject to change? Once formed and shaped in their best form, can we say that they are complete, fixed, definite, static, and fully determinate? Can we speak of discovering concepts? Or again, to reverse ourselves, as already noted, do we not speak of creating or inventing them?

If our concepts are discovered and unchanging, what is our ground for saying that this is so? Is it some higher rational being, such as, Plato's Good, the Christian God, or a divine principle of reason (*logos*) that is the ground for the existence of concepts? "In the beginning was the *logos*" as in Stoicism. The source of religion in this case, as with the Stoics' *logos*, must be a divine idea, the foundation and source of reason, law, and justice. To avoid such divine paradoxes and higher metaphysics about rational souls and their source in reason I prefer the skeptical suggestion that concepts are the products for the most part of the human imagination and not a result of divine inspiration.

Concepts develop from reflections on experience and not from religious revelations. My suggestion, then, is that concepts are subject to change, and they are not divinely generated fixed universals. And in this skeptical light concepts are not always amenable to strict definitions, but they are best considered in terms of the use *to which we put them*. Concepts in that case would be defined in terms of their *applications*. In other words, I am proposing to discuss concepts instrumentally, which thus reduces our concern with concepts to a problem about the adequacy of our concepts to how they get the job done.

Operational definitions are a type of pragmatic definition famously introduced and talked about in theoretical physics by Percy Bridgeman 1927. Empirical or measurable variables in physics were defined by the operations by which they were measured. Note the semantic overtones in calling someone "a big-time operator." Operators operate. Not only is Operations the place, as in the Air Force, where all the plans for actions are made, it is also the place where all plans of actions are initiated and carried out. Note that operators are those who make their machines do various types of work. Surgeons do operations. And in mathematics operations are what we do to make calculations. Note that most operations are rule governed, as in math. They end up being the defined procedures that need to be carried out to complete a task.

Note how operations are at heart a set of operations. They are the procedures that an operator puts in place. In simplistic terms operations are at the heart of everything we do. They are the processes where our tools are applied and how our applications in our jobs are carried out. They are the plans of actions that are actually working. And what makes a machine do its work is found in the scheme and details of its operations. Note we can talk about defining operations, not so much in terms of the terms used but in the sense of formatting plans to be carried out.

Operations, then, are defined by the order or sequence of operations that are being carried out step by step. Note too that the term *pragmatic*, unlike the term *operation*, has its root in Greek not Latin. Note the apparent derivative synonymy between pragmatic and practical, as these terms are used to mean the same thing in many contexts. Note again the positive overtones in both terms of suggesting something effective in doing the everyday tasks of life. It is pragmatic in that it works. It gets results. Definitions are pragmatic. They end up being descriptions of the operations that lead to achievements.

We can think of concepts as mental entities that can be created, reformed, changed, and projected into reality. In some cases concepts can act as ideals for reform and thus are normative and not just descriptive. Insofar as concepts are open to change and reform, they are relative to the perspectives of their creators and reformers in the historical circumstances within which they live. Thus, a concept of democracy or religion can be subject to definition or determination only in relation to historical human perspectives and developing ideals. And as such, a concept of democracy would be open to alteration or change in the ways we think of social policy. And again, a concept of religion would depend on how we think about consolation and death in different historical eras and cultures. Religion in its most dramatic forms of liturgy is about resurrection and salvation. It is mostly about saving grace. It provides consolation for a sense of ultimate dread and despair.

Note that we have different social, political, mathematical, scientific, and philosophical concepts. We have different concepts of space and time, different concepts of number, different concepts of democracy, and different concepts of religion. We evaluate the adequacy of these concepts by their ability to enable us to encounter our problems in this world. It is a mistake to think that the differences we have in talking about concepts results from the ambiguity of those concepts in our uses of language. Note that it was the aim of Descartes to have clear and distinct concepts as a test for truth.

In different disciplines concepts may have precise definitions to alleviate any possible ambiguity in talking about them. The epistemic question always is, do our concepts have any contact or touch with reality? Thus, is the concept of religion an ambiguous one, as we ordinarily think about it? Are our concepts of religion in touch with the reality of what goes on in different cultures? These are questions that have historical and social anthropological answers. Note that to say that Catholicism is a religion is not an ambiguous statement. Rather, we should think about what we say religion is in terms that fit certain contexts. Is animism a religion? Is money a religion for some people? Are we on the edge here of not being literal? Surely, to say Cheney's religion was oil is a metaphor. What, then, makes the word *religion* ambiguous in certain contexts? "He doesn't believe in God. He is not religious!" Such an explanation would be correct if by religion we mean only a belief in God.

Ambiguity occurs in the use of the term religion in what we say and do relative to situations. Note that behaviors as well as words may be ambiguous when someone analyzes what you are doing. But on other occasions behaviors can clearly be understood without question. Rather, we should in the end say it is the language we use to express or define a concept that makes any statement ambiguous. It is neither the term nor the concept, but rather it is the application of the term used that helps us decide about ambiguity.

Theologians do give us definite concepts of religion. And they give us many different definitions of those concepts. Their different concepts define the differences between their theologies. They are not necessarily ambiguous in what they say about what their religion is all about. If one's concept of God is Jesus Christ, one's concept of God is certainly not ambiguous.

But when one says, "My religion is the only true religion," then there is a presumption that your form of belief expressed is what defines religion. There is also behind such statements the presumption that what others believe in the name of religion is not truly religion. What others believe in is not true religion. What others believe in is superstition. "How can one who does not believe in my God be truly religious? They are superstitious, having false idols standing before them."

It is quite common today in philosophical discussions to hear philosophers seeking a definition of a concept such as religion. They do it in order to have a conceptual understanding of religion. But what is it to define or even construct such a concept? Again many philosophers derive from their common intuitions arguments to show that certain definitions of concepts would be inadequate. Their judgment is that we are incapable of having an intellectual grasp of what they think is in fact a true or pure concept, which is in their inner certainty about the concept that they think that they have.

Note, too, that there is a close connection between talking about concepts and talking about principles. What would be the difference between talking about a concept of knowledge and talking about the basic principles of knowledge? Note here there is a tendency to speak of principles as stating a theory and not having a concept unless you want to think of *a definition as a theory*. And I certainly think that giving a definition as a theory is a mistaken notion about the function of theories in giving explanations. Theories and principles, it should be noted, are stated in sentences, while concepts are expressed by terms. Thus, I ask, is it not a mistake to give a definition as a theory? Can we define theories?

My answer to the question is that it depends on how you relate a concept to a principle. Can we define principles? Some talk about the principles of the theory of free enterprise, which for most conservatives amounts to no more than a definition of a concept of a free market. But note the terminology shift in defining a concept of free enterprise and shifting our definition in terms of the principles of a free market. Would defining the theory in this case be the same thing as defining a concept? Note the ambiguities in talking about market freedoms as if markets are not governed by conventional restrictions on what we can and cannot do in free markets.

My contention, then, is that it is a mistake to think that theories can be explained by definitions. Theories may be defined, but in that case we are not logically defining definitions but explaining what we mean by a theory. For example, giving a definition as a theory runs counter to any notion of theory developed in the natural sciences. Theories in the natural sciences, for instance, seek evidence for invariance or evidence for certain ranges of probability that appear to be relative invariant patterns about what goes on in the world. But such theories differ radically from many proposed theories about history, religion, art, or literature, which are often discussed often by humanists as concepts.

But, then, can we define a concept of history, religion, art, or literature? Note that in this case we ought not to speak of these concepts as having essential properties, for concepts do not have properties. Nor, should we think of "the senses of a concept," for it is only our use of words that have senses. Thus, we see that conceptual definitions appear to relate to mental entities that can be formed or shaped by mental or rational beings talking about the world, talking about history, or even talking about fictions that have a created imaginary world all of their own. Or we may in logical or linguistic jargon be just talking about possible worlds, which, after all, is about what is not and thus consequently fictive.

Though I am not ruling out the existence of such a notion of pure and eternal concepts, I prefer the skeptical suggestion that our concepts are the products for the most part a result of the human imagination reflecting on our personal experiences of the world. Concepts in that case are not fixed and eternal notions, but mental entities created, shaped, formed, constructed, reformed, changed, or projected into reality, and when concepts create ideals, they can be acted upon and brought into contact with reality.

Insofar, then, as concepts are open to change and reform, they are relative to creators and reformers and their refinements of meaning. Thus, a concept of democracy or religion is subject to human perspectives and ideals. And, as such, a concept of democracy or religion as historical would be open to alteration, reconstruction, or change, dependent on contexts. As Clifford Geertz notes, "Where else could French politics exist but France?" (1973, 311). The concept of democracy and the concept of religion thus both have a history and do not have any timeless basis for any definable conceptual definition. They develop as a result of such cultural variances historically into being umbrella terms.

Sometimes we hear the term *constructs* for these structured notions; that is, they are often said to be *socially constructed concepts* (see Schiappa 2003 and

Brummett 2003, 2004). Note that we have different social, political, mathematical, scientific, and philosophical concepts or constructs, such as different concepts of space and time, different concepts of number, different concepts of democracy, and different concepts of religion. And note that some of the above-mentioned concepts or constructs can be given precise definitions that may be questioned as to their functional adequacy for practical applications.

Note, too, the use of the term "model" for such mental constructs. We model what it is to be a religion or what it is to be a democracy. The emphasis in this case is on the imaginative or creative source of such constructs. We develop models by which we classify, file, map, diagram, or catalog. We even use them to predict economic disasters. We can frame our concepts in mathematical and formal languages. We can schematize them graphically in flow charts, coordinate systems, and pictorial representations. All such models are used to structure or frame our concepts and ideas to make them applicable to the data and our experiences of the world.

It is a mistake, then, I repeat, to think of differences in our concepts as resulting from ambiguity in the use of language. Concepts are not directly spoken of as ambiguous. They may be vague in the sense that we have vague ideas about them. Some terms tend to be ambiguously used, but that doesn't make the term in itself ambiguous. Words may simply have many multiple senses and consequently different uses. And as for vagueness, concepts are vague just as terms are vague. But what makes them vague is that they are inapplicable in certain contexts. But vagueness can be eliminated if we are more precise and informative about what we are trying to talk about.

Note that a request for a definition of the nature of something that does not have a nature, such as a poem, an artifact, a unit of measurement, or a university, fails to recognize the social conditions under which these things come into existence. The difficulty in thinking of artifacts is that we want to think of them as real kinds of things, when in fact there is nothing natural about socially constituted artifacts. Artifacts by definition are products of art and not of nature.

Our language thus permits us to talk of things that are not just physical things. There are qualities and properties found in perception, such as dark, loud, and crooked. We have dispositions of persons and things such as virtues and vices. All are things in an abstract sense of being things. But in this abstract sense what it is to be a thing becomes almost meaningless unless we turn metaphysician and ask such questions as, "What is substance?" or "What is Being?" Note the emptiness of these abstractions about stuff. Any attempt to analyze them leads us endlessly into more and more empty abstractions.

There is something terribly empty about metaphysics. An old teacher, Charles Hartshorne, a quintessential metaphysician with whom in the past I was enamored as his student, talked about *important but empty concepts*. in his lectures. They were important for him, for they were the hopeful truisms and the redundancies that grounded his convictions about religious experiences. "*Dieu de l'amour a le besoin des créatures.*" It is an empty truism. How consoling to think that God might need us just as we need Him! It would nice to believe that sort of thing and to be convinced that is a reason for solace and assurance about redemption. Such analytically true conceptions derived from metaphysical and theological speculations especially about the concept of God I find as speculations are not exactly dependable methods for coming to terms with a lot of abstract notions and concepts about God that are hopelessly locked in aporia and dialectical tensions such as one always finds in any study of theology (see Hartshorne 1948).

But I leave my dismissal of metaphysics to another day. I found in such speculative philosophy an interesting exercise very much like my son's passion for chess. It is an endless labyrinth of speculation about things thought logically integrated that leaves endless paradoxes for us to chase in endless circles until the final hour of our death. Checkmate! Amen.

CHAPTER 15

Rhetorical Definition as a Generic Term

Talking and Walking the Talk

One can see that from an overall standpoint, from a big rhetoric point of view, that rhetorical definition as a rhetorical mode permeates the whole process of composing and also that definition and interpretation are the ways that we create meaning both in speech and especially in the way that we create and invent what we say in writing.

Definition initiates our first words in making manifest our incipient aims. And by various modes of defining, encapsulated under defining as an umbrella term, we progress from those aims. And there in the composition of what we would like to say we find that there are many senses of what it is to interpret and to define as we expand on that aim. It is this continuing expansion and elaboration of our aims by rhetorical definitions and by using definitional proposals that we are able to introduce new meanings that enact and aid us in the generation of the innovative things we would like to say that are both informative and persuasive.

And this enactment by interpretation and definition is a continuous development in the composing process. Composing in its creativity is a defining and an interpreting process that transforms aims progressively into the things that we want to say. It helps us present words about things that we can personally approve of. In composing, we create the patterns of words that we want to stand on. It is by interpretation and definition that we enact words that lead us into the successful rhetorical actions that we engage in while we are composing.

Often we can define our aims by sketching them first in an outline of what we want to do and say. The uses of outlines in rhetoric, it is worth noting, are twofold. We use them for invention. And many times we use them as summaries. Summaries are mnemonic devices to recall the gist of what we have said in a written text. Summary outlines function very much like abstracts. They are condensations of what someone has written or said.

But when outlines are used in prewriting, they become definitions and interpretations of intentions instead of summations. They become our guides to composing by helping us define what we want to say. A prewriting outline is a definition of intention that initiates the writing process. It is simply a tool for invention and a tool for composing. It is a guide to definitional expansion. In one sense it is a definition of a synopsis of a rhetorical action. As a synopsis it has the frame of a narrative. And as a frame of a narrative it is also an algorithm, which is no more than a definition of a procedure. And we narrate procedures.

Any schema or outline can be used as an initial representation that guides further the definitions and interpretations we make of our intentions. Such schemata of topics and themes are designs of patterns of the way we want to say things. As such they are talk about expressed intentions. And as such they are just one sort of definition. Terms like definition and interpretation are umbrella terms for many types and different senses of what it is to be a definition that have been historically developed to help us clarify what we are all about. And composing uses all these varieties of definition in many different ways as we develop what we want to say.

But we can also say that the definitions and interpretations involved in composition can be roughly divided into two types: rhetorical and logical. They are diachronic and synchronic respectively. One type summarizes historical usage, and the other type locates our meaning in a system of contrasting signs and their significations. And definitions and interpretations that are diachronic are based upon historical terms that are used for different types of clarification.

But as synchronic, interpretation and definition are terms for modes of discourse that examine terms in a system of language usage defined by their semantic contrasts with other words in our language. As synchronic, definition and interpretation can be thought of as correlative terms. And when we treat definition and interpretation as correlatives terms they are defined in terms of their interactive sets of synonyms and antonyms and their respective contrasts that take on different senses in our personal contexts of use.

For example, when we contrast synonyms with antonyms we are treating them as correlatives. Each involves the definition of the other. But note that synonyms as treated in dictionaries of synonyms are not strictly synonymous. Importantly, too, they are defined by their contrasts. They are terms with analogous uses and replaceable uses. They can be used for each other and interpreted to be synonymous in meaning in certain contexts, but they do not logically have the same meaning in all contexts (Urdang 1975). When we define usage, then, one correlative term contrasts with related synonymous terms, and all then in turn contrast with their antonyms in their usage. As such, interpretation of these interpreted and defined contrasts becomes generative of new meaning for different contexts and occasions.

And, too, we can also think of different senses of definition in different epistemic frames, either as nominal definitions, conceptual definitions, or real definitions. We can think of definitions of procedures, definitions of boundaries, definitions as classifications, definitions as statements about identities, and definitions as the basic axioms defining logical and mathematical frames; and finally, we can think of definitions as way of putting things in different perspectives. In synchronically looking at usage of the term definition it can also be noted that there are literal and figurative definitions, and even causal definitions. Note how all these different senses of definition lack any precise or rigid logical defining conditions.

Recently G. W. Bush described the events occurring in Basra as a *defining moment*. It is noteworthy that a *defining moment* is a moment in time when a thing will be defined. In this case Bush was suggesting at the time that the outcomes that he sought in Iraq were being determined. The events were said to be defining. It is this sense of definition in composing that there is a defining moment for what we wish to say in the process of composing. But what is important in that defining moment is that there is a shaping of a definition of what we want that outcome to be. But in the above instance, for Bush, the outcome of the military flare-up in Basra was not the defined outcome that he wanted realized. His aims were not translated into an achievement, which is our defining hope we have in composing.

Writing starts with questions that seek answers. But if we give answers without clarifying our questions, we can never achieve our initial aim, which is to find something to say about an incipient idea that we are developing. If we start by stating our answers to questions in writing, we are always backing up, looking for things to say, trying to find things to say about things that have already been said by someone else before. Such a mode of composing usually amounts to no more than a rationalization for what we have already said to be our intended conclusion. Composing is not simply finding someone else's reasons defending a conclusion. Rather it is a process of inquiry that moves forward toward a conclusion. And we move forward to conclusions by the clarifications of our aims. Composing is developing reasons for what we say in the very process of defining and explaining our own reasons for pursuing our aims.

Note that outlines for invention define in very much the same way that an algorithm defines. It is an outline of the steps in a procedure. They are very much like the steps in a computer algorithm. Note how, again, prewriting outlines and defines topics and headings, which are steps that invite other forms of definitional and interpretive expansions of these defined lists of topics and headings. Such definitional and interpretive expansions in writing are rhetorical acts of *refinement* on what we want to say. As modes of clarifications of aims and purposes they require disambiguation and the elimination of vagueness for both the composer and the reader with accurate definitional refinements on our meaning if we are to make clear what we want to say. And thus it is a mistake to treat a prewriting outline as a summary outline that states a finally defined conclusion without any developed preclarification of the issues raised in the beginning. As in classical rhetoric we begin with a narration of the problem, which amounts to a first attempt to define the problem.

Summary outlines in contrast are just that, nothing more than condensations. They lack the rhetorical fullness and completeness of what is needed to be compellingly clear and persuasive. They lack what is needed to adequately explain fully an author's intentions. Summary outlines tend to be abstract condensations full of ambiguities rather than a full-court press that moves forward and frontally in presenting a detailed complete statement of the case that is being made. Such summary outlines tend to look like models or schematic designs rather than elaborated forms of definition and interpretation that are needed in writing to make clear what one is saying.

Note how conceptual outlines require sentential expansions to define what we want to say. Note the advantage that conceptual outlines have over sentence outlines in composing and in speech. We are able to develop a conceptual point by elaboration, which prompts for the further things needed to be said to make points clear. It is common wisdom among speech specialists that conceptual outlines are better prompts for use in extemporaneous speaking. On the other hand, sentence outlines as tools of invention tend to inhibit oral invention and expression. They give statements that make points with closures. They invite laxity about invention and invite only reiterations of the points already being made in the sentence outlines. A sentence outline tends thus to act more like a summation than it does as an introduction inviting further amplifications and expansions of rhetorical aims and purposes.

A conceptual outline is a tool for definitional expansion. Conceptual outlines, as a consequence, unlike sentence outlines, thus are better tools for invention. Conceptual outlines act as starting points in writing, and, as in speaking, they invite extension. And that further expansion takes on sentential form from the need we have to enlarge on the concepts that we are engaged in using while we are explaining them. Concepts initiate the creative processes of trying to find the best things to say about them from new refined conceptual and redefined points of view. In other words, to paraphrase what I am saying in street talk, when we go from concepts into sentences, we are transforming our talk about our talk by walking out away from our talk and then continuing to walk further in our composing about the talk that initiated our talk.

What is important to note is that the act of writing, unlike speaking, is not simply a transcription of aim and purpose by putting into place a representation of our aims into a text in a truncated summary of it in writing. Rather, composing is a continuous process that makes progress in carrying out intentions into actions. As a cursory summary of this process, I would like to give the following figurative "street talk description" that I think is very much analogous to the process of invention in writing:

> First there is talk about the talk we want to write about, and then we talk about the walk that we want to begin to walk, and then we start to walk in our talking about our walk, and finally we walk the talk we talked about that no longer is just talk about talk. Finally it is the talk that is doing the walking.

It is illustrative to interpret these extended metaphors about talking and walking to see the analogies they have with the writing process. We need to see the continuity and the sort of progression we are engaged in when we invent and organize the way we are thinking about our writing in carrying out our writing. A common distinction made in contemporary philosophy and psychology is between a *prior intention* and an *intention in action*. Put in conventional rhetorical terms, this is the distinction between what we *mean to mean* and the *meaning of what we are saying in our act of saying it*. In meaning to mean, we have an intention to say something, but in saying it, we mean what we intended to mean when we express that intention in words.

Between these two states, for many, there appears to be a psychological discontinuity between what we want to write about and the getting down to the act of writing about it. How do we get across the gap between meaning to mean and in meaning of what we actually mean when we walk the talk that we talked about? In ordinary ways of speaking, writers speak of "being at a loss for words." They are unable to say what they want to mean, as if they were already aware of what it is that they wanted to mean before ever having gotten around to saying what they mean.

But how can what we want to mean, if it is not expressed, mean anything? In common parlance of English composition this inability to even begin to create the meaning of our meaning is called "writer's block." What makes for the disconnection in this double-talk about talking and walking the talk is the fact that we cannot find the words to say what we want to say. But importantly, rhetorically what you mean to say is something that can be defined. If we have the slightest iota of an idea of our intention to start with, we can then expand on that iota of thought and enlarge upon its meaning by interpretation and definition as we begin to express it.

As in painting, we put a number of lines on our verbal canvas. Those initial sketches are an invitation to what would complement and add to those lines to make a design that would fill the whole of the canvas. We write in the same way. We look to what will fill out a frame determined by our aim, by our context, and by our rhetorical situation. All writing just as with sentences, seeks closure in a sense of wholeness or an integrated sense of unity as in a painting.

All writing is essentially located in a narrative frame that has, like a drama, a beginning, middle, and an end. And that definition of what we aim at is our beginning. What we develop by discovery through definition is our middle, and the integration of that discovery with our initial aim is our end. We end our end in writing by completing our initial aim.

We see the continuity of expressing our aim and purpose in writing when we explore and use more and more words and use different words that interpret what we think our aims are. And that is the reason why we can cure our writer's block by putting into words interpretations of words and using expansive definitions of what we want to say in terms of those interpretations. In saying things by using definitions, we have arrived at a point where we can discover what we want to say in the very alternatives and the new frames that we use in defining what we want to say.

In this sense defining is at the very root of all communication. We define when we begin to form and shape words that fulfill our intentions. In a root sense of defining, we define when we make our aims definite. We define when we draw lines that circumscribe. We define when we formulate and bring together all the relevant distinctions we have in the past discovered, and then we add them up altogether with the distinctions that we have newly managed to create. Note that this sort of defining is not simply discovering distinctions that someone else has made, that is, using their usage to express ourselves. Writing is an act of self-discovery that expands and develops its words by using our own words.

Using the words of others to shape our thoughts is in a sense a kind plagiarism, as the thoughts in their words are not our own thoughts. Their words are not issuing out of our motivating intentions in wanting to say anything. Using their words, we do no more than say what they say. It is no more than George W. Bush saying the words provided to him by a speechwriter that he reads on a teleprompter. It is ersatz speech. Writing is always an exploration of our own thoughts on any matter. In writing, we are not scribes, that is, "scribblers." We do the writing. We do the composing.

Scribblers are no more than copyists. In copying someone else's words, we scribble to get some words thoughtlessly on the page and then hope our scribbling has some of the honorific status of an author that we admire for his gift of words. But what we have written are merely purloined words. Writing, on the other hand, is a personal exploration in which we use our imaginations to create and find distinctions for ourselves in our own vocabulary that enable us to create new lines of division, new formulations, and new ways of saying things. Definition is thus creative in making new word formulations thus making new definitions.

We find in the word meanings of other word meanings what we can expand on so as to be able to find in them a meaning that we want to call our own. Finding meaning is not a scholarly search for it in other people's words, but it is the making of meaning out of words by using our own words in ways that we may have never used before in that specific way. And when we do that, we often find that we are pleased to have said it that particular way. They are our words. That is the pure joy of writing. It is to see our own thoughts in our own words.

When we suffer a writer's block, we find ourselves accustomed to using what already has been said that is formulaic, and we find in our doubts about ourselves that we do not have the knowledge of the other writer's formulary in our repertoire to use them as well as they use them. We lack the words that others have used. Tongue-tied, we want simply to repeat them. Besides lacking the vocabulary they have, we are lacking any imagination to escape the prison of the conventional formulary of their particular word usages.

Many people lacking vocabularies compensate for their word deficiencies by using figurative language to see the meaning of their terms in the implications of their figures of speech. And in thinking figuratively, they thus fortunately see meaning differently. The secret of creative writing is psychologically to loosen up the imagination. It is to be motivated by curiosity that seeks out other unexplored alleys of meaning using different words to channel and reframe our thoughts.

Obviously, daydreaming is the world of the imagination. And for that reason much of creative writing is the stuff of dreams. Using the imagination is difficult when writing when we are overloaded and uptight with deadlines and preoccupied with multitasking. Multitasking divides our attention, thus making it difficult to float free of the tight timelines and the verbal constraints that often confine us in our speaking and writing. We are constrained by limitations and restrictions that are put on us when we think with other people's distinctions, when we think with their words and use their concepts. And sometimes we recognize with some despair that there is nothing to be gained in the way of clarity by simply circling over the same words used by others, repeating over and over what they say when we are trying to say something new and different on a subject that we want to call our own. At least, if it is part of our intent in writing to say something new, something truly informative or personally expressive to other people, then it suddenly becomes our problem to find different words and many different senses of already-used words to say things differently. And it is at that point that interpretation and definition is the way we can move on and move away from our aims to find and say something new.

When we try to bridge the gap from prior intentions to intentions in action in writing, we need to range over the problems of defining what is needed to bridge the gap. The gap is crossed by finding words to enact our intentions. And the way of doing that is to try to redefine our words or use them differently, and to say things in a way that makes clear to others that what we are saying is being said in our own way.

And one way of doing that is to use our imaginations to find new ways of interpreting the uses of our words. We can do that by using words from perspectives that are other than those that are normally used in using those words. We can do that by finding out how our words become salient with different senses in talking about our own experiences. Thus, a narrative about any unique experience has a way of creating contexts that help us give our words new meanings.

But the second way other than figurative to give new meaning to terms is to find technical ways of using words from different technical frames of reference. This requires some background knowledge in the sciences and the professional disciplines. Such a perspective depends on a search for strict definitions that make us see things differently from these specialist perspectives. To do this we can define new models, new frames of reference, and new perspectives in the way we look at things from new technical points of view that give us greater precision in the use of words.

But back to my major point, finding words to translate intentions into actions is all about finding applications of the meaning of words. And we can do this in composing by expansive uses of definitions. Definitions are one way of bridging the distance between the talk and the walk. We need to ask what are the rhetorical things happening when we use words to communicate complicated sets of intentions. We can only answer the question by making comparative and contrastive distinctions from definitions different from old senses found in conventional usage.

Note that it is a straightforward process of constant clarification as we go from wanting to say something that involves and requires definition and interpretation. And note that a search for definitions and interpretations in writing can be never ending. In using the two rhetorical modes of interpretation and definition, we clarify our aims and our purposes by expanding on them, by reframing them, and by introducing them into the perspectives that exist in the communicative situation that we share with our audience. It is a communicative situation that includes all the knowledge presumptions and assumptions held by both author and audience. These two rhetorical modes, interpretation and definition, can as a result be a grand search for meaning if given enough time, especially if you have time to write and revise your wording when you have something that you think important to say.

To do this, then, we first formulate in the sense of putting into a form of words what defines the larger issues about the aims and the purposes of other persons, that is, by understanding our audience with whom we are trying to communicate. We formulate in definitions words that create a new form or a new framework for our reader by which and through which we can fully express our prior intentions of seeking some sort of engagement with our audience that fits within our understanding of their situation and their motivations. Definition in this preliminary sense is an enlarging sense of what a definition does. It engages us with meanings that an audience can understand.

Definition in this sense gives us a precise focus by defining what is aimed at and defining the purpose of an aim that is found and located in the perspective of our reader in our rhetorical situation. Definition in this sense is finding and defining boundaries by either enlarging or restricting what we are talking about. It enlarges the compass of the discussion by expanding it into words that fit within defined boundaries within which we are writing situationally. Definition, in other words, helps us frame our discussion with our audience.

The meaning of what we say in a rhetorical situation is not directly dependent on meanings directly expressed with the conventional meanings of the words expressed. Meaning follows in communications from the pragmatics of the actions engaged in. But enacting prior intentions is only a first step in the composing process. Definition of frame and context are only a necessary step in defining and saying what we want to say, but enacted intentions must adopt rhetorical intentions in actions to be able to move on and further expand on what the speaker or writer is trying to do and say.

Intentions in composing are then like all intentions in action. They grow out of the steady revision of intentions that are active in guiding the actions in the act of composing. There should be no gap in such a transition that creates expanded intentions. Thus, many of our new, growing intentions follow from the definition of prior intentions enacted in the initial definitions of aim and purpose.

In the defined frame of reference we now adopt prior intentions in acting out our aims and purposes in writing. They have now become active intentions in the writing process. Important, then, is to see that the frame of rhetorical intentions that we use guides the continuous working through revised intentions that continuously guide us in the composing process. Note that the linear sequence of these statements above about the move from prior intentions to intentions in action.

The expression of a statement that has satisfactory closure is the original focus of rhetorical intentions. But once we open up in making that original statement of aim by definitional expansion, the writing process becomes rhetorically open and continuous. Rhetorical intentions bind our framing of sentences to carry out the complexity of intentions that further develop as we proceed to express or compose what we are saying. What is important to see is how interpretations and definitions help clarify and make straight what we are saying. Note that the use of logical definitions focuses on clarification of statements. And note in contrast, rhetorical definitions are important in the expansion and framing of what is said so the writer can make what is said clear and understandable to a reader within the common frames of our mutual cultural understandings.

What are these sorts of actions in composing that I want to call the rhetorical definitions that I am maintaining are so important to writing? It is a mistake to think that language mirrors our thoughts. The relationship of thought to language is not simple and transparent. Rather, what we want to characterize is how our thoughts emerge from our ratifications of them in the language that we create. It is characterized by our choice and our selection of certain words that we use to do our writing chore.

It takes courage to sanction our thoughts as existing in our words, for at that very sanctioning moment we are saying that our words are "our thoughts." In doing so, we have put into words what we think. It is an act of sanctioning our words. And that act puts us in the power of others to be critical of the stand that we have taken in our words. It especially puts us in the power of other people when our words are fixed. They can now be critical of our acting and taking a stand upon those words. When we write, we place our thoughts in words before the critical tribunals of others. They now can say, "If that is what you think, you are wrong."

Or they can also say, "If that is what you are thinking, you are having problems about yourself and your relationships with others." We need to see that our search for meaning is finding words that we would like to stand by. In a way, that is what written contracts are all about. It is only when the contract is written, printed, and certified that the contract is in force, that we have walked our talk. We are finished in writing in making our contracts. We are finally satisfied and want to stand by the words that we have put into them.

But it is sometimes difficult to find words that are not open to the multiple interpretations of others that we would want to stand by, especially when we find that others wish to deliberately misrepresent what we mean. This is the problem that creates the demand and the need for law. It defines both our rights and responsibilities. In the law there is every effort made by lawyers to use words that we are willing to stand by so that we will be willing to trust the courts to protect us from those who want to misconstrue our thoughts and intentions. Thus, we need sanctioned definitions for words that we want to stand on that lead to expected judicial decisions.

My claim has been that we deal with language within language. It is a mistake to think that language mirrors our thoughts. The relationship of thought to language is not as simple and transparent as it is commonly presumed to be for those who think of language as a code. Rather, I suggest that we characterize our thoughts by the meaning of our words. And we consequently find our thoughts in those words. We find our thoughts in the words we ratify as constituting our thoughts. It sometimes takes rational courage to sanction "our thoughts as being in our words." They become our depositions to others on what we would like or want to say on a given day. Any ratification of your words gives you your standing in court.

The moment we say that our words are our thoughts, we have put what we think in the power of others to interpret; they can decide for themselves what we think. They can now know what they think your thoughts are, whether or not that they are obscure, consistent, or whether or not they are to be seen as distorted or disengaged from any basis in fact. We place our thoughts in words before the tribunal of others. Others now can say, "If that is what you think, we think that you are wrong. If that is what you are thinking, you have problems about yourself and your relationships to others." We need to see that our expressions in words are in one way, then, finding words that we would like to stand by. Their clarity is necessary if we are to make commitments with no blurring and misleading ambiguities.

Rhetorically, definition is one of the traditional modes of discourse. It is one that is used especially in paragraph development. But it has not been one that has been described simply and formally in rhetoric as a primary mode of discourse. The traditional conception of definition as a mode of development has for the most part been thought to be auxiliary to the other modes such as argument, description, explanation, and narration. We see this in part when we think of definition as a mode of development within paragraphs, where definition relates to the overall aims of discourse, especially in defining the problem at issue or where definition is used to eliminate problems about clarity.

But definition, as I have been reframing the discussion here, is even a more fundamental and basic mode in composition than all those other traditional modes of paragraph and text development in that it is foundational in coming to terms with others. We need to see that rhetorical definition as a developmental mode in writing in the field of the humanities, where it is used primarily as a mode in expository essays that presents arguments and explanations. As expository, it contrasts dramatically with the processes of definition used in the sciences and mathematics, where definition functions primarily as a logical mode for stipulating and creating technical language. In the sciences it is a logical mode that provides abbreviations for mnemonic uses of language that facilitate attention to complex descriptions and operations.

Both in the humanities and the social sciences there are rhetorical aims other than just explanation and argument. Rhetorical definition is especially fundamental to aims and intentions that concern the definitions of values and definitions of policy proposals. We use logical definitions rhetorically insofar as they are fundamental to systems of classification and other modes of modeling and organization. Definitions in this respect are mnemonic. They are fundamentally mnemonic in fixing concepts, leaving for a listener a memorable definitive gist of what is being said. I like to think that a gist is a memorable sound-byte summation of what someone said. Much of what we remember of what others say amounts to no more than a gist that is usually no more than a simple paraphrase of what they said.

But definition as a mode of discourse, besides having a mnemonic function, does many other things. It interprets, and it clarifies. It précises terms to make them applicable. It removes ambiguities. It describes ideal and goals. It expands on our ideas and our concepts. But importantly, it creates language to make it easier to talk about complex affairs that certain things could not be talked about without those new forms of innovative language. Importantly, interpretation and definition as modes of development, besides formulating gists of lengthy statements, may eventually lead to us to make definitional proposals that are logical definitions for the purposes of logical precision for words that we want to stand on. But dependence on strict logical definitions does not occur in a great deal of explorative discourse where by interpretation you are able to trace out what might be the implications of using different senses of terms. In rhetorical modes of definition you can expand on terms, making them literally more descriptive and explanatory in discussing complexity. But such rhetorical expansions are always continuously open to further interpretive expansion.

There is an important distinction, then, to be made between discourse that defines our prior intentions and discourse in which our intentions are a part of our actions. Discourse in its final aim and purpose translates our intentions into our deeds. In other words, in our performances and in our deeds we walk the talk. We have acted and succeeded in saying what we wanted to say. Note the difference between discourse that states our intentions to act but does not end in action. It amounts to no more than a promise of action, whether it is sincere or not; such actions have to be tested and confirmed with actual deeds. And in that case what we have done in promising is merely to continue to talk about talk that sometimes never gets walked.

If we survey all the groups, all the lobbying organizations, every institution, every school, every small organization, and every business, we see that they all are famously creating *policy statements* that incorporate their values and their judgments on this and that. Sometimes such statements are called their philosophy. Sometimes they state their principles. Sometimes they are formal statements of institutional policy. Sometimes they describe the role that such organizations want to have in a community. Such statements are statements of intention. They are mission statements. They give meaning to what a group supposedly stands for and the role that group proposes to adopt within society. They are promissory notes about what actions they will support if called upon.

Such policy statements are statements of intentions that they promise that they will act upon or stand on in action. They are not intentions in actions. They are intentions incorporated in promissory notes about what such organizations will support and act upon if called upon. They are prior intentions being expressed or reported as intentions. As prior intentions to action they are defined and formulated purely for public consumption. They are just a part of the institution's public relations announcements. They are simply their PR.

Contrast these prior intentions to intentions that are initiated in actions that already are carrying out those prior intentions. Note that a corporation might announce their labor policies, but such announcements are not acting out the intentions of those stated public policies. They have no force except a moral one, and many institutions notoriously have no moral compelling force for acting upon them except to retain their good name and to keep public trust.

But note the difference when such stated intentions are carried out in actions such as negotiating and entering into civil contracts that are backed up by the law, whose enforcement can be compelled through the action of courts. Civil legal contracts are the formulation of intentions in action that can be used to carry through on statements of public policy by organizations. They thus define intentions in action in the stated rights and obligations that are written into contracts that produce predictable results before arbitrators and judges.

Public policy statements are not intentions in action but verbal promises about existing prior intentions. On the other hand, civil contracts are intentions in action. They are intentions that are put into action by placing the outcome of action external to any stated prior intentions. Intentions are acted out in the making of legal contracts, thus making intentions impossible to retract. Civil contracts thus are actions that become deeds. They put in place outcomes and fulfillments that are initiated by intentions that cannot be retracted, as they result in events that are no longer are in the power of those who make them to change them.

Note that this distinction is comparable in ways to the distinctions in speech act theory between the illocutionary force of a statement and the perlocutionary act that results from that statement. We can promise without fulfilling that promise in the perlocutionary sense of making a reality of that promise. It would be a promise not actually carried out. Policy statements are always open to question about their sincerity conditions.

But to make a promise as an achievement we need to accept the obligation to keep it. And a promise is never truly a promise in a sense of commitment until the promised deed has been performed in the act of promising. And that is why promises are usually given with tokens of good faith that put up hostages to fate. It is the same as earnest money in business transactions. It is a symbol of good faith.

Note that these distinctions are not simply ones that separate motive from act. Intentions in acts can be a necessary part of acts that are being carried out. Note that whether we are talking about motives or purposes, we need to see that we know them by interpretations. Even though someone defines their prior intentions, we do not necessarily know if those intentions are made in bad faith.

For instance, if someone declares their love for you, how do you know that they love you, even if they define precisely how much they love you? Whether they love you can only be known in how they act toward you. It can only be known in situations where their love is initiating actions that show love directed toward you. Sincerity conditions of love can only be interpreted from expressions that specify forms of feeling and evidences of actions that the feeling is supposed to be initiating. Only then can the expression of feeling be mutually defined as love.

Note we have the same parallels in writing. We have prior intentions to say something, and then we enact those intentions by carrying out those intentions in writing. Our intentions in writing are interpreted as we carry them out in action. Rhetorical intentions are a part of the writing process as we embody them in our rhetorical modes in saying what we are saying. And defining and interpreting are two rhetorical modes that we use to clarify and make straight what we are saying to an audience. They are modes that we use in achieving our intentions about what we want to say. Organizations by law walk the talk when they act out their intentions by creating the deeds talked about in their talk. And it is thus the same case in writing. We carry out our intentions by translating them into performances in our writing. We do what we say that we want to do. It is there being done in the very act of writing.

PART IV

*Logical Definition, the Language
of Control, and Rhetorical Criticism*

CHAPTER 16

Logical Definitions by Class and Differentia

Logical definitions aim at providing us with replacement rules by which we can exchange terms without changing the meaning of the sentences. They show us the logical or semantic equivalence of terms in a language. Logical definitions give us strictly synonymous language. Strictly synonymous terms in logical definitions, unlike dictionary synonyms, are substitutional equivalents that permit the substitution of the defining terms for the defined term.

We can be confident that the only problems we have in using formal languages and mathematical expressions that define terms strictly or logically are simple blunders and mistakes made in copying and in transcriptions. Such mistakes as mathematical errors, faulty derivations, transcriptions, and miscalculations are in general just errors in calculation and mistakes in using rule-governed logical operations.

Ambiguities are not a problem in logical and mathematical languages. Well-formed formal languages are free of ambiguity. But either way, as expressed in logic or math, or even if expressed in standard English, scientific definitions are logical definitions. In all such cases we find that the term defined is said to be functionally equivalent or equal in meaning to the meaning of the defining terms:

Term defined (=df) is equivalent in meaning to defining terms.

Defining terms (=df) is equivalent in meaning to the term defined.

Such a defined relation is why we think of strict definitions as precise and accurate in talking about experience. We cannot equivocate with terms that are uniformly interpreted to have the same meaning as the defining terms. But when terms are defined, sometimes with seemingly logical rigor in English, they do not always contain the stable required meanings of logical definitions. Some people attempt to use logical language to define terms that in many cases in ordinary English cannot be logically defined.

In traditional logic, then, *the term to be defined* is called technically the *definiendum*. And the *defining terms* of the *definiendum* are called the *definiens*. In a logical definition the definiendum is strictly and logically equivalent to the definiens and vice versa. But the terms definiendum and definiens in themselves are not strictly equivalent in meaning, but they are simply correlative terms where each term is definable in terms of the other. Words, however, that stand for other words in logical definitions are still said by definition to be *strictly equivalent*. What is named and what is described by definition are interchangeable in all contexts of their use. The following are logical definitions:

Definiendum (=df) is the term defined.

Definiens (=df) are the defining terms.

In these definitions what the term defined names is strictly equivalent to what is described by the defining terms. What is important to note is that logical definitions are used differently, depending upon what we are doing in the name of defining. But note again that we can make serious errors in giving logical definitions for terms in a natural language. And reporting on them can be semantically mistaken and positively misleading.

There are practically many different ways of asking for a logical definition. The words in our questions may not explicitly appear to be asking for a logical definition, yet the responses we make to certain questions are usually presumptively expected to be given in the grammatical form of a logical definition. But these expectations about a defining answer in words using natural language that are based on usage do not always permit us to give strictly logical definitions. Most such reports can be easily challenged by counterexamples that use other forms of correct usage of such words.

The very narrow and restrictive topic of logical definition sets up the correspondences, the contrasts, and the counterpoint with the other things that we do rhetorically in the name of definition. Very rarely in rhetorical defining is the rigor of logical definitions sought. And to demand logical rigor in defining words in many rhetorical situations is to ask for what is impossible. It is only under certain restricted conditions—for example, in the development of technical language in the sciences, technologies, and especially in the disciplines, especially those using mathematics—that we provide rigorous or strict logical definitions.

We can also contrast descriptive logical definitions with another kind of logical definition, for example, *procedural definitions*. They are in a sense more technical than logical definitions based on defining attributes. But they borrow very much of their rigor and strictness from logical and mathematical formulations of definitions. But there is a distinct difference between a logical definition that is rooted in perceptual and conceptual distinctions and a definition that is rooted in a list of procedures that can be expressed mathematically in the formal notations of algebraic equations that are expressing them as a type of algorithm.

One method of defining procedural definitions, then, is through the use of algorithms. Algorithms can define and formulate procedures innovatively. Procedures are steps in a narrative that become important in the implementation of scientific applications in both mechanical and electronic engineering. It is of note that the term algorithm has found its definite defining description lately in the uses made of algorithms in designing computer applications.

But strictness and rigor are relative to application. We find that the names of devices, instruments, and machines are defined descriptively and logically by patent rights and by the technical needs to identify products and names of parts manufactured through trade associations. Many of these devices are defined on the basis of design attributes. And many of these patented devices are defined by descriptions of the processes and the functions in their use that can be replicated and produced by machines. Many are no more than instruments and products invented to accomplish sequenced or ordered tasks.

Note, then, that there are two different types of logical definition, one *based upon descriptions* and another *based on the invention and the development of processes and procedures that are best defined by narratives*. Note that there are quarrels over the legal issues of patenting natural processes, as some are thought to be cultural discoveries not inventions. What constitutes innovation in securing patents depends on what we regard as grounds for meriting patent rights considered as intellectual property, that is, property that is the product of individual human invention. Many definitions of algorithms are very innovative and creative. We create and generate algorithms that can be judged more or less favorably for their efficiency and economy.

But some of these procedures may be nothing more than replications of natural processes. We do not create them but discover them in nature, such as those found naturally occurring as in the fermentation of cheeses, vinegars, and wines and those found commonly in food preparation and food production. The issue raised about natural processes in contrast to engineered procedures reveals the difference between algorithms that are creative and those that report procedures evolving naturally in the uses of tools and techniques already a part of our inherited pragmatic culture.

Many definitions are standardized in and through governmental institutions such as the National Institute of Standards and Technology, formerly the Bureau of Standards. Note the amendments that are needed from time to time in précising measurements to meet some of the new advances in technologies. Units of measurement of space and time are defined descriptively. We have seen that the need for precision in units of measurement as technology improves requires more precise definition and refinement. And from time to time we have consequently seen a need for refinement of the units of measurement to eliminate variability. Note that given the wobble and variations in the earth's rotation, solar time now lacks precision for certain types of measurements.

Now our time measurements are in nanoseconds; a nanosecond is one billionth of a second. A need for precision on that level was found in nuclear experiments and the measurement of radio frequencies. And now consequently the definition of time is more precise. It has been developed out of magnetic resonance measurements of the cesium atom that are now used in atomic clocks. As a result there now exists an internationally agreed-upon definition of the second defined based on the magnetic resonance spin of the cesium atom. Sun-based clock time thus has been replaced in some spheres of inquiry with atomic clocks. Note how such new definitions are defined by different operations, and thus they are, to be redundant, operational definitions.

Logical definitions can be formalized in both term logic and propositional logic. *Term logic* defines on the basis of *classes, sets, attributes*, or *properties*. *Propositional logic* defines on the basis of *necessary and sufficient conditions*. Sometimes we find that logical definitions can be interpreted in natural language using the categorical propositions of Aristotelian language. We need to use two categorical sentences compounded by conjunction to express definitions in Aristotelian language. But in the use of Aristotelian categorical propositions, it should be noted that logical definitions are a logical compound of two Aristotelian categorical sentences.

[All S are P] *and the converse* [All P are S] is a compound form of a logical definition in Aristotelian language. As a strict, definable, logical form, the compound Aristotelian logical sentence provides us with rules for strict substitution of terms using categorical sentences. Using Aristotle's example, "All men are rational animals, *and* all rational animals are men." The class of men and the class of rational animals are identical. Usually, in logical sentences the exchange is between grammatical subjects and predicate attributions.

Logical definitions thus aim at providing us with replacement rules by which we can exchange terms without changing the meaning of the sentences. They show us the logical or semantic equivalence of terms in language. Logical definitions give us strictly synonymous language. Strictly synonymous terms in logical definitions, unlike dictionary synonyms, are *substitution equivalents* that permit the substitution of the *defining terms* for the *defined term* and vice versa.

In logical sentences in the natural languages expressed in Aristotelian language, the grammatical subjects and predicate attributions in the definition are interchangeable, or in Aristotelian jargon they are said to be *convertible*. *Comparably, in definitions in English in physics using the copula "to be" we have the same interchangeability.* "Density is (=df) mass per unit volume, *and* mass per unit volume (=df) is density." Logical form of definitions in physics provides us with a rule for a strict substitution of terms.

A definition can also be treated by a logic of classes, or in set theory as a rule stipulating logical or semantic equivalence between "combinatory classes or sets" *and* "the class or set named by the term defined." This equivalence can best be illustrated visually in representations of classes or sets graphically using *Venn diagrams*, which is the name of a *formal graphic language* that can be used to interpret sentences in the natural language. By using Venn diagrams, we can visually display two overlapping classes, as in figure 16.1. The two overlapping classes A and B is the same as the class named by the term defined T.

A *negative class* (=df) is the class of all things not in a given class.

Let's indicate a negative class by a tilde (~) in front of the symbol representing the name of a class, as, for example, ~ A. The negative classes of A, B, and C are ~ A, ~B, and ~C. A conjunction of a class and its negation constitute everything in the universe; in class notation, this is expressed as A & ~A = 1. (See fig. 16.2.) Note that everything in the universe symbolized by (1) is either in a class

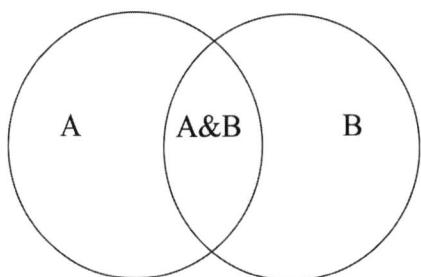

T=df A & B

Figure 16.1. Venn Diagram of Two Classes

174 • Politics & Rhetoric

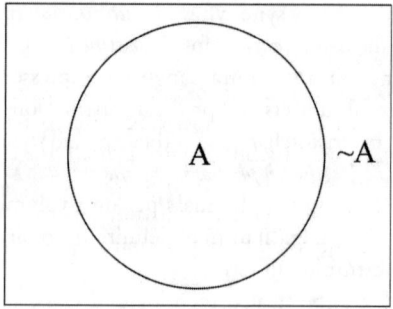

$$A \mathbin{\&} {\sim}A = 1$$

Figure 16.2. Venn Diagram of Complementary Classes

or in a class that is outside that class. Both the class of chickens and the class of things not chickens includes everything in the universe.

We can in mathematics also define the logical form of logical definitions in the logic of classes or in set theory. Thus, the class or set of things to be defined T is equivalent to the class or set of things that are defined by the class of the defining terms "both A and B" (A & B) (see fig. 16.3). By definition T has the same meaning (the same denotation) as things labeled by the class formed by the conjunction A & B. Note that a definition is commutative (convertible): not only is T (=df) A & B, but A & B (= df) T. Not only is a circle a line in a

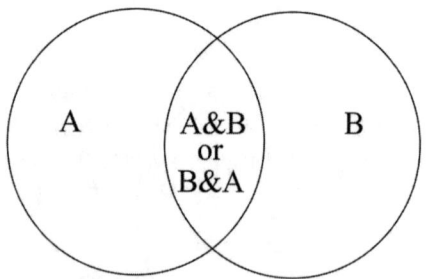

(T=df A&B) or B&A
T=species
Either A or B are Generic or
Differentiated but not at the
same time.

Figure 16.3. Venn Diagram and the Definition in Terms of Two Generic Terms

plane equidistant from a point, but a line in a plane equidistant from a point is a circle. Thus, figure 16.3 illustrates that the defined class T is the same or equivalent to the defining class A & B.

But, too, note that there are four classes exhibited in figure 16.4 by the two defining attributes A and B. They are (~A & ~B); (A & ~B); (A & B), and (~A & B). These four classes exhaust the possibilities of class membership in a universe that has only two classes. A Venn diagram by definition displays the conjunctive possibilities of overlapping classes labeled separately as *Class A, Class B, Class ~A,* and *Class ~B*. And these four classes conjunctively are equal to the sum of all the possibilities in that universe, as diagramed in figure 16.4.

Again in Aristotelian jargon the same relationship holds. *Species* (=df) is *the genus plus the differentia*, where T is the species, A is the genus, and B is the differentia. Species, genus, and differentia can all be interpreted as classes. It is important to note, then, that A and B are both genera, but not at the same time. But equally, the same holds as well for differentia, for both classes can be treated as differentia, but not at the same time. How we look at genus and differentia is a matter of perspective. It marks a contrast that is decisive in talking about the meaning of terms. This is a major distinction that, when noticed, changes our perspective about how we talk about and frame distinctions about terms.

In set theory conjunctions or equivalence relations are commutative. A & B is the same as B & A. In class and set theory, the notion of differentiating is thus again the same, a matter of perspective. Differentia are distinctions that allow us to divide a class into two classes. Class A is divided into (A & ~B) and (A & B). How you divide a generic term in a set of defining terms is totally relative

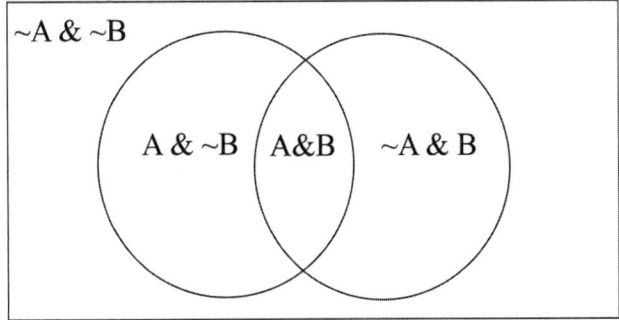

(A&~B) & (A&B) & (~A&~B) & (~A&~B)=1

Figure 16.4. Venn Diagram and Conjunctive Possibilities of Combinations of Two Terms and Their Complements

to the class you wish to divide by either a *distinction*, an *attribute*, or *differentia*. To define from an Aristotelian perspective we have to find a class of things A of which the species T is a subclass. We next find a class of characteristics B, the differentia, that distinguishes (differentiates) class A from the class, that is (A & ~B), leaving only (A & B) remaining in class A.

In Aristotle man (=df) is a rational animal. Man is the species. Animal is the genus. Rational is the differentia. We eliminate or separate all that is not the species, *man*, from the rest of the genus *animal* by showing that *man*, the species, is everything in the differentia *rational* that is also a part of the genus *animal*. Note that we can thus commute the genus and the differentia in "all men are rational" and come up with the same definition of the species. "Man is a class of beings belonging to the class of rational beings that are animals." In ordinary English a universal affirmative proposition "All S are P" is not commutative. Thus, *to be explicit*, we would have to add to the definition in English the commutative form of the Aristotelian sentence "all S are P"; that is, "all P are S."

All apples are fruit. But note that not all fruit are apples. It is therefore sometimes confusing to put definitions in the logical form of a universal affirmative "all S are P" for the simple reason that the terms of a logical definition, unlike those in a categorical universal affirmative, "all S are P," are commutative. In Aristotelian jargon, then, "all S are P" is not convertible. And it is only by presumption, and not by the logical form of the sentence, that we can convert terms in a definition that has the logical grammatical form of "all S are P." All men by definition are rational animals, which thus presumes that all rational animals by definition are equally men in Aristotle.

Note that in a logic of classes there is no distinguishing fact from fiction. To note that a class is not fiction, logic requires that a class have *at least one member that exists*. In logic such a notation that a class has members is called *existential import*. Existential import indicates that we are talking about classes that have *at least one* member. All men are rational animals, and there is at least one man that is a rational animal.

Note that all centaurs (=df) are men that are horses. But there are no centaurs, and there are no men that are horses. Note also that in saying that all men are rational beings in Aristotle there is a presumption that there are no other rational beings other than men. Note that if we were to define man as "a rational being" there would be the implication that presumptively there might be other rational beings such as we imagine in talking about faeries, angels, and devils. If God is a rational being and God exists, then it would follow that there would exist another rational being besides human beings. Man was created in the image of God as a rational being. "Being" and "existing" in these contexts are not strict synonyms. Note that like Bill Clinton, Aristotle believes there are different senses of "is," as he says in his *Metaphysics* (1941, 689). Saying that human beings are rational beings is nothing more than an attribution of a property to human beings, for there may be rational beings other than men. Thus, in that case, "men are rational beings" is not a strict logical definition.

Venn diagrams can be used to represent as many as three overlapping classes. Note in figure 16.5 that the Venn diagram represents three overlapping classes forming eight conjunctive possibilities of A, B, and C. Note that the conjunctive possibilities of any number of classes n can be calculated with the formula (2^n). In this case, with three classes, the number of possibilities of 2^3 is ($2 \times 2 \times 2$) = 8.

To define T as (A & B & C) means that we have three defining attributes of T. Note that a complex definition can have three or more attributes. The more attributes we have, the more rhetorically difficult it is to be clear in thinking about the rigor of definitions. In rhetoric there are psychological limits to how many items we can normally or easily attend to. And it is for this reason that when we start dealing with more than three items in a discussion we have difficulty in readily perceiving intuitively the large numbers of relationships overlapping classes higher than three would have.

When we have to compare and contrast large numbers of defining characteristics of a term, we need to overcome these constraints by using rhetorical definitions with no logical restrictions and limitations on interpretations. Rhetorical definitions are merely open-ended expansions of logical additions

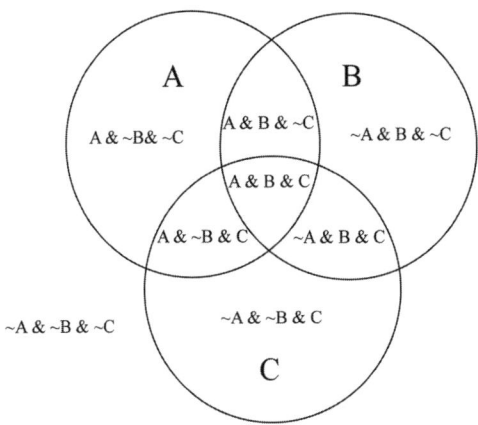

Figure 16.5. Venn Diagram and Conjunctive Possibilities of Three Terms and Their Complements

(a & b & c & d & e ... & n). But in contrast, psychologically, *dichotomies* are the easiest of the logical relationships to process mentally in our thinking. Next comes *trichotomies*, but things start to get too complicated when we compare and contrast four different attributes. When the human mind begins to compare and contrast four different items, the number begins to increase by the formula 2^n. Thus, when $n = 4$, the number of comparisons and contrasts is $2 \times 2 \times 2 \times 2$, which is 16.

When we try to hold more than five to seven items in short-term memory, the comparisons and contrast are difficult to image. Note that 2^5 equals 32, 2^6 equals 64, and 2^7 equals 128. Consequently, to deal with many items more easily in thought the human brain needs to chunk small numbers of items and then in turn to relate these chunks, using again small numbers of chunks. Note that counting is a simplistic way of chunking. Such is the rhetorical way we have of dealing with complexity. Such a method of dealing with large numbers of items is crucial to a rhetoric that wants to deal with complexity. Logically, we need to break up large numbers in chunks. Seven can be chunked into threes and fours. By this strategy we can reduce seven to three and four, reducing seven into two items, and in that way seven can easily be dealt with logically in short-term memory. Note that this is done in telephone numbers.

Note again that in logic a class and a negation are called *complements*. And it is easy to think in such binary terms. But logically, in our normal processes of logical inferencing, we much more easily assess the relationships existing between three terms, as we do in using the Aristotelian syllogism by relating two terms by means of the *middle term*. Thus an Aristotelian syllogism has three terms and only three terms. The middle term mediates the logical relationships between the two other terms. In Aristotelian logic this is called *mediate inference*, as opposed to *immediate inference*, such as we have when we convert the subject term and predicate term in definitions.

Mediate inference in syllogisms relates the subject term of the conclusion to the same term in the minor premise. And the predicate term of the conclusion relates to the same term in the major premise. The relation of the subject term in the conclusion is mediated in the two premises to show that the conclusion logically or necessarily follows from the premises.

All M are P

All S are M

Therefore, All S are P

The above illustrates the valid syllogistic form of mediate inference that traditionally has been called Barbara. Where definitions relate one term to two or more other terms, then logic can "mediate" between sentences containing many different terms.

However, traditionally, the logic of definition and what follows from definitions by logical transformations by logical substitutions of terms are called immediate inferences. We see this in the making of corollaries. We see it again in the grammatical transformations of indicative sentences when we substitute logically equivalent terms. We see this sort of immediate inference in the transformations from active to passive voice in grammar and vice versa.

But in mediate inference, logical implications are between sentences. Logical arguments aim to demonstrate that a given statement follows from other statements, and in Aristotelian logic mediate inference is always from two premises. Such a logical aim carried out by valid inferences is called *a proof*. In logic valid modes of reasoning from sentence to sentence are called *deduction*.

One can see that using definitions as premises in logical arguments, as in Aristotelian logic, we can derive statements expressing relationships between words or terms that are not easily viewed as intuitively connected. Consequently, it is important to realize that definitions are important, for they enter into our logical arguments. They importantly contribute to the logical grounds for the conclusions of arguments. And, importantly, it is a logical rule that we cannot shift the meanings of a term in an argument, for doing so makes an argument invalid. This logical mistake of using the same term with different meanings in an argument is called *equivocation*. And in this case we see that the definition of terms is all-important in determining the validity of a deductive argument.

However, when we try to use four or more classes using Venn diagrams, it is impossible to draw overlapping circles mapping all the combinatory possibilities of four or more classes in a two-dimensional plane. Logic to demonstrate a necessary or logical impossibility requires an exhaustive grid whereby we can logically eliminate possibilities to narrow the disjunction of possibilities, or even to show the necessity of the truth or falsity of one possibility as a conclusion.

Note the problem exhibited in figure 16.6. Our grid of possibilities in the overlapping classes does not exhaust the number of possibilities between the four classes and their negations. We have diagrammed four classes or four terms of attribution A, B, C, and D. Given our formula for logical possibilities between these term and their complements -A, -B, -C, and -D, we have 2^4 or $2 \times 2 \times 2 \times 2$ possibilities, or the 16 possibilities as listed below:

ABCD
ABC-D

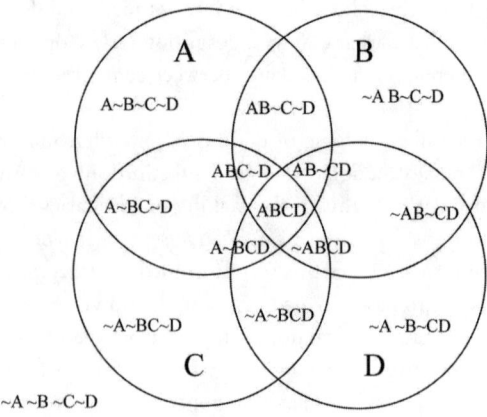

Figure 16.6. Limitations of Venn Diagrams with Four or More Terms

$$
\begin{aligned}
&AB{\sim}CD\\
&AB{\sim}C{\sim}D\\
&{\sim}ABCD\\
&{\sim}ABC{\sim}D\\
&A{\sim}BCD\\
&A{\sim}BC{\sim}D\\
&A{\sim}B{\sim}CD\\
&A{\sim}B{\sim}C{\sim}D\\
&{\sim}A{\sim}BCD\\
&{\sim}A{\sim}BC{\sim}D\\
&{\sim}AB{\sim}CD\\
&{\sim}AB{\sim}C{\sim}D\\
&{\sim}A{\sim}B{\sim}CD\\
&{\sim}A{\sim}B{\sim}C{\sim}D
\end{aligned}
$$

But note our diagram does not represent two of the possible classes listed above (~ABC~D) and (A~B~CD). They are missing in figure 16.6. It is for this reason that arguments with four possible terms cannot be illustrated in Venn diagrams. Moreover, in addition, it indicates that the language of Venn diagrams does not create an exhaustive matrix of possibilities over three terms, which means that deductive arguments using sets with over three terms are indecidable by the use of Venn diagrams.

And this grid with missing possibilities suggests that our logical intuitions are not reliable when we look at logical definitions with four or more defining classes and differentia in two-dimensional imaging. Definition in that case requires an alternative rhetorical mode, which I want to call rhetorical definition. Rhetorical definition as an expression is more descriptively additive than a logical definition. Rhetorical definition is a method of expanding on descriptive attributes. And as I have mentioned, the use of the term rhetorical definition as proposed is a generic term and includes logical definitions as a rhetorical species that focuses best within just three terms.

Logic that uses extended proofs with many premises requires a different and more complete matrix of possibilities than the one used in Venn diagrams to display the necessity of the inferences by an induction by enumeration or by some other process that systematically eliminates items in a complete matrix of possibilities. All logic thus is based upon different types of formally defined matrices and so displays all the distinct and defined possibilities. We use a matrix of possibilities by inputting premises into a logical frame to eliminate possibilities.

Premises thus in deductive logic function to eliminate possibilities in a logical grid or matrix and so enable us by elimination to arrive at conclusions. The display of logical matrices rhetorically necessitates for clarity about a great deal of complexity the use of models, such as symbols in print or in graphics as in mathematics or in visual diagrams. Note the importance of symbolic and graphical visual representations in math and logic. Such representations are tools for us to think with. And it is no accident that many of the elements of math and logic grew out of Euclidean geometry, which had its origins in diagrams and visual representations.

Logical conclusions are thus statements of remaining possibilities after we have eliminated as many possibilities as we can. Conclusions of arguments represent disjunctions of the remaining possibilities, or they represent a conclusion where there is only one possibility remaining; or alas, maybe there is no remaining possibility. Since our Venn diagram illustrated in figure 16.6 is not a complete matrix of possibilities, we cannot use it to eliminate and draw conclusions about remaining possibilities.

But nevertheless, any definition of T with four necessary attributes still can be defined by T (=df) (A & B & C & D). Note the complications, then, of definitions of over three terms, as in figure 16.6, with so many attributes. But another way to deal with such complexity is to use an ordered or a numbered code for each of the attributes in a set. We can thus define large numbers of defining attributes by ordered codes of letters or by numbers in an ordered set. This is the logic of bar codes that has made life so easy for merchants controlling their inventories.

What is essential in the definition of such codes is the significance of the order of the coded sequence. We can define an ordered set of defining properties by defining an ordering procedure, with each attribute to be defined separately so as to code each item in the given order. Essentially, this ordered coding is the practical value that bar codes have in identifying an item by its defined sequence in an ordered code. Obviously, we order words in dictionaries by an alphabetical code.

Ordinarily, the synonyms that we find in dictionaries are not strictly synonyms in the universal replacement sense of logical equivalence that defines logical definitions. But dictionary synonyms usually are terms that can be substituted to give a possible interpretation of the sense or meaning of the term as it is being used in a sentence in certain contexts. Sometimes we speak of them as having analogous meanings. The term *acute*, for example, is not strictly synonymous with *sharp*. We do not speak of knives as acute. Yet it is correct usage to say that "someone is sharp" is to say that "the person is acute." Acute in this context of speaking of a mental attribute is synonymous in meaning with saying that they are sharp.

On the other hand, when we say that "average velocity (=df) is the distance traveled divided by the time traveled," we can equally say that "the distance divided by time traveled (=df) is average velocity." Both subject and predicate expressions are strict semantic equivalents in elementary physics. Strict logical definitions by definition, as noted, are sentences that are commutative, that is, reversing the subject and predicate terms does not alter their correctness or the truth values of the derived sentences.

Note that many expressions in physics and mathematics are definitions and not mathematical descriptions of observable correlations. It is misleading to think that all the equations in physics are empirical descriptions of observable correlations. Many such equations are mere definitions. In chemistry the equation that the weight of reactants is equal to the weight of the products is an empirical generalization that was once basic to the conception of Dalton's atomic theory. It was a generalization arrived at by weighing the reactants and the products by experiment.

But density, on the other hand, in chemistry and physics is a definition. "Density" is (=df) "mass per unit of volume," that is, "$d = m/v$." Note that the presumption that the density of an element or a compound remains constant is itself an empirical generalization that for the most part seems true if a substance is homogeneous. That presumption again follows from observation that the density remains constant in the measurements of enumerable samples of materials.

And the fact that the density of a sample of matter varies indicates that the sample is not a homogeneous sample of a chemical compound or an element.

Such was the insight of Archimedes about the purity of a gold crown. *Eureka!* Thus, we should expect different granites to have varying densities, as they are fused mixtures of different types of metallic silicates with varying molecular weights.

Therefore "d = m/v" is a standardized definition. And also in mathematics pi (π) is (=df) "the circumference divided by the diameter," that is, "π = c/d" is a standardized definition. What makes each type of such definitions interesting is that from Euclidean geometry we can make deductions from definitions, for instance, that pi (π) is a constant that can be used to compute the diameters of circles if we know the diameter. Note we can reduce the measurement of the diameter of a circle to an algorithm that defines the procedure for calculating the diameter by first measuring the circumference and then dividing our measurement by pi (π; 3.14 or 22/7).

It is important to note that in physics, by combining definitions we derive equations that follow from primitive standardized definitions. These equations are thus logical derivatives of definitions and as such are themselves definitions. As definitions they follow from definitions that are simply said to be true by definition. Note that in physics that the distance an object travels S is the average velocity v_a times the time t. $S = v_a t$ is algebraically equivalent to $v_a = S / t$, from which it follows algebraically. And also by definition that the average acceleration is (=df) the rate of the change of velocity in a given period of time, that is, a (=df) $(v_f - v_i) / t$ where rate of change of velocity a (=df) $[(v_f - v_i) / 2]$.

From these equations that are true by definition we can logically solve for the equation $S = 1/2\ at^2$, which is again a definition that is logically derivative from the above definitions. But, if we were test to see if the rate of acceleration of falling bodies is *constant* by experiment at the surface of the earth, we can test the equation by experiment. We can test it to see if the rate of acceleration of falling bodies in a laboratory is a constant number. We call this the constant g. Substituting g for a in our definitional equation $S = 1/2\ at^2$, we have a statement of an observable empirical correlation, $S = 1/2\ gt^2$. This equation expresses a supposedly empirical observed correlation that can be tested in a lab, which is usually computed to be 32 ft/sec². The equation $S = 1/2\ gt^2$ can be algebraically transposed into $g = \sqrt{2S} / t$. The equation is no longer a definition. It is an expression of a description of an empirical observable correlation. It states that the rate of falling bodies at the surface of the earth is constant.

But note that the gravitational rate of acceleration theoretically changes with the law of gravitation. As a falling body approaches the center of the mass of a body by gravitation, the rate of acceleration changes. The rate of acceleration in that case is no longer supposedly the constant rate of acceleration that we are observing from experiments on the surface of the earth. Because of the inconsistency between the statement that the rate of acceleration is constant and the statement that the rate of acceleration is also changing, we need thus a new acceleration constant to determine by observation and experiment how all masses attract each other at a given distance. Thus, more observations and experiment are needed to calculate the forces that accelerate masses toward each other at different distances from the center of the earth. We can define that constant as the Newtonian gravitational constant. This new constant is called the constant of proportionality G.

Of course all this is elementary to any physicist. But the above observations about the use of algebraic equations illustrate the *elementary* importance in science of distinguishing between *equations that define terms* and *equations that describe functional correlations*, that is, the measures of changes in measurable experimental variables in experiments. There is a big cognitive difference, then, between a definition and empirical generalization in science. It is important to recognize this difference when we are trying to distinguish between the meaning of scientific terms and the use of those terms to get at the truth in scientific discovery about the regularities that we find in the ways of the world.

We should note, then, the interplay between scientific definitions and empirical correlations in tests by experiment. We should note carefully the role they play in talking about complex, observable descriptions of correlations between observable measurable events. What is important is the role that observation plays in physics and the difficulties we have in isolating and finding interesting factors that can operationally be defined and be subject to experimental control.

Mathematical definitions and definitions from chemistry and physics defined mathematically provide us with translational or substitutional equivalents that can to be substituted in one mathematical expression for another. Mathematics is a formal language. It is a formal way that we have of talking about complexity. But it should be cautioned, though, that we are interpreting these mathematical equations or expressions in English. We are using English as our metalanguage, and equally we are doing much the same thing when we interpret these technical definitions formulated in English in mathematics, which becomes a metalanguage for talking about English. It is important to recognize the dangers of *using English metalinguistically* to interpret the meaning of terms in formal languages. Such interpretations are fraught with all the ambiguities and the vagueness that ordinary English usage is heir to.

In many cases authors introduce very expansive definitions of their technical terms to make them applicable. What is important to note is that logical definitions are in the grammatical form of sentences. But definitions may require paragraphs or essays, not logical definitions, to be clear about many terms. To reiterate, talk about definitions has at times a wider and a more generic sense than talk just about logical definitions, and I have proposed to call this wider kind of definition rhetorical definition. Rhetorical definitions defined as such are a sort of the expansive explication (amplification) of the definiens that I have indicated we need to do in unpacking logically primitive defining terms. Primitive definitions are open to all sorts of ambiguities when the terms in the definiens are from the English vernacular.

There are several forms of logical definitions. In logic they are usually expressed by the operation (=df), which in algebraic notation in number theory can be expressed by the equal sign (=). In logic we can also express or define this definitional equivalence by class notation, that is, the class of the things defined by the defining terms is said to be *coextensive*, that is, it has the same members as the class of the term(s) defined.

But there are logical forms for talking about definition other than that of set theory or a logic of classes. We need now to move on and to explore another alternative logical way of formulating logical definitions using instead the logic of propositions, for in many ways the logic of necessary and sufficient conditions brings our thoughts of definitions better in line with the language of application and control.

CHAPTER 17

Logical Definitions by Necessary and Sufficient Conditions

Logical definitions can thus also be expressed in the logical form of *necessary and sufficient conditions* in the logic of sentences. We can interpret this language by interpretations using the logical terms in the formal languages of the *propositional* or the *sentential* calculus.

There are many forms and notations for these formal systems. There are various types of calculi with different notations. We can use these various sentential calculi and their symbols as a metalanguage to interpret the forms of the technical definitions that are expressed in the different logical or grammatical terms used in English to talk about the necessity and sufficiency of certain conditions. Keeping to the formal language of the logic of sentences, we can define the use of English terms such as "necessary and sufficient" by just one simple logical operator → (arrow), as used in one type of logical notation in the sentential calculus.

> By *arrow* in the sentential calculus we mean *by definition* (=df), [as interpreted in English,] that *the molecular sentence formed by arrow is not correct or not true only* if the statement that precedes the arrow, p, called *the antecedent*, is correct or true and that the statement that follows the arrow, called *the consequent*, q, is not incorrect or false. (In the sentential calculus a *well formed statement*—a grammatical correct sentence that combines statements to make a statement is said to be *a molecular statement*.)

This is all to say that the above statements are analytically true by definition, that the molecular statement "if p is true" and if q is false, it would be false that the molecular statement $p \to q$ is true. Another way of saying the above is that only when the antecedent is true and the consequent is false is the molecular statement $p \to q$ false. This can be interpreted in English to say that p is necessary to be q or p is a *necessary condition* to be q. And any other interpretation such as the consequent as false or the antecendent false and the consequent as true would make the molecular statement $p \to q$ by definition false.

Thus, the following truth table defines [$p \to q$]:

[p	→	q]
T	T	T
T	F	F
F	T	T
F	T	F

Arrow operator → is sometimes in logic called *material implication*. Normally we mean by *logically implies* in English that something *necessarily follows*. This sense of implication is sometimes called *strict implication*. Importantly, the two senses of implication *material implication* and *strict implication* by definition differ in their context of use. This is an important distinction in logic. Material implication is a relationship between sentences *within* a molecular sentence. But strict implication is a relationship *between* sentences as premises (especially molecular) and a conclusion in an argument (also possibly molecular).

Strict implication is in the *form of the argument* that if the premises are true, then the conclusion has to be true. Note strict implication can however be interpreted by treating the form of a valid argument as a molecular sentence whose the main operator is material implication →. The following form of argument, a strict implication, is called *modus ponens*. Sometimes this form of argument is described as affirming the antecedent of a conditional and thus necessarily affirming the consequent as a result.

$p \rightarrow q$
p
___
q

Let us introduce two more operators to our formal language, *the conjunctive* and the *disjunctive operators*. We need these operators when we talk about a set of plural conditions. We commonly use the ampersand for expressing the conjunctive operator "and" in English. But let us now substitute instead an inverted wedge (^) for an ampersand, and let us use the wedge (ˇ) for the disjunctive operator and define the meaning of molecular sentences that are conjunctions and disjunctions whose main operators (^) and (ˇ) using a truth table.

p	ˇ	q	p	^	q
T	T	T	T	T	T
T	F	F	T	T	F
F	F	T	F	T	T
F	F	F	**F**	F	**F**

A conjunction is true if the conjuncts are true otherwise false. A disjunction if false when both disjuncts are false; otherwise it is true. These definitions are unique descriptions of conjunction and disjunction. And we can go one more step forward by introducing the key logical transformation that is at the heart of the sentential calculus that allows for attachment and detachment of data in a computer. It is what is traditionally named as DeMorgan. It is the equivalence relation (biconditional) between conjunction and disjunction. The following truth tables display this equivalence. The truth value of the negation of a conjunction is equivalent to the negation of the disjuncts of a disjunction.

	~ (p ∨ q)			↔		~p ∧ ~q		
F	T	T	T		F	T	F	F	T
T	T	F	F		F	T	T	T	F
T	F	F	T		T	F	T	F	T
T	F	F	F		T	F	T	T	F
↑						↑		

With this amount of formal language let us continue our interpretation of *modus ponens* in the language of the sentential calculus. *Modus ponens* as illustrated earlier is defined by the form of argument in which asserting the antecedent of a conditional proposition in the premise makes the consequent of the conditional necessarily true. The form of the argument can be expressed as a molecular sentence $\{[(p \rightarrow q) \land p] \Rightarrow q\}$. The arrow is a symbol for material implication, and the "-->" is a symbol for strict implication. Material implication shapes conditional statements. Strict implication shapes proofs in logic.

This formal definition of a molecular statement that is generated by arrow (material implication) can now be used to state the correct form of logical definitions expressed in the logical form of *necessary and sufficient conditions*. To say that the statements of the defining conditions are *sufficient* (=df) is to say that if conditions are conjunctively false—for instance, p, q, and r are conjunctively false, ~ ($p \land q \land r$); that is, if one condition is not present—then the term t is defined incorrectly. And to say that the *defining conditions* p, q, *and* r *are necessary* is to say if any of one of these conditions, either p, q, or r are not met, then the term t is not being used correctly.

We can express sufficiency by a reversed arrow (←). And thus to say that a term is necessary and sufficient can be symbolized by what is called *equivalence* or the *biconditional* (↔). For a term to be correctly defined it is both necessary and sufficient that together that p, q, and r be correct or true, and that p, q, or r

be correct or true. Thus, the biconditional operator (↔) symbolizes the logical form of a definition in terms of necessary and sufficient conditions. It is to list the conjunction of things that are sufficient for something to be something, and as such the conditions in that list are the defining terms.

What is important, then, in the logical procedure of finding defining terms by necessary and sufficient conditions is to recognize what is necessary for a term to be used correctly and what is sufficient for that same term to be used correctly. We can thus interpret the logic of these conditions, not in the traditional language of Aristotelian logic that has been traditionally treated as by a logic of classes, but in the logic of the sentential calculus by using sentence schemata as placeholders for the statements of the defining conditions of a term showing that they are both necessary and sufficient for something to be what it is called. If, then, we have a set of necessary conditions sufficient for x to be t, then we can interpret the set of defining conditions as follows: *if not-*p *or not-*q *or not-*r, *then not that* x *is* t; *and if* x *is* t, *then* p *and* q *and* r *are the case*. In the sentential calculus this conjunction of necessary and sufficient conditions is thus called *equivalence* (*if and only if*) or *the biconditional*. Both notations are thus used to interpret logical definitions in terms of necessary and sufficient conditions for something to be strictly defined by a set of defining conditions.

In, sum, then a technical definition as a definitional proposal is by definition true by the logical form of a logical definition, which has the logical form of a definition either by class equivalence or by a set of necessary and sufficient conditions. We thus can state formally these substitutional, equivalent relationships either in the *logic of classes* or in a *sentential logic*. Technical definitions are incorrect logically insofar as they do not have a strict logical or grammatical form or insofar as the reported defining conditions are not the ones stipulated by those who propose them.

Thus, a definitional report of a technical definition is false if it is an inaccurate report of a definitional proposal that initiated it in the first place. It would be incorrectly reporting the specifications of the stipulated or standardized set of attributes accepted in the definition proposal of the technical definition. Note how circular it is to talk about logical and technical definitions. We can propose them or report them, but as statements they are still nevertheless proposals to use terms in an acceptable or approved logical or grammatical way.

Technical language arises from the need for terms to name and to talk about complex details that go into the complex affairs, patterns, arrangements, and assemblages that are found in the different disciplines and specialties. They function as tools for practical applications. We need them to carry on the communications within the disciplines, for example, such language as that of an oscillator, a Wheatstone bridge, a laser, a transistor, a carcinogen, a felony, manslaughter, the consumer price index, logical validity, and the binomial theorem; and the list goes on and on endlessly. All such terms are needed to meet the need for new terminologies in the emerging complex professions and disciplines. We use technical language to create and to name the important concepts and relationships in and out of this world to do the business of this world.

Technical language is the language of the disciplines, the trades, the marketplace, the arts, and the vocations and avocations; it has been adopted by specialists such as mechanics, tradesmen, physicists, engineers, economists, logicians, mathematicians, biologists, lawyers, doctors, merchants, and bankers, and this list will go on continuously as civilization advances. Logical definitions are practically necessary for work in all these specialties. It is a language that emerges from the division of labor that makes societies work together. And lastly, it is a language that has developed into a vocabulary that is bigger than what is found in any one dictionary. Let us not forget there are millions of trades and specialties that make up any advanced viable society or civilization. It is the politics of these disciplines (fields) that create new terms and that knits these disciplines (fields) together in a common language. As such these terms are socially constructed within these disciplines (fields; Bourdieu 1991).

CHAPTER 18

Pigeonholes and Rational Numbers

Note that we can label parts and put them into storage bins for easy access. The major analogy in talking about classifying is how we sort the mail. Mail has a mailing address so it can be directed to the proper box. Note that a filing system is based on different sets of attributes that allow us to store or access things with those specific attributes. Essentially, comparisons allow us to classify, to identify, and to locate. Such processes whereby we do these sorts of tasks are essentially just nominally position locators. They are pigeonholes with addresses. And on computers they are files and folders. And there is no end to how we use our imaginations to create names for files in our filing systems. And note how useful both cardinal and ordinal numbers are to name and locate anything within a system of codes. Note how locating things with attributes is the value of language defined by a code.

But it is simplistic to think that the value of numbers is only in their use as a code for locating things and putting them in order. I want to note that there are properties of numbers that escape many in the teaching of the elements of arithmetic. What has always struck me personally is that arithmetic was so confusing to me when I was in elementary school. It was only after I was in graduate school with a little logic under my belt that I began to understand what was so confusing to me when I was first taught algebra in high school.

Let me repeat a story I have told elsewhere that illustrates the important distinctions I want to make in studying the rudiments of number theory. And this simple story for me is a paradigm of the simplicity of the basics of number theory. And in talking about contrasts, it is only in my late dotage that I realized the importance of *rational numbers* in the development of science and mathematics. There is thus something of a childlike simplicity in the following story of what made me think of the simplicity of the continuity that there is between the teaching of elementary arithmetic and algebra in studying mathematics.

The beginning of my understanding of the elements of arithmetic and numbers started to dawn on me after a little friendly dialogue with my second son Steve, long before Steve started kindergarten. At the time I was aware that our definitions of numbers and our counting start from naming the cardinal numbers by defining each number named as a successor of a previously defined number by adding one. My concepts of arithmetic at the time had not progressed very much beyond that elementary definition.

I was sitting in the car with Steve, chatting with him one day, waiting for someone. And I was amazed that Steve was able to add at such an early age. Steve was demonstrating to me in the car that he was able to add simple whole numbers. I was surprised that he could do it, for I knew that Steve had not been exposed as yet to what were called "the number facts of addition."

It dawned on me after a number of right answers how he was doing it. He would pause, and then would give me an answer. The time delay indicated that something was going on up there in his head. Steve recognized that the addition of a number was nothing more than just counting up from a number, counting the counts until he reached a count equal to the number added. When I asked Steve what was five plus four, Steve simply counted up six, seven, eight, and nine, counting the four additions of one. Immediately I saw that subtraction was the reverse, that it was counting down instead of up, so 9 minus 5 would be 8, 7, 6, 5, and 4, counting five subtractions of one.

It dawned on me after that that multiplying, too, was comparable to addition in that it was best understood elementally as counting by adding tallies. *Tallies* is a less fancy word for *number sets*. I like the word *tally* because it can be used both as a noun and a verb. When you multiply, you are really then tallying a tally of tallies. First, you count items by making tallies of equal size, and then you tally the tallies by counting the tallies. To illustrate, multiplying three times five means that you take five tallies of three and count up from three by threes five times: three, six, nine, twelve, fifteen. Multiplication is revealed in our saying "five times three." Five times we add three. Note that once we understand times, we no longer think of it as a special kind of adding by counting. It is something new in name. We call it "multiplication" by definition.

Division seems a little more complicated than multiplications because dividing doesn't always come out even. But division is just the reverse of multiplication. We no longer sense it to be a special form of subtraction, but it certainly is when we think more about it. To divide a number you count backwards from that number by a number of tallies to see how many times you can subtract (take away that number) from it. We simply call it "take away." Dividing is finding out (subtracting) how many times you can take away a number. We take away five from thirty without remainder six times. In other words, you subtract a number a number of times from a given number, and that number of times you subtracted is the quotient, and if there is any number left over, that is the remainder.

But the major revelation came to me that division is the same thing as finding the number of fractions (parts, tallies, sets, subtractions) we can divide things into. It too is a new way of thinking of number counts. Division is the most interesting operation in mathematics in that the operation defines a type of number, namely *rational numbers*.

Note that all numbers can be expressed as divisions. Even cardinal numbers or whole numbers can be represented as rational numbers (fractions) with denominators of one. For example, 2 is the same as 2/1. A fraction as a ratio of two numbers is importantly a representation of division in algebraic language. And that was my big obstacle in moving from grade school arithmetic to high school algebra.

I did not understand fractions in grade school, and consequently I had great difficulty in making the transition into high school algebra. When I look back on how I was taught fractions, it is very understandable now why I didn't get algebra at first. I did not understand the logical grammar in algebra of fractions. Fractional notation or the ratios of numbers are an essential part of the grammatical syntax of algebra. It is important that we speak of ratios (fractions) *as numbers* so as to be clear about what we are doing, for a ratio can always be thought of as a division of two numbers, 3/2 is 3 divided by 2, which is the same as the mixed fraction 1 ½ that is (1 + ½). All are really numerical expressions for the same number.

We do not ordinarily think of the representation of a division as a number, but we do think of fractions as numbers. It sometimes becomes confusing how we think of numbers, for complex expressions of numbers are themselves actually numbers. Complex expressions of operations on numbers are, to repeat, numbers. Thus, the expression (1/3 × 3/1) is the same number as the number 1.

I had not considered in studying math the notion that operations on numbers are simply complex forms of numbers. It is the same as in propositional logic, where molecular sentences compounded from simple atomic sentences are just as much sentences as are simple atomic sentences. One puzzling shift in nomenclature from arithmetic to algebra was the shifting changes in mathematical operators. The symbol used for the operation of division in arithmetic (÷) was not used in algebra.

Moreover, the connection between division and multiplication is explicit in algebra. All divisions can be represented as multiplication of a multiplicand by a multiplier, that is, one number times another. We can always represent division, a ratio, or a fraction as a multiplication by multiplying the numerator of a fraction by the reciprocal of the denominator. The reciprocal of a number is one over that number, or that number divided into one. The reciprocal of 3 is 1/3. In other words, any fraction can be factored, that is, reduced to a binary multiplication of two ratios or rational numbers; for example, 3/2 is the same number as (3/1 × 1/2). And thus factoring, so important for algebra, enters into our operations with fractions.

But the important point to be made in all this basic simplicity is that rationalizing all numbers gives us a new and different conception of numbers, which helps us see algebra from a very different grammatical point of view than the mathematical schemata used in arithmetic that were devised for use in calculations that deal mostly with accounting and counting.

It was this key difference in the grammar of arithmetic and algebra then that gave me early trouble in the study of mathematics. Note that it was my own self-education in arithmetic that delivered me from my confusions and the damage that had been done in elementary school about how best to handle fractions. And today we are still making the same practical mistakes in teaching mathematics in making it sound more complicated than it is.

We teach computational and practical skills in doing mathematical problems with little understanding of the algorithms or the schemata that we are taught to use to make computations. In my day we used slide rules. Today we use calculators or computers. We need an understanding of the grammar of algebra to understand such computations and calculations, especially in solving the practical problems found on those standardized tests where we deal with problems in ratios, proportions, rates, percentages, and correlations and need to think of these things algebraically with ease and with facility in making practical calculations.

But it is only by understanding how numbers function in counting and ranking things that we begin to understand algebraic notation and manage to use it with any facility in dealing with complex problems of logic and modeling. Algebra is an artificial language that was created to understand how best we can describe things, and without that formal language those things cannot be described. Try describing the path of a fly walking across the ceiling without knowing the distances of all the points of the path measured from the walls and the ceiling. Math is a language that logically allows us to discover things that we would not ordinarily deduce from what we know if we talked about it simply in English. It would be all too complicated to talk about fly paths in the ordinary words of English.

The lesson I learned from Steve is that mathematics is simple if you try to understand it in simple terms as a formal language that has been created by definition. Note the following simple deductions from two equations: $1 + 1 = 2$ is true by definition and $2 + 1 = 3$ is true by definition. Logically, then, $1 + 1 + 1 = 3$ follows by substitution of $1 + 1$ for 2, and if you ask what $2 + 3$ is, logically, again by substitution of $1 + 1 + 1$ for 3, you end up with a tally of ones, $1 + 1 +$

1 + 1 + 1. You can simply count them as Steve did. There are thus five counts, which makes five. It is all so simple when you build up math cognitively from simples. That is the lesson that I learned from my four-year-old son Steve.

But there is a larger lesson still to be learned from my transition from arithmetic to algebra, where fractions are a way of representing a *contrast* between two different numbers, especially when we are trying to describe a correlation or a ratio between two contrasting measurements. The key to simplicity in thinking of fractions is that they are defined by an operation that tallies subtractions. And it is that relation between two elements, a numerator and a denominator, that makes it so obvious that technically *numerator* and *denominator* can be defined as correlative terms. They as correlatives are relating two different counts, or they are *correlating* two different measurements.

What is fundamental and simple is that the concept of a ratio, a proportion, a ration, or a fraction deals with the way we think in contrasts. A rational number does not pigeonhole something by a label based upon an attribute, but rather a rational number describes a contrast between two items with some seeming possible logical connections. Note how little it is noted that in mathematics, in talking about rational numbers, percentages are by definition rational numbers with denominators unstated but nevertheless presumptively understood. Sixty percent is understood to be 60/100. Note all the contrasts generated by pie charts and statistical graphs in making contrasts. They are ways of representing rational numbers.

What is important in ratios or rational numbers is the use of them in making comparisons. For example, in geometry we compare two ratios, and if they are the reducible to the same ratio, then we speak of them as a proportion. They are, in other words, comparisons of ratios where the ratios are the same. Note the language of double comparisons when we say a is to b as c is to d: $[a:b::c:d]$ as expressed in geometry or $[a/b = c/d]$ as expressed in algebra. It should be noted that it was in the early discovery of proportions and the simple comparison of ratios that we found the beginnings of modern experimental science and the early developments in science that tested for correlations, especially in early chemistry and physics.

But in contrast, what was important in the early developments of ancient sciences, which was especially the case in biology, was the coming to terms with labels. They defined by traits or by counting or by ordering with numbers which allowed them to name, classify, pigeonhole, file, and categorize in magnificently orderly ways, but such labeling did not give them a way to describe contrasts, ratios, or differences, which is what gives contrasting terms the power they have today to talk about our controlling events. Categorizing does not give us the language of sharing or rationing, nor does it give us the ways of dividing up the goodies of life according to any just or judicious calculation, as many say we should properly do in ethics, politics, and business.

Note that politics is all about dividing and sharing responsibilities and providing fair shares of the ratios that make up the ways we distribute goods and control the world. Politics is about making up the ways that we can live together with fair and agreed-upon commitments. And note that contracts and commitments are about the agreed-upon ratios, balances, and accounts of equilibria that are important to buying, selling, and living and sharing in different ways the good life with other people.

Note, then, the importance of correlatives in coming to terms with terms that are defined relative to each other. Such terms create a language that allows us to talk about reason in terms of rational numbers and rationally defined terms. It may be a play on words, yet there is some basic wisdom to saying, "Rational numbers are rational because they make things rational by helping us define the ratios of justice." And that is one of the basic axioms, to my way of thinking, that govern the language usage that we use in politics.

CHAPTER 19

Coming to Terms with Terms about Application and Control

Aristotle's taxonomy of causes formal, final, efficient, and material are essentially explanations of what makes something the way it is. Things are defined by form or by the essential properties that make that thing what it is. The way things are made are explained by ends and purpose. The way things are made by the agencies and causes that bring that thing into being are understood. And finally, things are made up of the stuff that they are made of.

Aristotle's four causes then are explanations about how things are made. It is a causal language that amalgamates our language of description with application and control. The shape and form of the pots are what pottery is all about. The potter organizes and includes all the essential properties of what makes a pot a pot in the making of pots. The ends and purposes for which a pot is used define the way we use pots. The potter with the use of his wheel and with his kiln brings pots into being. The clay is the material from which the pot is made. For Aristotle all four causes are then the things that make a pot the way it is. Note, then, we can from Aristotle's perspective say that all these causes are what make a pot a pot. And equally again, we can say all these four things cause a pot to be what it is. We can know pots by their shape, by the purposes they serve, by those agents and processes by which we make them, and we know them by the stuff that they are made of.

But then, when we move into the questions about human actions, it has also always impressed me about Aristotle in his *Ethics* that our acts in doing things issue out of personal qualities that we have and that make a person what he or she is. They are what makes a person the way he or she is. And in turn, those personal qualities as habits translate into the actions that issue causally out of them. But in Aristotle's *Ethics* this raises the puzzle in ethics about how being good so as to be good or doing the right and good thing in order to be good makes choosing to be good so difficult when one is so bad. Something more is needed than mere dispositions toward virtue.

Practical and rational modes of decision and action seem to be part of what it is to be moral. Dispositions lead to actions, and yet rational actions define good dispositions. It was, then, a part of early ethical thought and religion in classical and early Christian times that we do good things because we are good. Though we gain paradise by action, we importantly gain paradise by being good. And note here again, as in the Aristotle's notion of science, that we define virtue by character traits, and we do that by a logical definition in terms of properties of what we do in being good.

My likely interpretation here of Aristotle's views on human action in terms of the logic of properties and the logic of conditions illustrates my view that application and control are connected by the way we view the logic of definition in terms of properties. And in turn, we view in this connection the logic of definition again in terms of causal conditions and causal agencies. How do we keep rhetorically straight in our minds this division of ethical praise of individuals as persons for their qualities and in turn affirm and evaluate the importance of their choices and their deeds?

And when I think about this question, what has always struck me is that Aristotle's language about causes runs smoothly from form to function. His language moves easily from defining characteristics in terms of definitions of causes to the language of causation. It merges the language of descriptions of what our terms mean to causal language about the control and function that these defined structures have in making and creating and bringing things into being.

With the rise of science in the Enlightenment, Aristotle's sciences that stressed formal and final causes were rejected by the new sciences that stressed material causes and efficient causes about agency. As touted by the new advocates of the sciences in the Enlightenment, efficient and material causes were the "in thing" in the sciences, and formal and final causes were ruled out in scientific explanation. Note that this changed emphasis of the new Enlightenment sciences moved science away from essential definitions or logical definitions in terms of classes that explained functions. And their new scientific explanations no longer depended upon a logic of observation of the true causes and the forms and ends of things found in nature. The new logic of the sciences instead was based on conjectures about and refutations of the true correlations between the things happening in nature. The new logic was about hypothesis testing rather than the descriptions of things. The new science rejected a logic of essential properties, formal causes, and essences.

But this transition in the Enlightenment, I suggest, was all about a difference in logical focus on definition. And I suggest it was a difference that emerged from the change in the way we represent the logical form of definitions. Note, however, that the logic of necessary and sufficient conditions can be applied equally as well as a logic of classes both to causal explanations and to a logic of descriptions. What makes a circle when defined in terms of essential properties is that it is constructed and produced by drawing a line in a plane that is equidistant from a point in that plane. The description gives us a mode of production. Greek geometers thought of their geometry in terms of construction, and note that the essential description of a circle allows us to know how to construct a circle. What makes a circle is a compass that allows us to distend and to rotate a point along a line that is equidistant from a point in a plane. But note that we can equally use the language of necessary and sufficient conditions to apply our definition of a circle to the construction of a circle, and that also tells us how to make things go in circles. We know by definition how to make things circle. We define "around" in a frame of reference, and that is the kind of circle we make.

But let us use similar language to apply to the logic of definition that uses language to describe physical change. We can logically define combustion. We describe combustion of a fuel as being ignited and combining with an oxidizing agent. Again, we can see that the logic of definition in terms of necessary conditions allows us to apply this definition in causal language. It allows us to explain how we can start and control fires. The necessary and sufficient conditions for a fire, which logically describes what it is to be a fire, are what make a fire a fire. What makes a fire are a kindling temperature, a fuel, and an oxidizing agent. Fires are a flaming release of heat and light caused by the sudden burst of chemical energy released under certain conditions. And, of course, these conditions are the defining conditions of combustion that create a fire.

Note thus that the logical description of the defining conditions of what it is to be a fire can be applied in our formulation of the factors that allow us to start a fire, to cause it to burn, and above all to control the fire and even to snuff it out. We start fires by finding fuel, using combustible material, and supplying it with air. We know all these properties when we build furnaces, design firebombs, and deal with arsonists. It is all about application of our knowledge of what a fire is by definition, and it is all about the translation of that knowledge of application into command-and-control behaviors whereby we cause things to happen.

What fire language lacks for the most part is the precision and accuracy of the technical language that we use in physics and chemistry to make our fire talk much more understandable in terms of technical language. Note that in chemistry water is defined as a compound with certain chemical properties made up of atoms, two atoms of hydrogen and one atom of oxygen. Note that it is only a feeble attempt at humor to ask for a cup of H_2O. Our ordinary experience of water is not of water as a gas but as a liquid, and as a result, in our ordinary talk we distinguish between ice and water in speech. "What I saw was ice in the road, there was no water there." And note that it seems to be a play on words when we contrast chemical language with ordinary language and ask the question, "Is ice water?" Suddenly we note that our language is out of joint. Our notion of water is surfeited with all the notions of water turning to ice. And with the entrance of our technical language of chemistry into ordinary ways of speaking, the puzzle of ice being water is relieved of its puzzling opposition of meaning in everyday speech by everyone conceding that ice is water.

But note that there is a great deal of difference in ordinary language in how we think and visualize water as a gas. It centers on the problem as to what is being called *steam*. Is it a gas, or is it the condensing visible water vapor arising above the boiling water source? At least we see steam condensing and then evaporating as it disappears. But the presumption coming from science about water vapor is that it is a gas. Steam is something invisible. But what we see as steam visibly is only a condensation of tiny small droplets of water. But water vapor is invisible as a gas coming off of boiling water, and that makes it so damned hot. But note that physically, the temperature of water vapor actually, as we do in talking about dew points in talking about humidity, depends upon the atmospheric temperature. The temperature of water vapor is variable. Note that these are not things we observe and see, as we do not see water vapor. But we do assume the temperature of the water vapor is the same temperature of the air that it is in.

But I would like to carry this discussion about what we observe and see one step forward. Before chemistry developed as a science, we really did not have a concept of carbon dioxide. Note that in this case carbon dioxide is one atom of carbon and two atoms of oxygen by definition. Carbon dioxide is a name that has backed into ordinary discourse from developments in chemistry. And note that since we do not have ordinary experiences with carbon dioxide, there were no words that were developed out of our ordinary applications of words in dealing with it. Carbon dioxide is viewed from what happens with it in our talking about various chemical and physical technologies that are now said to be so important in our talk in dealing with it. It is from science and technology that the language we use to talk about carbon dioxide developed into practical applications in our present-day uses of it.

Under normal conditions carbon dioxide has no liquid state, as does water. We know it only technically as an invisible gas, and maybe for some by its frozen solid state as "dry ice." Note that we would not ordinarily speak of dry ice as frozen carbon dioxide. But note the chemical and physical properties of carbon dioxide are what we apply in our using it and talking about it practically. We can condense it into a liquid under pressure, but in doing so we never see it in inside fire extinguishers in its liquid state. And we can use carbon dioxide in various ways to make carbonated beverages. Carbon dioxide is absorbed in water, and that is the great danger now as to why our seawater is environmentally becoming acidic; carbonic acid is being formed by the ionization of the gas from the atmosphere into the sea water. And we know that if the sea warms up, less carbon dioxide will be absorbed into the sea and more will enter into the atmosphere from the sea.

Environmentally, the topic of carbon dioxide gets complicated, and thus we should note how environmentalists have a need to resort to so much metaphor in talking about the chemical compounds of carbon. Note their need to talk about the problem of global warming in terms of "a carbon footprint." Such metaphors tend to simplify the chemistry of carbon and oxygen in the biosphere and especially in the oceans and the atmosphere. But note that now, when we transcribe all these conceptions about what carbon dioxide is and use those definitions of it in terms of its physical and chemical properties, we can study the problem of global warming in terms of the causes and effects that too much carbon dioxide has in the atmosphere and the oceans. And once we have those definitions, note how easy it is to see how we can translate our definitions of our experiences of atmospheric conditions and the chemistry of seawater into technical language.

Note that now we do not have, as a result of the developments in physical science, all the puzzlement we might normally have in speaking of things from the terms we have that only evolved from the natural languages and that we have used confusingly about things that we touch and see. Everyday terms involved in the practical processes of everyday life are not readily applied to all the newly discovered technically described processes. Everyday terms do not easily translate into a language that talks easily about command and control.

What I am suggesting in this analysis is that definitional language and our causal language gets out of whack in everyday talk. It becomes dualistic and disjunctive in everyday speech, such as when we reify terms and reify causes into objective entities. We create powers and things that are said to be working outside our language with no explanatory connection to be made within our language. The result is empty and mythical terms that lead us far astray. But our language can be reformed and redefined. And terms and causes by definition can be used to describe the ways we actually deal with the world, and we can redefine our language in such a way that we learn about the meaning in our new language from our interactions and deeds in using the new developing language of science in dealing with the world.

But here again, I believe we see that in history there was a definite division in the way the ancient world looked at ethics and how they connected their actions with their language. The ancients focused on the ethics of being a good person.

It was all about virtues, about how their personal qualities were related to justice and how reason is based upon moral principles. It was essentially an ethics about being, an ethics about acquiring virtue, and essentially it was not an ethics that focuses on doing what is right and practical in the politics of everyday living. Thus, moral language of the Christian Enlightenment in Italy has its parallels in its developing scientific language for causal explanation, where we go from a definition in terms of properties to definitions in terms of causal conditions, which then allows us to apply terms to issues about command and control.

The key terms of Christian moral enlightenment were *love* and *duty*. To be good we needed to show our love and acknowledge our responsibilities to ourselves and to others by deeds and actions. To do that, we needed to interpret and define ethical terms such as love and duty, not in terms of mental states of feeling and attitude, but in terms of agency and causality. Love and duty are displayed in actions aimed at deeds.

What I have sketched above is my own historical perspective on the modern mind in its search for personal and private meaning in order to understand and to be able to do the right thing, which I believe to be the major project of the humanities. Humanistic study reframes how we look at both personal love and patriotic or civic duty. The language used in the humanities is the same used in talking about both private and public virtue. But in terms of word and deeds, the terms of the language used in the humanities are also about words that are applied in making decisions. It is a language about terms that are about agency. It is a language of words that enable humanity to bring about personal happiness and public achievement guided by such notions as love and justice.

Thus, in my view there is no dualism in either the sciences or the humanities between what we mean by words and what we mean about their application for command and control. And equally, in moral language there is no dualism between being good and doing good. We understand being good in terms of what we do (our deeds) to be good. Definitions of meaning thus rest upon applications that allow us to make transitions from notions of what makes things what they are into the language of command and control. It is about control over our own lives and control over how we should best relate to others, especially in the name of morality and politics.

What I have sketched is only a rough outline of moving from definitional language to causal language in the living out of our lives. The details about these applications are in our histories and in our humanistic studies. They are mostly about the rise of the intellect and about the advance of civilization. In humanistic studies it is easier to see in history a forest of progress than it is to see progress in the growth of individual trees. But in my view the hope of civilization is now not simply a matter of progress in the sciences, it is equally as well about the progress we have to make in humanistic studies. We need it for civilization to continue to exist. The humanities are about the success of politics in guiding people in concerted action through personal intelligence (Dewey 1938).

And that for me is why rhetorical studies are important. We need rhetoric as an adjunct that focuses on the language of the humanities. We need rhetoric to revise the language that we need to confront the problems we face that are retarding the advances of civilization. We need to see how the language of application and control is intimately tied up with the language of politics that sanctions our uses of language that we together adopt as usage.

CHAPTER 20

Interpretations as Hypotheses and the Contexts of Interpretation in Rhetorical Criticism

I was a radar operator in World War II on a B-29. The radar oscilloscope was called a planned position indicator (PPI scope). The sweep produced a ground return that reflected an image of the earth below. It required a great deal of inferencing from navigation logs and maps to *interpret* what it was one was *seeing* in the scope of the ground return coming up from below. To the uninitiated it was a scattered blob of orange, slowly changing globs of light of varying intensities, with a great deal of dark shadows, and there were even spots with no light at all.

Weather returns had to be separated from the blurbs of light returns from mountains and cities. Mountains and giant nimbocumulous clouds, for instance, had huge shadows behind them. Being able to read a scope required a great deal of experience to see the geographical features and to identify the rivers, lakes, and the towns that lay below. Water did not reflect the radar waves, so that the shapes of bodies of water were iconic and visible, with well-defined shorelines. It was easy to locate yourself around seacoasts, large rivers, and lake shores.

What struck me was the difference between *seeing* and *interpreting* what I was able to identify, and what eventually the differences between seeing and interpreting came to be called. Often it was said that we were "reading" those radar ground returns. My experience with radar was very analogous to a specialist in diagnostic imaging who are said to be reading an MRI, a CAT scan, or an X-ray, but sometimes instead, some speak of the reading as interpreting, or sometimes just simply actually "as seeing" directly the internal anatomical structures that are within the body.

At what point in the experience in our seeing of such images would we be accurate in calling our seeing an interpretation? At what point is the experience best called reading? At what point is the experience simply "seeing something as," as we would say in the seeing of someone or of something, as we do in pictures as in photographs?

From a psychological perspective, what the brain does in all these activities can be described as interpretation. But that use of interpretation is too narrow for what went on in my thinking about what I was seeing in that radar scope. I was well aware of the inferencing that I was doing from my navigation maps and logs in carrying out my interpreting of what I was seeing in that scope. On many occasions I simply confirmed what I was seeing from knowledge from my navigation log of my relative location, my range and bearing, to what I was able to identify.

Note we interpret photographs at times to see in them things that are sometimes not previously noticed. Noticing is a major point of *seeing as*. It requires directed attention to things not noticed before in our usual ways of looking at things. And the same thing occurs when we speak of our interpretation of the faces that we see in photos. We begin to see expression in faces not noticed before. And again, sometimes we say that we see emotions or feelings in a face. Sometimes we see the ardent look of love in someone's eyes when our attention is called to it. Sometimes it simply turns out to be only your interpretation, as someone else may not see it as you do. And possibly, what we see in the expression in faces is simply acting or mimicking. Facial expressions can be feigned. Note, then, the interchangeable way sometimes we say we see, interpret, or we read. How do we go about clarifying the differences in these meaning shifts about noticing and seeing?

Note the shift from what we think of as interpreting and what we think of as analyzing. Note again the shift from what we think we are seeing from what we see as a result of our thinking. Whether it is a true look of love or not depends on our knowledge of the context and the situation, upon our background knowledge, and on the causal factors that we are able to notice and to isolate in our analysis of the situation. Can we be confident about what we see when we interpret and judge what we think we see, especially where someone is feigning? Note that these issues are part of Geertz's discussion of the problems of the interpretation of ethnographic patterns in cultural studies in anthropology.

And the same questions can be asked about listening and reading what someone is saying. How do we have confidence about understanding about what is being spoken, or again about understanding what is being written down on a page? Sometimes we need to understand thoroughly the situation of writing if we are to interpret and analyze and to be a judge of what is being said. On the other hand, most of the time in our reading we do not need to slow down to reflect on what is being read, nor do we in our listening have time to check back and recheck in our memories about what was actually said, nor do we need at times to examine carefully what is being said.

One difficulty about listening compared to reading is that in reading we can shift our attention away from what is being said by looking back in the text to reflect back upon what was said. And interpreting and analyzing while listening tends to be a distraction, and thus it tends to make a listener into a poor listener. But in reading, we can check on what we think we understood by stopping and going back to what was previously read. We can check back to see what the words were that we might have missed while reading a previous passage. Nevertheless, there is frequently an issue about how much time we can spend on a text. Glancing back makes a reader a slow reader. I heard a book review editor explain how under time constraints he could give only so much time in previewing books to see if they were bad, mediocre, or good.

But note that the radar operator and those specialists who read X-rays and other imaging, despite their heavy responsibilities, have similar time constraints placed on them in their interpretations of images. And consequently, these specialists, if they are not careful, can, like busy editors, make great big mistakes. But again, when one thinks about it, for a scholar to be a good scholar or for a critic of visual or sound recordings to be a good critic, he or she needs to spend sufficient time to make sure their interpretations and judgments are correct by carefully rechecking to see if their interpretations have any validity. As a reliable interpretive critic one should not be under any time constraints about how much interpreting is needed to understand fully what is seen and heard. But equally, the same can be said for a literary or a historical scholar whose reading needs to be extensively extended and repeated to make certain there are no mistaken interpretations being made.

Thus, we see that the phenomenon called interpretation is integrated with seeing, hearing, and reading in the performances of tasks. And consequently, there is a strong tendency among psychologists to speak of *all awareness* as interpretation. But that sort of assimilation of concepts of seeing, hearing, and reading to acts of interpretation ignores the fact that when we speak of interpretation we do it usually as distinct and adjunct to our talk about seeing, hearing, and reading. And it ignores the fact that interpretation can actually interfere with different acts of seeing, as in the appreciation of art and literature (Sontag). It can interfere with our having trust in messages, and it can undermine trust in people with whom we have to deal closely when we are constantly having suspicions in examining and reexamining them.

Too much rhetorical interpretation prevents us from having closure when we talk and relate to people. Certainly, it is psychologically a mental health problem to be overly suspicious and paranoid in dealing with other people. To be overly critical can cause people to focus on peripheral points at issue. And again, we can see the same in skepticism and cynicism. These attitudes can amount to character disorders when people obsess too much on one thing only. Important then are the motives and needs we have for excessive amounts of interpretation. Some decisions that depend upon interpretation cannot be postponed. There are times when we need to act, and there are times to think about our actions. Note the limits we have on how much time we have, when we need to go about our daily business, to make up our minds about how to vote.

There are two levels of interpretation, *holistic* and *microscopic*. Holistically, we need to look at interpretations top down in construing what a sentence is saying, rather than trying to work up from the sentence to the meaning found in the text as a whole. What I am proposing, then, in this first instance is that interpretation, in order that we may look at the overall intention, be directed and focused on the overall context of the text as a whole. To read well, first one ought practically to scan and then later to scrutinize. And from that point of view we need to view the text in a context of overall presumptions about what the text is doing in that rhetorical situation. *Macroscopically*, we look at a text as a structure of sentences and terms making contributions to an overall text. Important on this level are both the semantic content and the overall contextual implications of presenting such a large amount of semantic content to a reader. What words mean in specific passages relates to what we are interpreting about what is going on in the overall presentation of a text in the context of its use. We shape hypotheses about what a text is doing in the overall context of use.

But a *microscopic* level interpretation, on the other hand, begins with words and sentences. Essentially, sentences are speech acts. We thus interpret what each speech act is doing and saying. And for that, we need to analyze grammatically and semantically how words are contributing to the speech act performances in the way they are said. When we begin from the word and sentence level, we view a text as additive. We build up what is being done and said as conjunctive, as a serial addition of distinct and separate thoughts. Thus, both holistically and microscopically, we interpret by using hypotheses on both levels of interpretation, macroscopic and microscopic. Let me now propose a technical definition of interpretation that hypothesizes about what is done and said on both levels:

> A *hypothetical interpretation* (=df) is a statement that is put forth as an empirical hypothesis that someone is doing or saying something in a statement or in an overall text.

However, I need to note that I use the term hypothetical interpretation in this proposal as the name for a type of hypothesis that tries to resolve differences of opinion about what is going on in a statement or in a text. It is a testable assumption about what is being said or done on both levels of a text. 'Hypothetical interpretation' as I am using the term is being proposed as a *technical term* for an activity that can also be technically called *interpretive criticism*, which goes on carefully in the examinations of communications on the basis of a careful set of observations and interpretations. Interpretive criticism thus equally comes in two flavors, macroscopic and microscopic interpretive criticism.

I am in making these proposals restricting the use of the term interpretation technically to narrow the sense of the term interpretation to avoid all the ambiguities that we find in many other technical and ordinary senses of the term interpretation found in critical literature. I am not using it to speak of actions in general, nor am I using it to speak of resolving ambiguities of nonverbal actions, but I am using it to speak of what is being done and said in communicating with someone in a rhetorical situation where the primary mode of communication is the use of language.

Of course, when we say something to derive the implications that an audience might make from what we say, we do it by indirection and suggestion, and, as I have already pointed out, it is not always clear to a reader what the intended implications suggested or implied by the author are. Thus, any interpretation of what implications anyone might want to leave with an audience is extremely difficult at times to determine. But if they were intended, it is again a matter of interpretation. On a microscopic level the intentions behind locutionary and illocutionary acts present us with a much more solid foundation of evidence for interpreting speech acts as having a determinate meaning. There are grammatical tags and markers that directly reveal what sort of speech acts are being performed. "I *promise* that I will never do it again." "I *compliment* you on your achievement."

If we describe the psychological process as interpretation, we are in danger of thinking that ordinary perceptual reading is as inferential as is analytic reading. In analytic reading we are logically inferring implications made from statements made. As I have described, analytic reading is reading in which interpretations are made in slow time. Analytic reading as a form of interpretation attempts to resolve what a statement is doing and saying after we have carefully weighed all the evidence and carefully thought about what is being literally said by the words said.

What I am distinguishing at this point is what goes on comparably with beginners in reading a foreign language, where they need to translate, not simultaneously but after reflective consideration, what is being said in one language by reflecting about what is being said in the other language. Such, unfortunately, was my conception of what it was to read a language when I took Latin in high school. Such translations were interpretations in the technical sense in which I speak of translations as bilingual interpretations.

But it is dangerous to think that the cognitive processing by the brain in the perceptual uptake of reading follows from the same sort of inferential process that goes on as I have been just describing in talking what the words mean in translation. However, for pragmatic purposes we do need to assume that something is taking place that is analogous to what I am technically defining as interpretation. But importantly, we need to note that different speeds of unconscious inferencing in reading takes place so rapidly that it seems to be almost immediate uptake. It all happens in a fraction of a second, so quickly that we cannot be conscious of the sequences or processes that occur in the brain, as we do in interpretation in the slow, analytic, and careful ways that we do in weighing of evidence to support interpretive hypotheses.

As we have seen, once we carefully peruse a written statement, constantly revisualizing it, there is no limit on the processing time available for the inferencing that is so necessary to determine what would warrant hypotheses about its meaning. But in linear perceptual reading, the time constraints on short-term memory limit the processing time, and we had better get it right or lose it before we forget it and then end up never knowing what was said, as our short-term memory lapses.

What I am recommending for the first stages of learning to read are the tested ways that confirm the strategies that are needed to improve our cognitive processes that take place in the perceptual uptake of the meaning of a passage as we read it quickly. But I will leave that formidable task for the most part to those dedicated to teaching reading skills in the language arts on the elementary level. What I am interested in here is that reading that involves reflection and reexamines reformulations and paraphrases. It is a slow time inferencing about the facts and evidence that are entertained by the interpretation and considered analytically. It is reading that takes place using interpretive hypotheses that can take days or weeks to confirm. And it is this kind of reading I speak of as analytic reading.

Critical reading is reading that makes judgments. It is reading that requires time for the reader to think about what is done and said. It is reading that tries to grasp fully all that is intended—and even much more than that, to grasp even what might be inadvertently said and done without any awareness by the author of what he or she has said and done. Critical reading is reading that needs to come fully to terms with a text, either to improve it in writing or to be able to deal with it as a statement or a commitment that is coming from someone else. It is to take up the challenge to see the text as others with good evidence might see it, or how we or someone else might personally see it in terms that reflect our or their own interests and beliefs. It is reading that requires an expanded awareness in the complete light of one's own understanding of one's own integrated frames of knowledge and one's own history, culture, and system of values.

Interpretation beyond the sentence level I have proposed to call *macroanalysis*, and interpretation on the sentence level *microanalysis*. The integration and refinement of these two levels of analysis in terms of each other is the hermeneutic circle. One level is used to interpret the other and vice versa. The hermeneutic circle goes on and on until interpretations are judged sufficiently adequate on both levels. The hermeneutic circle is merely an expression of the contention that interpretation is always open. And in that context of circling we need to see that in one way words in themselves are not ambiguous or vague. Ambiguity and vagueness are context dependent. We need to see that, although we speak of words as being vague and ambiguous, we carefully need to consider the ways in which we come to think of a word as vague or ambiguous.

If we carefully note, we see that words are vague or ambiguous only indirectly or derivatively from sentences and texts that are ambiguous and vague. Words are thus vague or ambiguous derivatively. We indirectly say they are ambiguous from the fact that they are embodied as words in a context that is ambiguous or vague. They are the words that are said to create or cause us to be vague in contexts thought vague and ambiguous. But a reader can try to get outside the context of a text, as often takes place in various types of literary criticism.

In *reader-based criticism* the text is interpreted from outside of its historical context. It is reading functioning now in a new set of presumptions about culture and belief. These new sets of cultural presumptions drive the reader into making new sets of interpretations. What is said by indirection and contextual implication are radically transformed by a contemporary reader's interpretations. The presumption behind reader-based criticism is the radical contextual historicity of all scripted texts that exist at the present time. If there is any validity to this position about our presence, interpretation takes place always in a particular space and time, and that location is what determines the outcomes of our interpretation of written texts. Such a view explains at least the historical transformations in Platonic and biblical scholarship, and it explains how these forms of scholarship have appeared to be open and endless as time has passed.

We need to look to the contextual implications of texts, to questions about style, and to questions about the role that *persona* plays in affecting contextual implications and affecting the style of a text. We need to do this both from the perspective of *intentional criticism* and *reader-based criticism*, especially if we are looking at a text historically. Reader-based criticism must be first and above all looked at as a literary theory of interpretation. Insofar as I am primarily interested in rhetoric by which an author communicates directly with readers, the text is not easily stripped of its historical rhetorical context as I deal with it. For that reason, reader-based criticism is not a justifiable form of criticism if the perspective we take is treating a text as a piece of rhetoric. It abandons any criteria for evaluating the rhetoric in the text's original rhetorical situation that by nature is always a unique situation.

Of course, a reader may look on himself or herself as not a part of the audience that is presumed to be contextualized in a text. In this case the reader stands above the rhetorical situation and views the text externally as a piece of rhetoric in a cultural context different from his or her own. Thus, rhetorical criticism can stand historically apart from a text and assess it from values and norms that are contemporary with the rhetorical critic. In this case we are not judging the rhetoric of the text internal to its own rhetorical purposes. Rather, what we are judging is the value of its rhetoric from contemporary moral and political points of view.

Thus, we see that rhetorical criticism that is anchored in contemporary moral and political viewpoints abandons what might be thought neutral rhetorical criteria for assessing the value of a piece of rhetoric as rhetoric with an aim or purpose. It takes sides for or against the author from contemporary perspectives and not from aims and purposes within the author's perspective. The basis of interpreting ambiguities, vagueness, and omissions thus in the final analysis keeps shifting with changes in our historical perspectives about what we read and write. And to adopt that view of interpreting we necessarily have to take a stance on our own personal concept of ourselves and the culture and language that we live in with the recognition that historically our culture and language will in the end eventually change.

References

American Psychiatric Association. 2000. *DSM-IV-TR: Diagnostic and statistical manual of mental disorders*. 4th edition. Arlington, VA: American Psychiatric Association.
Aristotle. 1941. *The basic works of Aristotle: "Categories," "On interpretation," "Prior analytics," "Posterior analytics," "Topics," "On sophistical refutations," "Nicomachean ethics," "Politics," "Rhetoric," "Metaphysics," and "Poetics*. Ed. Richard McKeon. New York: Random House.
Austin, J. L. 1962. *How to do things with words*. Cambridge, MA: Harvard University Press.
———. 1970. *Philosophical papers*. Ed. J. O. Urmson and G. J. Warnock. 2nd ed. Oxford: Oxford University Press.
Bacon, Sir Francis. 1955. *Novum organum*. Chicago: Encyclopedia Britannica.
Barthes, Roland. 1988. *The semiotic challenge*. Trans. Richard Howard. New York: Hill and Wang.
Baudrillard, Jean. 1968. *Le système des objets*. Paris: Gallimard.
———. 1981. *For a critique of the political economy of the sign*. Trans. Charles Levin. St. Louis, MO: Telos Press.
Bayard, Pierre. 2007. *How to talk about books you haven't read*. Trans. Jeffrey Mehlman. New York: Bloomsbury.
Beardsley, Monore C. 1950. *Thinking straight: A guide to readers and writers*. New York: Prentice Hall.
———. 1958. *Aesthetics: The problems in the philosophy of criticism*. New York: Harcourt, Brace, and World.
———. 1966. *Thinking straight: Principles of reasoning for readers and writers*. 4th ed. Englewood Cliffs, NJ: Prentice Hall.
———. 2007. *Thinking straight*. Amherst, NJ: Oliphant Press.
Bitzer, Lloyd. 1968. The rhetorical situation. *Philosophy and Rhetoric* 1 (January 1968), 1–14.
Black, Max. 1949. *Language and philosophy: Studies in method*. Ithaca, NY: Cornell University Press.
———. 1962a. *Models and metaphors: Studies in the philosophy of language*. Ithaca, NY: Cornell University Press.
———, ed. 1962b. *The importance of language*. Englewood Cliffs, NJ: Prentice-Hall.
Bloom, Allan. 1987. *Closing of the American mind*. New York: Simon and Schuster.
Bloomfield, Leonard. 1933. *Language*. New York: Henry Holt.
Booth, Wayne. 1961. *The rhetoric of fiction*. Chicago: University of Chicago Press.

———. 1978. *Modern dogma and the rhetoric of assent.* Notre Dame, IN: University of Notre Dame Press.

———. 1979. *Critical understanding: The powers and limits of pluralism.* Chicago: University of Chicago Press.

———. 2004. *The rhetoric of rhetoric: The quest for effective communication.* Oxford: Blackwell.

Bourdieu, Pierre. 1991. *Language and symbolic power* Cambride, MA: Harvard University Press.

Bridgeman, P. W. 1927. *The logic of modern physics.* New York: Macmillan.

Brooks, Cleanth. 1947. *The well wrought urn: Studies in the structure of poetry.* New York: Reynaland Hitchcock.

Brummett, Barry. 2003. *The world and how we describe it: Rhetorics of reality, representation, simulation.* Westport, CT: Prager.

Bruner, Jerome. 1990. *Acts of meaning.* Cambridge, MA: Harvard University Press.

———. 2002. *Making stories: law, literature, life.* New York: Farrar, Straus, and Giroux.

Burke, Kenneth. 1965. *Permanence and change: an anatomy of purpose.* Indianapolis, IN: The Library of Liberal Arts.

———. 1966. *Language as symbolic action: essays on life, literature, and method.* Berkeley, CA: University of California Press.

———. 1969a. *A grammar of motives.* Berkeley, CA: University of California Press.

———. 1969b. *A rhetoric of motives.* Berkeley, CA: University of California Press.

Butchvarov. 1970. *The concept of knowledge.* Evanston, IL: Northwestern University Press.

Carnap, Rudolph. 1935. *The logical syntax of language.* London: Psychical Miniatures.

———. 1948. *Introduction to semantics.* Cambridge, MA: Harvard University Press.

———. 1969. *The logical structure of the world and pseudo problems of philosophy.* Berkley, CA: University of California Press.

Cassirer, Ernst. 1979. *Symbol, myth, and culture: Essays and lectures of Ernst Cassirer, 1935–1945.* Ed. Donald Phillip Verene. New Haven: Yale University Press.

Cicero, Marcus Tullius. 1986. *Cicero on oratory and orators.* Trans. J. S. Watson.

Cole, Peter, and Jerry L. Morgan, eds. 1975. *Speech Acts.* Vol. 3 of *Syntax and semantics.* New York: Academic Press.

Corbett, Edward P. J. 1999. *Classical rhetoric for the modern student.* 4th ed. Oxford: Oxford University Press.

Croce, Benedetto. 1963. *Aesthetics and science of expression and general linguistic.* Trans. Douglas Ainslie. New York: Noonday Press.

Crystal, David. 2008a. *Think on my words: exploring Shakespeare's language.* Cambridge, UK: Cambridge University Press.

———. 2008b. *By hook or by crook: A journey in search of English.* New York: The Overlook Press.

———. 2005. *How language works: How babies babble, words change meaning, and languages live and die.* New York: Penguin Group.

———. 1997. *The Cambridge encyclopedia of language.* 2nd ed. Cambridge, UK: Cambridge University Press.

Davidson, Donald. 2001. *Inquiries into truth and interpretation*. 2nd ed. Oxford, UK: Clarendon Press.
Derrida, Jacques. 1974. *Of grammatology*. Baltimore, MD: John Hopkins University Press.
———. 1978. *Writing and difference*. Trans. Alan Bass. Chicago: University of Chicago Press.
Dewey, John. 1929. *The quest for certainty: A study of the relation of knowledge to action*. New York: C. P. Putnam's and Sons.
Dewey, John. 1938. *Logic: The Theory of Inquiry*. New York: Henry Holt and Company.
Ducrot, Oswald, and Tzvetan Todorov. 1979. *Encyclopedic dictionary of the sciences of language*. Trans. Catherine Porter. Baltimore, MD: John's Hopkins University Press.
Eco, Umberto. 1992. *Interpretation and overinterpretation*. With Richard Rorty, Jonathan Culler, and Christine Brooke-Rose. Ed. Stefan Collini. New York: Cambridge University Press.
Empson, William. 1930. *Seven types of ambiguity*. London: Chato and Windus.
Fowler, Henry Watson 1926. *A Dictionary of Modern English Usage* (1st ed.). Oxford: Clarendon Press.
Frankfurt, Harry G. 2005. *On bullshit*. Princeton, NJ: Princeton University Press.
Gadamer, Hans-Georg. 1994. *Truth and method*. Trans. Joel Weinsheimer and Donald G. Marshall. New York: Continuum.
Gaonkar, Dilip P. 1993. The idea of rhetoric in the rhetoric of science. *Southern Communication Journal* 58:258–95.
Geertz, Clifford. 1973. *The interpretation of culture: selected essays*. New York: Basic Books.
Goffman, Erving. 1959. *The presentation of self in everyday life*. Garden City, NJ: Anchor Books Edition.
———. 1974. *Frame analysis: An essay on the organization of experience*. Cambridge, MA: Harvard University Press.
Gove, Philip Babcock, ed. 1961. *Webster's third new international dictionary of the English language unabridged*. Springfield, MA: Merriam-Webster Inc.
Grice, Paul. 1989. *Studies in the way of words*. Cambridge, MA: Harvard University Press.
Habermas, Jürgen. 1987. *The philosophical discourse of modernity: Twelve lectures*. Cambridge, MA: MIT Press.
———. 1991. *The structural transformation of the public sphere: An inquiry into a category of bourgeois society*. Trans. Thomas Burger. Cambridge, MA: MIT Press.
Hartshorne, Charles. 1948. *The divine relativity: A social conception of God*. New Haven: Yale University Press.
Heidegger, Martin. 1962. *Being and time*. Trans. Jody Macquarrie and Edward Robinson. San Francisco: Harper.
Hirsch, E. D. 1967. *Validity and interpretation*. New Haven, CT: Yale University Press.
———. 1981. *The philosophy of composition*. Chicago: University of Chicago Press.

———. 1988. *Cultural literacy: What every American needs to know*. New York: Vintage Books.
Hume, David. 1739. *A Treatise of Human Nature*. Oxford: Oxford University Press.
Huxley, Aldous. 1940. *Words and their meanings*. Los Angeles: Jake Zeitlin.
Johnson, Ralph H. 1996. *The rise of informal logic: Essays on argumentation, critical thinking, reasoning, and politics*. Newport, VA: Vale Press.
Joseph, Sister Miriam. 2002. *The trivium: The liberal arts of logic, grammar, and rhetoric*. Philadelphia: Paul Dry.
Kant, Immanuel. 1781. *Critique of Pure Reason*. Cambridge: Cambridge University Press.
Kennedy, George. 1980. *Classical rhetoric and its Christian and secular tradition from ancient to modern times*. Chapel Hill: University of North Carolina Press.
Kinneavy, James L. 1971. *A theory of discourse: The aims of discourse*. Englewood Cliffs, NJ: Prentice-Hall.
Kirsten, Malmkjaer, ed. n.d. *The linguistics encyclopedia*. London: Routledge.
Kneale, William, and Martha Kneale. 1962. *The development of logic*. London: Oxford University Press.
Korzybski, Alfred. 1933. *Science and sanity: An introduction to non-Aristotelian systems and general semantics*. Lancaster, PA: Science Press.
Kripke, Saul A. 1980. Naming and necessity. Cambridge, MA: Harvard University Press.
Kuhn, Thomas S. 1996. *The structure of scientific revolutions*. 3rd ed. Chicago: University of Chicago Press. (Orig. pub. 1962.)
Lakoff, George, and Mark Johnson. 1980. *Metaphors we live by*. Chicago: University of Chicago Press.
Langer, Suzanne. 1942. *Philosophy in a new key: A study in the symbolism of reason, rite, and art*. Cambridge, MA: Harvard University Press.
Leff, Michael. 2000. Rhetorical disciplines and rhetorical disciplinarity: A response to Mailloux. *Rhetoric Society Quarterly* 30 (4):83–93.
McDowell, John. 1994. *Mind and the world*. Cambridge, MA: Harvard University Press.
McKeon, Richard. 1987. *Rhetoric: Essays in invention and discovery*. Ed. Mark Backman. Woodridge, CT: Ox Bow Press.
McLuhan, Marshal. 1967. *Understanding media: The extensions of man*. New York: Bantam Books.
Mead, George Herbert. 1932. *The Philosophy of the Present*. Ed. Arthur E. Murray. Chicago: Open Court.
———. 1934. *Mindself-and society: From the standpoint of the behaviorist*. Ed. Charles W. Morris. Chicago: University of Chicago Press.
Mailloux, Steven. 2000. Disciplining identities: On the rhetorical paths between English and communication studies. *Rhetoric Society Quarterly* 30 (2): 5–29.
McCloskey, Deidre. 1997. Big rhetoric, little rhetoric: Gaonkar on the rhetoric of science. In *Rheorical Hermeneutics: Invention and Interpretation in the Age of Science*, ed.

Alan Gross and William M. Keith, 101–12. Albany: State University of New York Press.

Menand, Louis. 1997. *Pragmatism: A reader.* New York: Vintage.

———. 2002. *The metaphysical club: A story of ideas in America.* New York: Farrar, Straus, and Giroux.

Morehead, Philip D. 2002. *New American Roget's college thesaurus in dictionary form.* New York: Penguin.

Morris, Charles W. 1938. *Foundation of the theory of signs.* Vol. 1, no. 2 of *Encyclopedia of unified science.* Chicago: University of Chicago Press.

———. 1946. *Signs, language, and behavior.* New York: Prentice-Hall.

Ogden, C. K., and I. A. Richards. 1947. *The meaning of meaning: A study of the influence of language upon thought and the science of symbolism.* New York: Harcourt, Brace.

Palmer, Richard E. 1969. *Hermeneutics: Interpretation theory in Schleiermacher, Dilthey, Heidegger, and Gadamer.* Evanston, IL: Northwestern University Press.

Panofsky, Erwin. 1955. *Meaning in the visual arts.* Garden City, NY: Anchor Books.

Peirce, Charles Sanders. 1960. *Collected papers of Charles Sanders Peirce.* Vol. 1, *Principles of philosophy*, Vol. 2, *Elements of logic.* Ed. Charles Hartshorne and Paul Weiss. Cambridge, MA: Belknap Press of Harvard University Press.

Perlman, Chaim, and L. Olbrechts-Tyteca. 1968. *The new rhetoric: A treatise on argumentation.* Trans. John Wilkenson and Purcell Weaver. Notre Dame, IN: University of Notre Dame Press.

Petraglia, Josep. 2003. Identity Crisis: Rhetoric as a pedagogic and as epistemic discipline. In *The realms of rhetoric: The prospects for rhetoric education.* New York: State University of New York Press, 151–70.

Pinker, Steven. 2007. *The language instinct: How the mind creates language.* New York: Harper Perennial.

Plato. 1969. *The collected dialogues of Plato: "Republic," "Euthyphro," "Phaedo," and "Phaedrus."* Ed. Edith Hamilton and Huntington Cairns. Princeton, NJ: Princeton University Press.

Polanyi, Michael. 1958. *Personal knowledge: Towards a post-critical philosophy.* New York: Torch Books.

Popper, Karl. 1959. *The logic of scientific discovery.* London: Hutchitson.

———. 1963. *Conjectures and refutations: The growth of scientific knowledge.* London: Routledge and Kegan Paul.

Quine, Willard Van Orman. 1953. *From a logical point of view: Logico-philosophical essays.* Cambridge, MA: Harvard University Press.

———. 1960. *Word and object.* Cambridge, MA: MIT Press.

———. 1981. *Theories and things.* Cambridge, MA: Harvard University Press.

Richards, I. A. 1965. *The philosophy of rhetoric.* New York: Oxford University Press.

Rorty, Richard. 1982. *Philosophy and the mirror of nature.* Princeton, NJ: Princeton University Press.

———. 1998. *Truth and progress.* Vol. 3 of *Philosophical papers.* Cambridge, UK: Cambridge University Press.

Saddock, Jerrold M. 1974. *Toward a linguistic theory of speech acts*. New York: Academic Press.

Safire, William. 2003. *No uncertain terms: More writing from the popular "On language" column in The New York Times Magazine*. New York: Simon & Shuster.

Saussure, Ferdinand de. 1972. *Course in general linguistics*. Trans. Roy Harris. LaSalle, IL: Open Court.

Schiappa, Edward. 2003. *Defining reality: Definitions and the politics of meaning*. Carbondale, IL: Southern Illinois University Press.

———. 2001. Second thoughts on the critiques of big rhetoric. *Philosophy and Rhetoric* 34 (3): 260–74.

Scott, Robert L. 1967. On viewing rhetoric as epistemic. *Central States Speech Journal* 18:9–16.

———. 1976. On viewing rhetoric as epistemic: Ten years later. *Central States Speech Journal* 27:258–66.

Searle, John. 1969. *Speech acts: An essay in the philosophy of language*. Cambridge, UK: Cambridge University Press.

———. 1995. *Construction of social reality*. New York: Simon and Schuster.

Sontag, Susan. 1966. *Against interpretation*. New York: Dell Publishing.

Sperber, Dan, and Deirdre Wilson. 1986. *Relevance: Communication and cognition*. Cambridge, MA: Harvard University Press.

Stevenson, Charles L. 1944. *Ethics and language*. New Haven, CT: Yale University Press.

Tarski, Alfred. 1941. *Introduction to logic and to the methodology of deductive sciences*. New York: Oxford University Press.

Toulmin, Stephen E. 1984. *An introduction to reasoning*. 2nd ed. New York: Macmillan.

———. 2001. *Return to reason*. Cambridge, MA: Harvard University Press.

Trask, R. L. 2007. *Language and linguistics: The key concepts*. 2nd ed. Ed. Peter Stockwell. New York: Routledge.

Urdang, Laurence, Walter W. Hunsinger, and Nancy LaRoche. 1991. *A fine kettle of fish and other figurative phrases*. Detroit, MI: Viking Ink Press.

Urdang, Laurence. 2008. *The last word: The English language, opinions and prejudices*. Detroit: Omnidata Research.

———. 1998. *Suffixes and other word-final elements in English*. Old Lyme, CT: Verbatim.

———, ed. 1986. *-Ologies & -Isms*. 3rd ed. Anne Ryan and Tanya H. Lee, editors. Detroit: Gale Research Inc.

———. 1983. *Literary, rhetorical, and linguistics terms index*. Frank R. Abate, managing editor. Detroit: Gale Research Company.

———. 1975. *The basic book of synonyms and antonyms*. 2nd ed. New York: Signet.

———, managing ed. 1966. *The Random House dictionary of the English language* [unabridged]. First edition. New York: Random House.

Vygotsky, L. S. 1962. *Thought and language*. New York: Wiley.

Walton, Douglas. 2001. Persuasive definitions and public policy arguments. *Argumentation and Advocacy* 37 (3):117–32.
Waismann, F. 1965. *The principles of linguistic philosophy*. Ed. R. Harre. New York: Macmillan.
Whitehead, A. N. 1929. *Process and reality*. New York: Macmillan.
———. 1938. *Modes of thought*. New York: Macmillan.
Williams, Bernard. 2002. *Truth and truthfulness: An essay in genealogy*. Princeton, NJ: Princeton University Press.
———. 2005. *In the beginning was the deed: Realism and moralism in political argument*. Ed. Geoffrey Hawthorne. Princeton, NJ: Princeton University Press.
Winterowd, W. Ross. 1985 Kenneth Burke: An Annotated Glossary of His Terministic Screen and a "Statistical" Survey of His Major Concepts. *Rhetoric Society Quarterly* 15 (3–4): 145–77.
Wittgenstein, Ludwig. 1922. *Tractatus logico-philosophicus*. London: Kegan Paul, Trench, Truber.
———. 1958. *Philosophical investigations*. Trans. G. E. M. Anscombe. Oxford: Basil Blackwell.
———. 1960. *The blue and brown books*. Oxford: Basil Blackwell.
———. 1970. *Lectures and conversations on aesthetics, psychology and religious belief*. Ed. Cyril Barrett. Oxford: Basil Blackwell.
———. 1972. *On certainty*. Ed. G. E. M. Anscombe and G. H. von Wright. New York: Harper and Row.
———. 1980. *Culture and value*. Trans. Peter Winch. Chicago: University of Chicago Press.
Wollheim, Richard. 1980. *Art and its objects*. 2nd ed. New York: Cambridge University Press.
Wordsworth, William. 1904. *Poetical works*. Oxford: Oxford University Press.
Worf, Benjamin Lee. 1956. *Language, thought, and reality: Selected writings*. Ed. John C. Carroll. Technology Press of Massachusetts Institute of Technology.
Yoos, George E. 1966. Some reflections on titles of works of art. *The British Journal of Aesthetics* 5 (October): 351–364.
———. 1967. A work of art as a standard of itself. *The Journal of Aesthetics and Art Criticism* 26 (Fall): 81–89.
———. 1968. On being literally false. *Philosophy and Rhetoric* 1 (Fall): 21–227.
———. 1971. A phenomenological look at metaphor. *Philosophy and Phenomenological Research* 32 (September):78–88.
———. 1975. Review of *The concept of knowledge*, by Panayot Butchvarov. *Theory and Decision* 6 (March): 371–75.
———. 1975. An analysis of some rhetorical uses of subjunctive conditionals. *Philosophy and Rhetoric* 8 (Fall): 203–12.
———. 1978. An Evaluation of E. D. Hirsch's *The Philosophy of Composition*. *Rhetoric Society Quarterly*, 8 (Fall): 57–62.
———. 1979. Rules, Conventions, and Constraints in Rhetorical Action. *Rhetoric Society Quarterly*, 9 (Winter): 28–34.

———. 1987. Rhetoric of appeal and rhetoric of response. *Philosophy and Rhetoric* 20: 107–17.

———. 1994. Style, invention, and indirection: Aphorisms. In *Composition and context: Festschrift for Don Stewart*. Carbondale: Southern Illinois University Press.

———. 1995. Pragmatics and critical thinking. *Inquiry: Critical Thinking across the Disciplines* 14 (Summer): 19–28.

———. 1996. Logos. In *Encyclopedia of rhetoric and composition*. Ed. Theresa Enos. New York: Garland.

———. 2003. Review of *Truth and truthfulness: An essay in genealogy*, by Bernard Williams. *Rhetoric Review* 23 (1): 77–93.

———. 2003b. Review of *Making stories: Law, literature, life*, by Jerome Bruner. *Journal of Advanced Composition* 23 (2): 459–63.

———. 2007. *Reframing rhetoric: A liberal politics without dogma*. New York: Palgrave Macmillan.

Young, Richard E., Alton L. Becker, and Kenneth L. Pike. 1970. *Rhetoric: Discovery and change*. New York: Harcourt, Brace, and World.

Index

Adam's language, 76
advanced literacy, 142
aggregates, 125–27. *See also* umbrella terms
Allah's language, 76
allegory, 26, 103
allusion, 26, 103. *See also* reminding
ambiguity, 19, 32, 41, 78–79, 151, 169
analysis, 119; contrastive, 133–35; logical, 5–8
analytic philosophy, xv, 7, 8, 119
antinomies, 27, 36, 110–13
antinonyms, 134, 154
appeal, 52, 55, 60, 80, 88
argument, 79–80
argumentation, xv, 33
Aristotle, 26, 37, 199–200
arts, 55–56, 109, 120, 142
attention, 9, 26, 39, 60
Austin, J. L., 51, 74

background knowledge, 26, 100–102. *See* presumption
basic semantic axiom, 22
Beardsley, Monroe C., 106–7
belief, 18, 38. *See* trust and faith
big rhetoric, xvi-xvii, 21, 33, 55, 153. *See also* little rhetoric
boundaries, 63, 86, 120, 155, 161
Brummett, Barry, xi, 49, 151

Carnap, Rudolph, 38, 77
categorical terms, 68
causal language, 67, 199–204
cause-effect, 131
chunking, 78

common sense, 23
communications departments, xiii
conceptual definitions, 143–44, 146
conceptual metaphors, 104
conceptual outlines, 156
connotation, 97
connotative definition, 97
contracts, 62, 72, 162, 165, 198
conversation, 30–31
conversational implicatures, 33, 99
conservativism: language, 88, 91, 96; political, 125–26
contrasts: correlative terms, 27–29, 128; figures, 5; rational numbers, 193, 197
cooperative principles, 30–31
correlative terms, 4, 26–29, 131–37, 154
creation of langauge, 24, 54–55, 77–78
creative writing, 61, 159
critical analysis, xv

dead metaphors, 109–10
definiendum, 170
definiens, 170, 185
defining an aim, 153–56
defining as an act, 74
defining a point, 122
defining terms, 26, 69, 169–70, 173–75, 185, 190
definition: of algorithms, 155, 171; of boundaries, 120, 161; as a formulation, 74, 159; of intentions, 120, 154, 164–65; of logical operations, 170–71; of narrative, 118, 154, 171; of procedures, 147, 155, 171; of values, vii, 164–65

definition and interpretation: as clarifying modes, 118–19; as rhetorical modes, 80, 123, 141–42; as umbrella terms, 23, 154
definition of reality, 24–25, 49–50, 56, 148, 150
denotation, 26, 96–97
denotative definition, 67, 97
Derrida, Jacques, 27
Dewey, John, 73, 132, 205
dialect, 96
dictionaries, 73, 81–82, 86–88
dictionary synonyms, 169, 173, 182
differentia, 175–76
diversionary strategies, 32, 49
dyadic contrasts, 26, 29

English departments, xiii
enthymeme, 80
episodic memory, 70, 109. *See also* memory: semantic
equivocal, 16–17
essential definition, 132, 200–201
ethos, 55
exemplary example, xv, 9
explanation, 128
exposition, 61
extemporaneous speech, 59, 156. *See also* impromptu speech

faith, 11, 18, 38–40. *See also* belief and trust
fictive, 49
figures, 70, 83, 103–6
foundations, 6, 33, 36

genera, 26
gist, 84–86, 153, 164
grapholect, 96
Grice, H. P., 31–33

hermeneutic circle, 6, 213
hermeneutics, 6, 21, 87, 119
Hirsch, E. D., 95

history: of cultures, xiv, 150; of language, 22, 89–90; of rhetoric, xiii, xvi, 124
humanities, xii, xvi, 21, 24, 142, 164, 204–5
hypothetical interpretation, 210

ideolect, 95–96
ignorance, 9, 14, 18, 50, 152
illocutionary acts, 166, 211
implicatures, 30, 33
impromtu speech, 59
informal logic movement, xv, xvii
intention in action, 157
interpret: sense, meaning, language use, 22. *See* basic semantic axiom, 22
interpretive commentaries, 52, 212
interpretive summaries, 73, 214
intuition, 145, 149
irony, 3, 39

Kant, Immanuel, 36, 145

legitimatization, 65, 83, 95, 140
linkng correlatives, 29
little rhetoric, xvi, 21. *See also* big rhetoric
language as a cage, 77–78
language usage, 48, 62–63, 73, 91
language use, 48, 51, 63–64, 96
liberal, 125–26
limits of knowledge, 18, 71
literalization, 83
logical grammar, 68, 195
logos, 146–47

macroscopic analysis, 210–11
manifest presumption of intent, 98, 153
meaning: as a personal affair, xi; as refinement, v, xi-xiii, 4, 22, 158, 172; as socially constructed, xi, 127, 150–51
meaning of meaning, 3, 8, 23
means-ends, 131
memory: episodic memory, 70–71; long term memory, 70, 85; semantic

memory, 70–71; short term memory, 85, 178, 212
metalanguage, 77–78, 187
metaphor, 70–71, 87, 90, 103–13
microscopic analysis, 210–11
misplaced concreteness, 50
mutual understanding, 25, 55, 75, 82, 98–100, 120, 123–24

narrative, 118, 154, 158, 160, 171
natural language, 70, 83, 170, 203
negation, 71, 129, 133, 173, 178–79, 189
neologism, 82, 88–89
nominal definitions, 143, 155
nothing, 11, 15–16, 71
noting, 25, 111

operational definitions, 69, 147
ordinary language, 28, 32, 83, 85
ostensive reference, 25, 97–98
oxymoron, 106

paradigms, 60, 67, 73, 99
paradoxes, 35–40
paraphrase, 27–28, 140
perceptual metaphors, 108
pejorative terms, 82, 126, 130
perlocutionary acts, 28, 166
Peirce, Charles Sanders, 6
personification, 70, 103
Plato, 40, 67, 141
Popper, Karl, 132
précising terms, 78–79, 92–93, 140, 160–61, 172
prejudice, 98, 102
prescriptions, 51, 75
prescriptivists, 92, 95–96
presumption, 13, 31–32, 40–42, 53, 70, 97–99, 135
prior intention, 160–66
private language, 53, 204
probabilities, 14
promising, 165–66

propositions: as points of argument, 69; as statements, 69, 145
persuasive definitions, 143
principles: concepts vs. principles, 149; moral, 204; political, 126
prewriting outlines, 155

quasi-literal, 110

real definitions, 143, 146
reductio ad absurdum, 37. *See also* Aristotle
redundancy, 5, 16–17, 111, 121
reification, 50, 143
relativism, 29
relevance, 33, 98–101
religion, 146–51
religious language, 18, 38, 105
reminding, 25, 79–81, 111
responsibilities, 27, 132, 198
rhetorical frames, xii, 30
rhetoric of appeal, 26, 52, 60
rhetoric of response, 26, 60
Rhetoric Society, xiv
Richards, I. A., xii, xv, 33
rights, 13, 131

sanctioning our thoughts, 162
Saussure, Ferdinand, 6–7
scanning, 210
Schiappa, Edward, xi, xvi, 150
science, 150, 184, 200
scrutiny, 210
sense: meaning to say, 35; meaning of what is said, 35
seeing as, 139, 104, 208. *See* Wittgenstein
seeing plus a thought, 104
sentence outlines, 156
sociolect, 95–96
Sperber and Wilson, 39, 97–98, 101
stipulations, 84–85
strict synonymy, 169
subjunctive conditionals, 49, 103
summary outlines, 156
synecdoche, 70, 84, 108–13

synonyms, 29, 87, 154, 169, 182

tautologies, 121
technical language, 28, 69, 78, 83, 85, 164
term defined, 26, 136, 169–70, 173
terministic screens, 94
theories, 96, 149–50
theory of verification, 22, 67, 128
translation, 29, 64, 184, 211–12
triads, 178–81
tropes, 106, 112–13

United States Constitution, 171, 173
unwarranted presumption, 198, 110

vagueness, 32, 78–79, 151, 213–14
Venn diagrams, 173, 177–81
visual metaphors, 112

war on terrorism, 108
well formed sentences, 187
Wittgenstein, Ludwig, 22, 37–38, 53, 76, 104, 125–27, 144–45
writer's block, 159